KEEPING AN OPEN MIND IN A CLOSED SYSTEM

David Alva Personett

Dedicated to my family and all the "truthers" out there, those who seek the truth, true journalists, true writers.   Truth will set you free. Keep the light on, so the world can see.
All glory to God!

CONTENTS

INTRODUCTION

"Things that will destroy man: Politics without principle; pleasure without conscience; wealth without work; knowledge without character; business without morality; science without humanity; worship without sacrifice." -- Mohandas (Mahatma) Gandhi

"To be GOVERNED is to be watched, inspected, spied upon, directed, law-driven, numbered, regulated, enrolled, indoctrinated, preached at, controlled, checked, estimated, valued, censured, commanded, by creatures who have neither the right nor the wisdom nor the virtue to do so. To be GOVERNED is to be at every operation, at every transaction noted, registered, counted, taxed, stamped, measured, numbered, assessed, licensed, authorized, admonished, prevented, forbidden, reformed, corrected, punished. It is, under pretext of public utility, and in the name of the general interest, to be place under contribution, drilled, fleeced, exploited, monopolized, extorted from, squeezed, hoaxed, robbed; then, at the slightest resistance, the first word of complaint, to be repressed, fined, vilified, harassed, hunted down, abused, clubbed, disarmed, bound, choked, imprisoned, judged, condemned, shot, deported, sacrificed, sold, betrayed; and to crown all, mocked, ridiculed, derided, outraged, dishonored. That is government; that is its justice; that is its morality." — Pierre-Joseph Proudhon (1851)[1]

E very day, we are bombarded with subtle and sometimes not-so subtle reminders of who is in charge. The demise of most is a reality of powerlessness and economic oppression, carefully orchestrated by political insiders and mass media with inane distractions and educational perversions. Time

---

[1] *General Idea of the Revolution in the Nineteenth Century*, translated by John Beverly Robinson (London: Freedom Press, 1923), pp. 293-294.

marches on to a New Global Empire. These are the modern-day bread and circuses so effectively utilized by Roman authority millennia ago and carried on by papal royalty through the Middle Ages. Into the Age of Enlightenment, Western societies struggled to seek a new order based on liberty and peace, usually with acknowledgements toward a creator and Natural Law.

The principles of Liberty - as defined by modern day liberals, progressives and conservatives alike - have become a hodgepodge of meaningless, flag-waving jingoism. To liberals and progressives, liberty cannot be realized without economic equality. No one is free as long as people cannot have the same opportunities and distribution of wealth, thereby denying liberty of those who are forced to involuntarily distribute their wealth to others. Conservatives, on the other hand, want freedom for themselves but not necessarily for their neighbors. Hence, while supporting selective constitutional rights, such as gun ownership, they destroy other rights and force taxpayers to pay for adherence to vice laws and other social prohibitions of victimless acts, forcing, as well, their extreme violence, sometimes against innocent people, through warrantless searches and non-judicial-mediated property seizures. Modern conservatives (neoconservatives) support giving up constitutional protections to "better fight" terrorism and the war against certain drugs they do not like.

Freedom is simply defined as having the absence of coercion and force. To the Left, freedom means nothing more than the lyrics of a Kris Kristofferson song implying that "freedom's just another word for nothing left to lose." Freedom from want, hunger, poverty, illness and, above all, fear was President Franklin Delano Roosevelt's mantra. Because they are afraid, they need the nanny state to protect and nurture them. Most Americans are happy to have the freedom to go to church or shopping. Of course, the same could be said of the Germans during Hitler's regime where citizens, other than Jews and select others, had most of the same accommodations we have today.[2] Until, of course, it got really ugly.

Freedom is morality. It is the way in which we treat each other. When we deny others their freedom, we commit an immoral act. When we put people in cages (jail) for possession of a plant, selling raw milk to willing customers, or other non-violent acts that hurt no one, we commit an immoral act. Freedom is the lack of aggression from others, especially those who align with the power hungry. As James 1:25 of the Holy Bible reassures, "But he who looks into the perfect law, the law of **liberty**, and

---

[2]   Mayer, Milton, *They Thought They Were Free: the Germans 1933-1945* (The University of Chicago Press, Chicago, 1955)

perseveres, being no hearer that forgets but a doer that acts, he shall be blessed in his doing." This perfect law of liberty (being right with God) is rooted in Mosaic Law and the Golden Rule, both requiring people not to commit fraud and force on others. A libertarian, anarchist, or anyone (a doer) who lives his life as a non-aggressor is the moral arbiter of a sociopolitical oligarchy of thieves and murderers. They will serve justice by removing themselves from the corrupt system. Controllers of none no longer control. People cannot call themselves free and then be an accessory to state violence by supporting political policies that abuse the fundamental rights and liberties of others! They are not free. They are delusional slaves, or worse, slave masters.

George Washington University law school professor Jonathan Turley notes:[3]

> I am still amazed that we have come to this point of rapidly declining feelings of freedom and widespread dissociation with our political system. It is not the failure of our constitutional system and only partially the failure of our leaders. **It is largely a failure in ourselves that we have become such grumbling drones — powerless, passive, and frankly a bit pathetic. Our government is openly trying to strip away core privacy protections and increase police powers at every level. Yet, we have fallen victim** to the "blue state" and "red state" mentality — allowing politicians to constantly deflect criticism by referring to the other side as the greater evil. The result is predictable and ... incredibly depressing.

One of the most ridiculous arguments made by statists is that if a society was totally free, and the various governments were shrunken down to their constitutional compulsions, then the statist would not be free, that the statist would be *forced* into a life where he is responsible for his own decisions and actions. This, in their minds, would result in chaos. Of course, this argument from statists is fundamentally wrong, both on principle as well as democratically. For one, we have mass economic and social chaos now with one of the largest and most meddling governments this world has ever seen. Would a slave be oppressed to be *forced* into a life of freedom if given a chance?

Recently, a state senator from Utah, a Republican, arguing for a resolution that would prohibit pornographic content available on public computers such as libraries and even private such as McDonald's said that viewing pornography (apparently by accident) "is violating his First Amendment right to not view it." Oppressing others

---

³   Turley, Jonathan, http://jonathanturley.org/2014/07/03/gallup-poll-satisfaction-with-their-freedoms-has-record-drop-among-americans-2/

to justify one's own "freedom from" is a *modus operandi* of all tyrants throughout history. Simple computer programs and techniques are available to address concerns by anyone who doesn't want to accidently see pornography, from timeout programs built into the operating system to simply allowing private business to police their own computers.

If you are in America, and if you are smart enough to understand that you are losing your personal sovereignty, and by extension your community and country, this is a guidebook for those who seek an explanation from this libertarian's viewpoint as to why your civilization is becoming unhinged – and what you can do about it. Libertarianism, besides meaning living one's life based on Liberty, or the Non-Aggression Principle, could also be defined as tolerant anarchism. History has shown that people function best in societies as decentralized, loosely connected, and geographically designed confederations. A society dependent on a central government, and more suppressed by its growing totalitarian state, is always destroyed by the sheer weight (actions) of its own oppressors.

Libertarian philosophy is grounded on Natural Law. Plato (although no libertarian) in his Socratic dialogue *Republic*[4] describes the ideal community as, "...a city which would be established in accordance with nature." The monotheistic religions of the Fertile Crescent are founded on the Law of Nature. The ancient Mosaic edicts of the Ten Commandments are founded on the simple concept of property rights and respect for an authority higher than the state or other humanistic power. You do not steal. You do not murder. You do not covet your neighbor's property or spouse. These are a number of the earthly edicts people should embrace as a civilized society. They are simple rules that are the basis of a civil and moral society, a libertarian tenet that you do not commit force and fraud (theft) on your neighbor. Everyone has a right to their *space*. Liberty means people have a right to their own property, *i.e.*, their own money, their own belongings, and that the government or your neighbor must sue to infringe upon them. We are given our freedom by our very nature. Whether you believe in revolution or God, we were not put on this planet to be slaves.

In his book *Guns, Germs and Steel*,[5] Jared Diamond, usually the embodiment of a quintessential progressive university professor, describes analytically a sterling example of the benefits societies receive from a decentralized, diffuse authority. Counter to centralized control over the means and benefits of production, Diamond

---

[4]   Plato, *The Republic*, 428e9, ca. 380 B.C.

[5]   Diamond, Jared, *Guns, Germs and Steel* (WW. Norton & Co, New York, 1997, 1999).

reports that populations on the smaller Polynesian islands were more egalitarian, where tribal leaders dressed the same as the other tribesmen and went out on hunts with them. On larger islands, authority was centralized, where tribal leaders are pampered, and the populations are stratified according to power. The populations on larger islands lived to serve their tribal leaders.

People who become disgusted with the hideous, odious display of governmental hubris and tyranny tend to gravitate to alternative sociopolitical leanings such as the libertarian or anarcho- "green" movements outside of the left-right paradigm. It is not so much that these people hate government. They just despise the present state, which has become far too indifferent to the original intent of the various constitutional states established to respect and foster individual rights. The early Founders agonized over the ugly stain of slavery, sanctioned by greedy mercantilists and their representatives in government. It was a time of prosperity for those who set out to earn it, where people weren't chained to the ancient curse of taxation and centralization. Earlier arrogant and imperialistic regimes represented evil, and the Founders would have nothing of it. In North America, they expanded west, explored, discovered and prospered. The individual had little to do with driving Native Americans off their lands. That was the job of the U.S. Calvary and their corporate mercenaries.

The chapters in this book are sectioned into different iconoclastic problems within the American society perpetuated by decades of governmental perversions to our fundamental right to life, liberty and the pursuit of happiness. The modern security state has swept up our liberties and thrown them into the ashbin of history in exchange for keeping people "safe." It has always been about keeping the peasants, peons and paroles "safe." Even prisons have safety rules. These chapters will define under each XYZ-Industrial realm and paradigm how authority expands to meet the ever-growing (or –changing) challenges of the day to keep the voting, taxpaying mundanes safe and happy.

And so, now, we have a plethora of institutions draining trillions of dollars from a quasi- private economy to protect us from terrorists, guns, food, the climate, even ourselves. We no longer belong to us. Most have become children of the nanny state.

Science (taken on in the first chapter of this book) has changed considerably in the past few centuries, but not so much as the past 30 years. Science has become big business, with not just research and development of novel technology, but in a way in which to be packaged as commercialized modern miracles, or even as modern social movements (e.g., environmentalism). Even biologics and experiments are packaged and commercially available for the laboratory, science making money off science. Years ago, scientists and their assistants developed their own reagents, e.g., antibodies or DNA plasmid vectors, and wrote their own computer programs for data analysis and statistics.

Nowadays, to pay for this commercialism, scientists spend more than 90 percent of their time in their offices writing papers and grants, government grants encouraged, in a desperate, endless, Sisyphus-like process of securing their livelihoods for another few years. Many of them burn out early and either change professions or move into faculty positions at community colleges where funding matters are easily resolved by coercive extraction of taxes by the state. Science purely for the sake of science possibly no longer exists.

Funding is now driving science, instead of the other way around, more so for the sake of funding than for perpetuation of science, medicine, and technological advances. Many in science, those who refuse to compromise their principles, are seeing this phenomenon every day, as pseudo-scientific "theories," such as human-implicated global warming or the amyloid theory for Alzheimer's disease that generate billions of dollars for the theorizers.

Congressman Billy Tauzin (R-LA) noted in testimony before the Commerce subcommittee on Health and the Environment (March 26, 1998) that "when we do target funds...toward a disease...we can make it [gains] happen a lot sooner. [I]t's no coincidence that because we targeted funds at AIDS research that there has been a 70 percent drop in AIDS deaths this last year. That's remarkable and we know that's possible."[6] Of course, simple education dissemination towards safe-sex, so-called "AIDS awareness," and cheap drugs already available in other countries, but banned by the FDA, had little to do with a sharp reduction in AIDS deaths.

Nowhere has the distinction of political correctness and lobbyist misadventures invaded our most fundamental personal liberties as to what we eat than our federal government's development of a nationally recognized food pyramid.[7] The Federal government changed the food pyramid, after decades of promoting an emphasis on the wrong food group!

---

[6] Testimony before the Institute of Medicine Committee on the NIH Research Priority-Setting Process

April 3, 1998, National Academy of Sciences Auditorium, Washington, DC. Report by Alastair T. Gordon.

The Islet Foundation. http://www.islet.org/35.htm

[7] http://en.wikipedia.org/wiki/Food_Pyramid

So, people say living in the US is better, with more freedom, than any other country. But that is all relativism with no absolute principles to ground the argument. In a truly free country, the only possible role for government would be to protect the rights and liberties of its citizenry from force and fraud. But government is force and fraud. So how could a government whose sole existence is maintained by force and fraud ever protect anyone from force and fraud? No government, even the American government supposedly constrained by a constitution, is never limited to respecting the rights and liberties of its citizenry.

Generally, I found most people who talk about freedom have no idea what freedom really is. No one can say we live in a *free* country and then demand people cannot freely exercise their freedom. Comparing freedom of various countries is like comparing a nice, firm defecated stool to a puddle of diarrhea. This means that one must think in terms of *relative* freedom. Governments exist to control the resources, businesses and wealth for a small sub-population of elite over the rest of the population. It always has been that way and, unfortunately, will probably be that way for a long time to come. The American experiment has been a complete failure, as is the fate of all governments and societies that evolve into mass co-dependence on empire. America was bound to fail because its population allowed the elite few to pervert the Constitution and control the economy,[8] and by extension society, through an expanding security force by its state.

An argument was made on a website message board one day that Americans have the responsibility to occupy conquered countries like Japan and Germany, because the governments of those countries want the US there, despite the fact that an overwhelming majority of their citizenry wants the US gone. How can the politicians of these countries possibly say with a straight face that their countries are democracies and not just another American conquered colony?

Elitist Corporatism

In the early stages of every corrupt, tyrannical government, state control of the food supply is essential for controlling its population. Thomas Jefferson said, "If people let government decide what foods they eat and what medicines they take, their bodies will soon be in as sorry a state as are the souls of those who live under tyranny."[9] Communist countries in the 20th Century enslaved or murdered the

---

[8] Griffin, G. Edward. The Creature from Jekyll Island: A Second Look at the Federal Reserve (American Media, 4th ed., 2002)

farmers and took possession of their farms first. Ricardo Walther Oscar Darré, a leading Nazi "blood and soil ideologue, and who served as Reichsminister of Food and Agriculture (1933 to 1942) campaigned for big landowners to part with some of their land to create new farms, and promoted the controversial Reichserbhofgesetz, the state Hereditary Farm Law, requiring any farm of 7.5 to 125 hectares to be *Erbhof* , "the size needed to maintain a family and work as a productive unit. Larger farms were subdivided." [10] At first glance, this may seem like a good idea, breaking up larger farms and sharing the joy, so to speak, but if it was forced upon the larger landowners against their will, then the natural order of change was disrupted, creating animosity and eventually feuds and violence. History has shown that nation building does not promote peace and prosperity.

A Modern Parable, very sad.

A Japanese company (Toyota) and an American company (Ford Motors) decided to have a canoe race on the Missouri River. Both teams practiced long and hard to reach their peak performance before the race.

On the big day, the Japanese won by a mile. The Americans, very discouraged and depressed, decided to investigate the reason for the crushing defeat. A management team made up of senior management was formed to investigate and recommend appropriate action. Their conclusion was the Japanese had 8 people rowing and 1 person steering, while the American team had 7 people steering and 2 people rowing.

Feeling a deeper study was in order; American management hired a consulting company and paid them a large amount of money for a second opinion. They advised, of course, that too many people were steering the boat, while not enough people were rowing. Not sure of how to utilize that information, but wanting to prevent another loss to the Japanese, the rowing team's management structure was totally reorganized to 4 steering supervisors, 2 area steering superintendents and 1 assistant superintendent steering manager.

They also implemented a new performance system that would give the 2 people rowing the boat greater incentive to work harder. It was called the 'Rowing Team Quality First Program,' with meetings, dinners and free pens for the rowers. There was

[9] Thomas Jefferson. The quote above is a paraphrase taken from Jefferson's Notes on Virginia, Query XVII (1781-1785).

[10] Schoenbaum, David. Hitler's Social Revolution: Class and Status in Nazi Germany, 1933-1939, (Garden City, NY Doubleday, 1966). p 164 Referenced in: http://en.wikipedia.org/wiki/Richard_Walther_Darr%C3%A9

discussion of getting new paddles, canoes and other equipment, extra vacation days for practices and bonuses. The pension program was trimmed to "equal the competition" and some of the resultant savings were channeled into morale boosting programs and teamwork posters.

The next year the Japanese won by two miles.

Humiliated, the American management laid-off one rower, halted development of a new canoe, sold all the paddles, and canceled all capital investments for new equipment. The money saved was distributed to the Senior Executives as bonuses.

The next year, try as he might, the lone designated rower was unable to even finish the race (having no paddles,) so he was laid off for unacceptable performance, all canoe equipment was sold and the next year's racing team was out-sourced to India.

Sadly, the End.

Here's something else to think about: Ford has spent the last thirty years moving all its factories out of the US , claiming they can't make money paying American wages.

TOYOTA has spent the last thirty years building more than a dozen plants inside the US. The last quarter's results: TOYOTA makes 4 billion in profits while Ford racked up 9 billion in losses. Ford folks are still scratching their heads, and collecting bonuses.[11]

So, what is a society to do with this deliberate destruction of an industry what was once the envy of the world? Apparently, the CEOs of American automobile manufacturers didn't believe the self-interest of the American consumer was stronger than some patriotic duty to "buy American."

After World War II, United States had an interest in building Japan's industrial base to serve the US's needs in Korea during the Korean War. After that war, Japan introduced those vehicles into the American market, where it was quickly taken as a joke compared to American cars, which were larger and more stylish. After the disastrous economic policies of the Nixon administration in the early 1970s, gas prices skyrocketed due to Nixon's price controls causing a shortage of gas, and long lines at the gas station in the United States in 1973 that lasted for years. Smaller, gas-sipping foreign cars and trucks began taking over the U.S. market.

---

[11] http://www.tensionnot.com/jokes/office_jokes/american_vs_japanese_management

Corporate America is destroying our way of life, possibly only second to the state. But when carefully analyzed, corporations have become the state and the state has become a giant corporation, financed by a "private bank," the Federal Reserve, controlling nearly every aspect of our economy and personal lives. The US media reports nothing but drivel and misinformation from state bullet points to elicit fear at every moment of the day. It is no wonder newspaper media is losing subscriptions at an unprecedented speed, but also fewer people even want to stay engaged in democratic exchanges because of topical absurdities or for fear of alienation. Society's moral infrastructure is crumbling to dust around us. Whatever is not rotting our minds with corporate-state propaganda is gunking it up with depravities of commercialism, sex and violence.

Getting my daughter off the van and taking care of her in the afternoons, I had the opportunity to see late afternoon TV shows kids around the country are exposed to every weekday. Subtle nuances are directed to young, impressionable pre-teenagers and older filled with nothing more than sexual innuendos, debauchery and bathroom humor. This is what passes as after-school babysitting and play time for kids under 15 years old. Kids are subtly given subliminal cues to disobey and mock their parents. Parents on these shows are shown to be not too bright, sometimes with eccentric or self-absorbed personalities. Feminism has taken over Disney for years. Young girls are nearly always the alpha character, the ones in control, mature, and more intelligent, while young boys are foolish, immature and ridiculed. Consider the fact that executives from the top eight production companies in Hollywood control the social and political perspectives of millions of impressionable minds. It is mind-boggling.

For instance, people generally will say they prefer freedom to a totalitarian state-controlled existence. But after careful examination of most people's perception of freedom, you will find out their freedom is close to being the opposite of what freedom really means. A good number of Americans, and even many foreigners, I've discussed of these issues, say they love America because they say they are free, but believe that certain social behavior, such as illicit drug use, should be regulated or prohibited. No one who is really free would accept state control of personal behavior. No one is free who cannot choose what he does or doesn't do with his own body. There is no such thing as state-allocated liberties. The best the state can do in a truly free society is to arbitrate justice to murderers, thieves and rapists.

For decades Americans have been conditioned by the state institutions and sycophantic corporate media to believe that freedom comes to the people through their government. It only seems logical to most, because they, the constituency, choose their representatives to look after their best interests (freedom, collective security from invaders, even prosperity). It never occurs to them that the political class could have another agenda. This agenda is counter to the authority explicit in the constitution. Most people believe they are free because the "constitution gives them certain rights." Of course, this is not the purpose of the constitution. They just believe the constitution gives us rights because they believe we derive our rights and liberties from government. But the constitution was written to control central government powers, and not to control the governed. The Founding Fathers had to explicitly amend their constitution they had just created with a Bill of Rights to protect the governed. This Bill of Rights required the government to respect the Natural Rights of all people, citizen or not. In fact, nowhere in the Constitution will you find the word citizen, except in the requirement that elected representatives of the federal government be either natural born citizens (Presidents) or a set number of years (Representatives and Senators), and that the Supreme Court respect the rights of *all* citizens, foreign or domestic, in other words, *all* people. The Founders understood that *all* people have inalienable rights not defined by boundaries or other exceptions.

Conservatives talk a lot about freedom, but most do not believe in it. No one can promote "freedom" and then deny freedom to others. Most conservatives support the War on Drugs, which has been a miserable failure, and which has done nothing to promote freedom. They invade other countries under the guise of bringing freedom to the countries they invade while supporting some of the most draconian domestic policies of the so-called "free world." In actuality, as seen in Iraq and other occupied states in the Middle East, liberation wasn't intended to liberate the liberated but only from their properties and bodies!

Marijuana is a plant that grows naturally around the world, although that alone is not justification for decriminalizing the drug. Drug warriors will argue that poison ivy also grows naturally around the planet, but people do not "toke up" poison ivy and ironically, although it can harm people far worse than marijuana, the presence of poison ivy on your property will not cause you to forfeit your home, your car and your bank accounts to the state! Marijuana has a number of medicinal qualities, many of which have not been well explored, primarily because the federal government prohibits access to the plant for experimental purposes.

The corporate media has brainwashed people into believing political discourse is right vs. left, Republican vs. Democrat. Newscasters, political pundits and talk show hosts have made literally billions pitting people against people in a fallacious left-right paradigm. But people are waking up. People of all stripes are joining various freedom movements (or The Freedom Movement), because they now understand, and reality has shown them, that it's really about us vs. them, them being the politically connected elite. Neither the Republicans nor the Democrats have any interest in defending liberty, and they certainly do not have an ounce of respect for the supreme law of the federal government, the U.S. Constitution.

The Republicans showed their real colors the past decade, during the George W. Bush's two presidential terms in office, when the Republicans were in control of both the House and the Senate. Republicans could have shown us more than empty patriotic jingoism by cutting federal budgets and blocking the federal government's capacity to interfere with the rights of individuals and the states. Instead they tripled the size of government, spent trillions on occupying the resources of Central Asia and tore up the Bill of Rights with their infamous PATRIOT Act and war on terrorism.

Corporate media is polluted with CIA ops, has been for decades. Years ago, former CIA Director William Colby admitted that "the Central Intelligence Agency owns everyone of any significance in the major media."

The purpose of this literary excursion is to shed light on what is increasingly becoming the single-most destructive man-made disaster on the planet: state authority, and its power to establish modern-day serfdom. This author's hope is to leave such a malodorous taste in the reader's mouth for government that a clear understanding of anarchy will be a near-religious experience, or spiritual awakening. For over a century, gargantuan governmental destruction of our rights and liberties by the hideously manipulative ruling class in the United States has spread throughout the world rivaled only by the communist movement, which may soon be realized by convergence into one ominous force. State institutions, especially education bureaucracies, have indoctrinated people to fear freedom. Democracy creates an environment where governments become the means for one group to overpower, or even eliminate, another group by virtue of an implied authority by sheer numbers, no different than long ago what so-called "barbarians" did. Anarchy, with its underlying principle of non-aggression, is something so alien to Americans now that even slaughter *en mass* in an attempt to bring about social order is justified at the drop of a hat.

SCIENCE-INDUSTRIAL COMPLEX

"The prospect of domination of the nation's scholars by Federal employment, project allocations, and the power of money is ever present and is gravely to be regarded." Dwight Eisenhower farewell speech, 1960[12]

"Science driven by politics and funding is not science at all; it is just propaganda wearing a white lab coat instead of a priest's robe." Michael Rivero ~ radio, graphic engineer and entrepreneur

The History of Science Funding

Science, today, is all about funding. A case in point, recently unfolding before our eyes, is the push by environmentalists, and their lapdogs in the media and the political class, to pour more public money into "climate change" research, and to begin taxing economic and personal output based on one's "carbon footprint." Carbon dioxide, a fundamental molecule for life's cyclic existence, was recently ruled[13] by the Supreme Court to be a toxic air pollutant that demanded societal attention and micromanagement. The bizarre idea that democratic

---

[12]   *http://www.scienceofsociety.org/inbox/res2.html*

[13]   Proposed Endangerment and Cause or Contribute Findings for Greenhouse Gases under the Clean Air Act, April 2009. http://epa.gov/climatechange/endangerment.html

collectivism could manage the intricacies of a life-sustaining planet is discussed in depth later in this chapter.

A consensus for funding in the public sector is decided by a culture of dogma-believing organopoliticians. One of the best of examples, and a good example of political interference in science, comes from a so-called "climate expert" on the Weather Channel calling for MSA decertification of all meteorologists who believe climate change is a natural phenomenon.[14]

As meteorologist Marc Morano points out:

> "I have been in operational meteorology since 1978, and I know dozens and dozens of broadcast meteorologists all over the country. Our big job: look at a large volume of raw data and come up with a public weather forecast for the next seven days. I do not know of a single TV meteorologist who buys into the man-made global warming hype. I know there must be a few out there, but I can't find them. Here are the basic facts you need to know:
>
> "Billions of dollars of grant money is [sic] flowing into the pockets of those on the man-made global warming bandwagon. No man-made global warming, the money dries up. This is big money, make no mistake about it. Always follow the money trail and it tells a story. Even the lady at "The Weather Channel" probably gets paid good money for a prime time show on climate change. No man-made global warming, no show, and no salary. Nothing wrong with making money at all, but when money becomes the motivation for a scientific conclusion, then we have a problem. For many, global warming is a big cash grab."[15]

People who study these things are publishing data that suggest climate change is occurring on Mars[16] and Jupiter[17] as well.

> Just as Darwin discovered the law of development or organic nature, so Marx discovered

[14] Morano, M . "Weather Channel Climate Expert Calls for Decertifying Global Warming Skeptics"http://epw.senate.gov/public/index.cfm?FuseAction=PressRoom.Blogs&ContentRecord_id=32abc 0b0-802a-23ad-440a-88824bb8e528, January 17, 2007.

[15] Spann, James. 2007. "The Weather Channel Mess." http://epw.senate.gov/public/index.cfm?FuseAction=PressRoom.Blogs& ContentRecord_id=3a9bc8a4-802a-23ad-4065-7dc37ec39adf marc_morano@epw.senate.gov

[16] Webster, G. and Beasley, D. "Orbiter's Long Life Helps Scientists Track Changes on Mars."Jet Propulsion Labortory, California Institute of Technology, http://mars.jpl.nasa.gov/mgs/newsroom/20050920a.html, September 20, 2005

[17] Marcus, P.S. "Prediction of a global climate change on Jupiter." Nature **428**:828-831. http://www.nature.com/nature/journal/v428/n6985/abs/nature02470.html, April 22, 2004.

the law of development of human history: the simple fact, hitherto concealed by an overgrowth of ideology, that mankind must first of all eat, drink, have shelter and clothing, before it can pursue politics, science, art, religion, etc.; that therefore the production of the immediate material means, and consequently the degree of economic development attained by a given people or during a given epoch, form the foundation upon which the state institutions, the legal conceptions, art, and even the ideas on religion, of the people concerned have been evolved, and in the light of which they must, therefore, be explained, instead of vice versa, as had hitherto been the case.

But that is not all. Marx also discovered the special law of motion governing the present-day capitalist mode of production, and the bourgeois society that this mode of production has created. The discovery of surplus value suddenly threw light on the problem, in trying to solve which all previous investigations, of both bourgeois economists and socialist critics, had been groping in the dark.

Two such discoveries would be enough for one lifetime. Happy the man to whom it is granted to make even one such discovery. But in every single field which Marx investigated -- and he investigated very many fields, none of them superficially -- in every field, even in that of mathematics, he made independent discoveries.

Such was the man of science. But this was not even half the man. Science was for Marx a historically dynamic, revolutionary force. However great the joy with which he welcomed a new discovery in some theoretical science whose practical application perhaps it was as yet quite impossible to envisage, he experienced quite another kind of joy when the discovery involved immediate *revolutionary changes in industry, and in historical development in general.*[18]

People should realize that nearly all funding for climatology is funded by government agencies. When the private sector funds studies, especially ones that could refute climate change/warming dogma, those studies are immediately attacked by the Left with its army of climate change purists. Even when the study has irrefutable data showing contradictions to climate dogma, the attacks become *ad*

---

[18] Frederick Engels' speech at Karl Marx's gravesite funeral (in English). https://www.marxists.org/archive/marx/works/1883/death/dersoz1.htm

hominem attacks on the researchers and their source(s) of climatology funding, despite the fact that most funding for science in general comes from private funding sources (see below). In recent years, the credibility of climate science has increasingly become a target, as reports of "cooking the books,"[19,20]politicization or democratization of science,[21,22,23] and misrepresentation of the data[24,25] come into the light.

At the same time, other so-called experts have been saying the planet on an average has been cooling since about the turn of the century (ca. 1998). Therefore, the consensus is anything but unanimous amongst people in the field of climatology and meteorology.

Today most of the funding and resources for scientific discovery, about 65 percent, comes from the research and development departments of private industry, while the rest comes from government funding to universities (20%), other government agencies (10%) and private charities (5%).[26] Of government funding, about 35 percent goes to medical research while most goes to military R&D (See Figure 1).[27] So-called "soft sciences" such as social studies and the humanities are nearly totally funded by the government, where it suits its purpose to shape and control the future interactions of its society, as Frederick Engels, Karl Marx and a select other economists would have it.

---

[19] Bastasch, Michael (2015) "NOAA Fiddles with Climate Data to Erase the 15-Year Global Warming 'Hiatus'", The Daily Caller June 4, 2015 http://dailycaller.com/2015/06/04/noaa-fiddles-with-climate-data-to-erase-the-15-year-global-warming-hiatus/

[20] Booker, Christopher (2014) "The Scandal of Fiddled Global Warming Data." The Telegraph June 21, 2014.   http://dailycaller.com/2015/06/04/noaa-fiddles-with-climate-data-to-erase-the-15-year-global-warming-hiatus/

[21] McCright, A.M. and Dunlap, R.E. (2011) "The Politicization of Climate Change and Polarization in the American Public's Views of Global Warming," 2001-2010. The Sociological Quarterly 52:155-194.

[22] Gauchat, Gordon. "Politicization of Science in the Public Sphere: A Study of Public Trust in the United States." Am. Sociological Rev. 77(2), April 2012.

[23] Jotterand, Fabrice. (2006) "The Politicization of Science and Technology: Its Implications for Nanotechnology." J. Law, Med. & Ethics, 34(4):658-666

[24] Spencer, R.W. and Braswell, W.D. (2011) "On the Misdiagnosis of Surface Temperature Feedbacks from Variations in Earth's Radiant Energy Balance." Remote Sensing 3: 1603-1613.

[25] Taylor, James, "New NASA Data Blow Gaping Hole in Global Warming Alarmism. Forbes, July 27, 2011.   http://www.forbes.com/sites/jamestaylor/2011/07/27/new-nasa-data-blow-gaping-hold-in-global-warming-alarmism/

[26] Wikipedia.org http://en.wikipedia.org/wiki/Research_funding

[27] Dooley, J.J. "U.S Federal Investments in Energy." R&D: 961-2008. U.S. Department of Energy. PNNL-17952

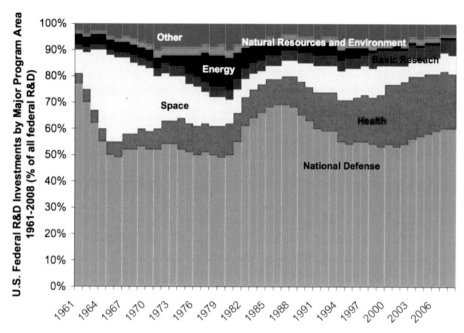

Figure 1: U.S. Federal Government Investments in R&D by Major Area of Focus

Decades ago, before the government got involved with funding non-military science and technologies, scientists were financed by private endowments and wealthy individuals. Scientists and their technical staffs made, purified and analyzed for quality nearly all their reagents. Nearly everything was prepared in the lab. Analysis of data was done without computers. Yet vaccines and antibiotics were developed, synthetic fibers were discovered, and the U.S. put men on the moon, the latter with the help of fledgling computation machines (proto-computers). Today, technicians use kits developed by other scientists and technicians, optimized to work like Hamburger Helper under normal working conditions. Some of the time, I saw technicians doing experiments that they had absolutely no idea how the chemistry of the reaction(s) really works, and because some of these kits have proprietary "ingredients" in them, the technicians had no idea what chemicals were in the kits.

Today's science is becoming something of a joke. Central Dogma drives funding, while funding bankrolls Central Dogma. Climatology, oceanography, health and medical research, all have been recipients of generous bureaucracies of the State and its taxpaying minions for many decades. But taxpayers and benefactors are getting wise to a system that rakes in billions of tax dollars every year for putative scientific theories, such as Global Warming or Cholesterol Theory of Cardiovascular Disease, without definitive results that help the health and well-being of humankind. Cracks in the amyloid theory of dementia began forming in the late 1990s, coming into the public eye when a few articles questioning amyloid's role in dementia began appearing in scientific journals and major newspapers.[28],[29]

As an August 14, 2015, article by Makia Freeman points out, much of the scientific research today is untrustworthy and outright fraudulent.[30] Researchers are calling the amount of fraudulent scientific research "epidemic," while pharmaceutical companies rake in billions flooding the market with medicines that have marginal benefits and sometimes dangerous or even lethal effects.

Science and health industries make billions of extra profits vying for a piece of the "free money" coming from both state and federal government funding sources (i.e., the taxpayers). The result of this corporate dependency on public funding, scientific supplies, like medical costs inflated by generous health insurance payouts, become increasingly expensive as public funding skews market factors in both supply and demand. A simple tube of Crazy Glue one could find at a grocery store in the 1990s for 99 cents, sold for fifteen dollars in a popular science and technology supply catalog. Some research environments, such as universities, require funding to be spent from specific supply companies contracted to sell to laboratories for a discount. Technicians cannot simply go to the nearest store and buy that Crazy Glue for 99 cents unless they pay out of their own pockets!

Pop science is taking over serious studies by the media distorting the importance (or sometimes unimportance) of a study. In England, £300,000 were spent to determine that "ducks like water."[31] In the abstract of the paper published, we are

---

[28] Begley, Sharon, "Scientists World-Wide Battle a Narrow View of Alzheimer's." The Wall Street Journal, April 16, 2004. http://www.wsj.com/articles/SB108206188684384119

[29] Mandavilli, Apoorva, "The amyloind code." Nature Medicine 12:747-751 (2006)

[30] Freeman, Makia, "Most Scientific Research of Western Medicine Untrustable & Fraudulent, Say Insiders and Experts." Activist Post, August 14, 2015. http://www.activistpost.com/2015/08/most-scientific-research-of-western-medicine-untrustable-fraudulent-say-insiders-and-experts.html

[31] Morris, Steven, "Ducks like water study "waste of £300,000 taxpayers' money" The Guardian Wednesday 20, 2009. http://www.theguardian.com/science/2009/may/20/research-proves-ducks-like-water

[32] Jones, T.A.,*et al.*,2009. "Water off a duck's back: Showers and troughs match ponds for improving duck welfare." Applied Animal Behaviour Science 116(1):52-57.

[33] Cancer Statistics, National Cancer Institute. April 27, 2018. https://www.cancer.gov/about-cancer/understanding/statistics

confronted first to the humanitarian impact of making the soon-to-be dead ducks' lives better if given showers until fattened before slaughter! "The impact of production systems on the welfare of ducks grown for meat is becoming increasingly controversial. In the UK, approximately 18 million ducks (Anas platyrhynchos) were reared for meat in 2006."[32] Certainly the farmers and meat industry that have a vested fiduciary interest could have funded this study for far less than extracting funds from a seemingly bottomless pit afforded by taxpayers.

Worldwide, about 14 million people receive a positive diagnosis for cancer (2015), estimated to increase 68 *per centum* to 23.6 million by the year 2030.[33] Much of a rise in cancer is attributed to the fact that humans are living longer. Of the estimated eight billion inhabitants of Earth, this calculates to ~ 0.295 percent of the world population will develop cancer yearly by the year 2030. A little less than three-tenths of one percent worldwide! Much of these cancers could be averted by simple changes in lifestyle or diet. It hardly seems reasonable to spend billions of tax dollars every year for cancer research! And much of this research has developed chemotherapeutic drugs that increase patient survivability by only a few months, with some realization that some chemo drugs actually hasten mortality.

Science Funding Scam

Science funding has become a universally obscene source of income for research institution bureaucrats and administrators. Indirect costs are the infrastructure support for an institution not related directly to the actual research project funded. Direct costs are linked to the actual operation of the laboratory conducting the funded project. Indirect costs have skyrocketed compared to direct costs for laboratory research. The federal Government Accounting Office reported that "...for the fiscal years 2003 to 2012, indirect costs increased notably faster than direct costs, at 16.9 percent and 11.7 percent, respectively.[34] Indirect costs have become the golden goose for most cash-strapped institutions, both private companies and universities, as less and less money from funding actually goes to the laboratories.

It appears that the ice bucket challenges have raised nearly $80 million. Much is going to the ALS Association. Last year, only less than a third ended up in research and a fifth to community services (for patients), with the remaining 53% going to primarily salaries and advertisements. I saw this for years: Money being syphoned off research for administrative (indirect) costs, such as landscaping and bureaucratic

---

[34] GAO-13-760 report to the Ranking Member, Committee on the Budget, U.S.Senate "NIH Should Assess the Impact of Growth in Indirect Costs on Its Mission." September, 2013

boondoggles. The $1.9 million in administrative costs is primarily for about ten $100k+ salaries, the highest being around $350k. I hope the $80 million gets to research.

The National Aeronautics and Space Administration

The policies and many examples of military-corporate interests involved in space exploration obviate the fact that NASA has always existed for the purpose of militarizing space, or to propagandize the US state, such as the primary reason for going to the moon (to beat the Soviets). Writes Dr. Kathryn Muratore:

> *... the US is going to go to the moon (again) to prove what, exactly? If NASA makes it to the moon (again), will that somehow prevent China from going to the moon? (And what about India?)*
>
> *... NASA faces a five-year gap between the retirement of the space shuttle in 2010 and the first launch of Orion, the six- person craft that will carry astronauts to the International Space Station and eventually the moon. Obama has said he would like to narrow that gap, during which the U.S. will pay Russia to ferry astronauts to the station.*
>
> *While Russia is ferrying astronauts, Orbital and SpaceX will be ferrying cargo. I believe that, previously, private contractors built the rockets, but didn't oversee the missions, whereas Orbital and SpaceX will now run the missions.*
>
> *In regular lapses in common sense, pro-science people fail to connect federal spending on space missions with the warfare state (and isn't Obama the peace candidate?). And now, they cheer this spending as a way to save the economy. Why don't we pay these companies to buy a load of plasma TV's and take them to space to float away?*

Misinformation has Gone to Pot

> *The U.S. government believes that America is going to pot – literally.*
>
> *Earlier this month, the U.S. National Institute on Drug Abuse announced plans to spend $4 million to establish the nation's first-ever "Center on Cannabis Addiction," which will be based in La Jolla, Calif. The goal of the center, according to NIDA's press release, is to "develop novel approaches to the prevention, diagnosis and treatment of marijuana addiction."*
>
> *Not familiar with the notion of "marijuana addiction"? You're not alone. In fact, aside from the handful of researchers who have discovered that there are gobs of federal grant money to be had hunting for the government's latest pot boogeyman, there's little consensus that such a syndrome is clinically relevant – if it even exists at all.*
>
> *But don't try telling that to the mainstream press – which recently published headlines worldwide alleging, "Marijuana withdrawal rivals that of nicotine." The alleged "study" behind the headlines involved all of 12 participants, each of whom were longtime users of pot and tobacco, and assessed the self-reported moods of folks after they were*

randomly chosen to abstain from both substances. Big surprise: they
weren't happy.[35]

Accusation about marijuana's role in causing cancers and other health problems are based on assumptions that the war on drug tactics in Central and South America have not included introducing chemicals with known carcinogenic and immunomodulating properties. The fact is that we don't really know what the US government is spraying on the plants illicit drugs are derived. Reports of herbicides and a pathogenic fungus sprayed on plants cannot be confirmed due to layers of government security measures to obscure what it is really doing to the drug crops. But in "The largest study ever conducted on marijuana relevance to lung cancer," researchers found that "smoking marijuana does not cause lung cancer," no "matter how much or how often it is smoked."[36,37]   A University of California Los Angeles pulmonologist, Donald Tashkin, whose 30 years of research established a putative link between smoking pot and deleterious health effects, found recently that even with heavy smokers the incidence of the three cancers studied was not clearly significantly higher than those who didn't smoke cannabis.

The FDA Kills

The Chinese put melamine in the baby food shipped to the US and other countries. The Chinese regime, which essentially controls most means of production, quality control, and dispersal, must have known melamine was present in the baby food its manufacturers produced. Yet, people in the United States want more regulation to keep us "safe"!

Recently, our government suggests mercury for the youngsters is acceptable as long as it is in vaccines. Possibly if the US military quit dumping batteries and other junk in the oceans, we wouldn't have such a problem with mercury in our fish.[38, 39]

The Corrupt Center for Disease Control and Ebola

---

[35] Armentano, Paul, "Setting the Record Straight on Marijuana and Addiction"
http://www.lewrockwell.com/armentano-p/armentano-p24.html

[36] Acuff, Justin Study Demonstrates Smoking Pot Doesn't Cause Lung Cancer, No Matter the Frequency or Amount," May 15, 2013. http://www.addictinginfo.org/2013/05/15/study-smoking-pot-cause-lung-cancer/

[37] Kaufman, Marc, "Study Finds No Cancer-Marijuana Connection," Washington Post, May 26, 2006.

[38] Bluemink E. "Pollution runoff is eroding Alaska coast."   Anchorage Daily News January 19, 2008 http://www.adn.com/news/environment/story/287529.html

[39] Green, H. "BU prof and alum pioneer in coral reef ecology studies." The B.U. Bridge. October 19, 2001.

Government funding is a cash cow for technocrats. The recent Ebola fiasco during late summer and early fall of 2014 showed the world the nefarious nature of one more of the hundreds of entrenched federal bureaucracies. As Ebola slowly infiltrated and nearly spread through the United States, the CDC Director and others were complaining before Congress about the "lack of funding" from a previous sequestration of the federal budget. But investigators with the Washington Times revealed that while CDC officials complained about lack of funds, they had been given six billion dollars in salaries and 25 million dollars in bonuses over a period of seven years.[40]

Genetically Altered Food:

Millions of tax dollars are being paid to scientists and government researchers to understand why 90% of the honey bees in the US has been wiped out in a relatively short time. The hypothesis of this is based on the fact pollen containing the genes that encode resistance to insects transfected into food crops is consumed or carried by the bee. This genetically modified (GM) pollen is then transferred to the natural microflora residing in the gut of the bee. The microflora then has the ability to produce the insecticidal compound that kills its host, the bee, or infect other bees, in turn killing them.

A study in England has shown material from GM plants have been found in the honey of beehives located as far as two miles from plots used to study GM plants.[41] And there is reasonable concern about the effects pesticides have had on bee populations, which the FDA appears to "basic failure of regulatory bodies such as the EPA in representing the interests of the public," as netizen Kimberley Mok remarked on her website[42]

The giant chemical company Monsanto has been in the forefront of public investigations and exposures for years.[43] Recently,[44] Monsanto has been lobbying Congress to support bills that would destroy organic farming.

---

[40] Riddell, Kelly. "CDC doled out $25 million in bonuses while blaming cuts for Ebola outbreak." The Washington Times, October 16, 2014 http://www.washingtontimes.com/news/2014/oct/16/cdc-blames-cuts-for-ebola-response-pays-millions-i/

[41] The Sunday Times, September 15, 2002
http://www.timesonline.co.uk/tol/life_and_style/article1151919.ece   and
http://www.gmfoodnews.com/st150902.txt

[42] Kimberley D. Mok, .   "Photo Essay: Bees and Beekeepers In Crisis" http://www.treehugger.com/files/2008/12/bees-colony-collapse-disorder-kate-kunath.php   December 2, 1008

The Global Warming Hoax

> A mathematical model is neither a hypothesis nor a theory. Unlike scientific hypotheses, a model is not verifiable directly by an experiment. For all models are both true and false.... The validation of a model is not that it is "true" but that it generates good testable hypotheses relevant to important problems. (R. Levins, Am. Scientist 54:421-31, 1966)

There may be no bigger hoax perpetuated by scientists, primarily climatologists, as a lobbying tool for more government research funding, than the global warming (GW) theory. Of course, climatologists have a vested interest in an increase in this area of research.

Possibly, one of the most fitting rebuttals of an inane CNN[45] article that "informs" us about global climate change (warming, this week) that is causing a 0.006% increased global mortality comes from "Garrett":

> Global warming is happening! The Dinosaurs killed themselves due to global warming because the Brontosaurus and the T-Rex failed to negotiate climate treaties in Kyoto. Lets [sic] face it. T-Rex ran all over the place expelling greenhouse gases and the Brontosaurus ate all the green leaves off the trees. All of the other developing dinosaurs had to eat leaves and expel gases too!!! We are doomed! I wonder if there is a way to tell just how hot earth gets in its natural cycle over billions of years. Look at planet Venus. What was that planet like 3 gazillion trillion years ago? And what will it be like a bizillion million years from now? Nobody knows!!!!! This whole thing is a joke!!!. Global hoax. Shut up and go home I dont want to hear about it!!!! Let me know when the ice age starts I want to go bob sledding and hang out with the Abomidible [sic] Snowman. Oops sorry I meant Snowperson.

It is mind boggling to think people actually believe that so-called "experts" could really micromanage a planet's climate. They could no more do that than they could micromanage the universe! Governments around the world are plotting to

---

43   Jane Akre, "The Fox, The Hounds and the Sacred Cows," in, *Into the Buzzsaw: The Myth of a Free Press*, ed. Kristina Borjesson (Amherst, NY: Prometheus Books, 2002), pp. 37-63.

44   Linn Cohen-Cole, "Monsanto bills being rushed through Congress, set to destroy organic farming." Op Ed News online,   http://www.opednews.com/articles/Monsanto-bills-being-rushe-by-Linn-Cohen-Cole-090217-758.html

45   Whiteman, Hilary, "Report: Climate change crisis 'catastrophic'." CNN online May 29, 2009. http://www.cnn.com/2009/WORLD/europe/05/29/annan.climate.change.human/index.html

subject the world's economies to an international "carbon" tax, to collectivize our economies by governmental edicts and fees. To believe they could actually develop governmental programs to control as complex a system as global climate, even with the most powerful minds and computers, is seriously approaching the collective madness of kidnapping the moon for ransom. Is there, in fact, any governmental program that has ever succeeded in solving the societal problem the program was implemented to accomplish? Name one. Did the drug war get drugs off the streets the past 50 years? Did the War on Poverty improve prosperity for the poor? Or did it just trap the poor on the plantations of state assistance?

As President of the United States Barak Obama prepares for a 2015 climate convention in Paris, science politicians at National Aeronautics and Space Administration as well as National Oceanic and Atmospheric Administrations (NASA/NOAA) were "fixing" the data (what we call "messaging the data" with sardonic perturbation in real science circles) to fit the global warming propaganda being used to globally usher in a system of carbon taxes and trading, essentially creating a carboncentric economy based on a carbon currency standard.[46]   Writes Morgan Wright at Steven Goddard's blog at wordpress.com:[47]

> Some of the scientifically illiterate writers used by the Obama administration think that CO2 absorbs photons of IR and re-emits them, and calls "reflection." I saw Al Gore use this brain fart in his Inconvenient movie. He is a complete moron and anybody who thinks this actually happens is not a scientist. Not even close.

The war on poverty is failing miserably, as the rot of inflation and increased dependence on social programs, for both recipient and social worker, continue to impoverish more and more people every generation. Housing projects are now breeding grounds for vice, further expanding the need for law enforcement and the justice system required to enforce the ever-expanding laws to combat vice. Generations of families are trapped in an endless cycle of government subsidies, illegitimate kids, and the ghetto culture. As governments grow to "tackle these problems," inflation grows to pay for them, trapping the poor into chasing higher prices for simple necessities, like food and utilities. The United States is beginning to look more like the former Soviet Union every day.

[46] Rose, David, "Exposed: How world leaders were duped into investing billions over manipulated global warming data." Daily Mail, U.K., February 4, 2017. http://www.dailymail.co.uk/sciencetech/article-4192182/World-leaders-duped-manipulated-global-warming-data.html

[47] Goddard, Steven, "Biggest Fraud in Science History – The NASA/NOAA Surface Temperature Record." July 25, 2015 https://stevengoddard.wordpress.com/2015/07/25/biggest-fraud-in-science-history-the-nasanoaa-surface-temperature-record/

These are just a few examples of the horrible failures of government trying to micromanage society. So, what makes anyone think a massive program to reduce the "carbon footprint" and make the world all butterflies and rainbows would work? It wouldn't.

Fortunately, common sense is still thriving in the scientific community.[48] Carbon dioxide is an essential molecule for nearly all life to exist. Nature has a remarkable ability to regulate CO_2 by regulating the dynamics of conifer populations, for example.[49,50]

> Over 31,000 scientists have united against the political agenda of global warming. The scientific consensus, which includes over 9,000 scientists with Ph.D.s, supports the necessity of carbon dioxide and sheds light on the agenda of global warming, which includes industrial energy rationing, central economic planning, and global taxation schemes. These scientists are now _speaking out against the_ hoax of global warming and how global agreements to limit greenhouse gases are actually destructive to all plant and animal life on the planet.

Even seventh graders are getting wise to the GW myth. This is not necessarily a predicted phenomenon considering the constant bombardment of GW misinformation since day one of kindergarten. Writes a Boulder, Colorado, seventh grader Vivi Gregorich for her class presentation _Is Global Warming Real?_

> My purpose is to expose the tendency of people to believe what they're told without really thinking, using global warming as an example. And to offer solutions through raising awareness and educating the public. Now, more than ever is the time to think for ourselves, in this time of war, in this time of economic chaos, and in this time of environmental destruction.
>
> One of the main problems faced by the whole world is our unwillingness to think for ourselves. We just believe and accept what we're told by the government and the media. But have any of us considered that maybe what they tell us isn't really true? Probably not. Global warming is a huge example of that.
> ...
> According to Christopher Booker, in his "Review of 2008," temperatures have dropped considerably in the past few years. Also,

---

[48] Johnson, Lance D. "Over 31,000 scientists say global warming is a total hoax; now they're speaking out against junk science." Natural News. September 21, 2017

[49] Teatman, C.W. "CO2 enriched air increased growth of conifer seedlings." Forestry Chronicle 46(3):229-30, 1970.

[50] Tangley, Laura. "High CO2 Levels May Give Fast-Growing Trees an Edge." Science 292(5514):36-37. April 6, 2001.

North America received its greatest snow cover since 1966 (Christopher Booker). Arctic web site, Crysophere Today, reported that the Arctic ice volume increased 500,000 sq km from 2007 to 2008. Additionally, Antarctic sea-ice this year reached its highest level since satellite records began in 1979. Polar bear numbers are also at record levels (Crysophere today). And, Nasa's Goddard Institute for Space Studies, a respected research center in New York, made an analysis of surface air temperature measurements, and concluded that December 2007 to November 2008 was the coolest year since 2000. Their data also shows [sic] that the hottest decade of the 20th century was the 1930's, not the 1990's (Nasa's Goddard institute for space studies).[51]

Simple research - looking up the facts - brought this seventh grader to the conclusion that global warming probably is not occurring and that she has been misled by her authorities and the media.

Of course, Hollywood has jumped on the bandwagon with various alarmist movies and documentaries extolling the virtues of environmentalism and government solutions.[52] John Coleman, founder of The Weather Channel, called global warming science the "greatest scam in history."[53] For years environmentalists have been crying about warming of western Anartica as another proof of GW. Yet, British scientists that study the polar caps reported that there may be a "possible natural explanation found for West Antarctica's warming":

South Pole - In 2008, scientists from the British Antarctic Survey reported a layer of volcanic ash and glass shards frozen within an ice sheet in western Antarctica [the same place the one degree Fahrenheit warming has been reported]. The volcano beneath the ice sheet "punched a hole right through" due to its heat and force. This geologic event (a volcano) may prove to be the source of the recent warming seen in West Antarctica in what has otherwise been reported as a 50-year cooling trend seen in East Antarctica.

Dr. David G. Vaughan of the British Antarctic Survey said, "This is the first time we have seen a volcano beneath the ice sheet punch a hole through the ice sheet."[54]

---

[51]   Gregorish, V. "Is Global Warming Real?"   Blog at World Press. January 21, 2009 http://salonesoterica.wordpress.com/2009/01/21/is-global-warming-real/?preview=true&preview_id=3595&preview_nonce=5a51ec5587

[52]   Morgan, Gwyn. "Time to fight back against Hollywood's misinformation." The Globe and Mail, Inc. March 26, 2017

[53]   Sheppard, N. "Weather Channel Founder: Global Warming 'Greatest Scam in History'" IN; ICECAP   http://icecap.us/index.php/go/joes-blog/comments_about_global_warming/   November 11, 2007   and   http://newsbusters.org//blogs/noel-sheppard/2007/11/07/weather-channel-founder-global-warming-greatest-scam-history?q=blogs/noel-sheppard/2007/11/07/weather-channel-founder-global-warming-greatest-scam-history

[54]   Chang, K. "Scientists find active volcano in Antartica". January 12, 2008. http://www.nytimes.com/2008/01/21/world/21volcano.html?_r=2&refer=science

Because energy-efficient bulbs are more "complicated and energy-intense" they require four times the energy (4 kW) to produce than incandescent bulbs at one kW. Writes Kathryn Muratore, PhD about incandescent *vs.* the newer halogen bulbs:

> *Who wins in this battle of the politically-correct? Climate change, of course. The incandescent light bulb ban that I* <u>*blogged*</u> *about before is being fought by advocates for the* <u>*blind*</u>*. But, says the all-knowing bureaucrat, the blind can switch to (costly) halogen lights (which she fails to mention would require installing new fixtures) without losing the benefits of incandescent bulbs. She assures us that "the price will come down and technology will improve." Here I thought that prohibitions cause price increases and slow innovation.*[55]

---

55   http://www.lewrockwell.com/blog/lewrw/archives/025000.html

MEDICAL-INDUSTRIAL COMPLEX

*We're going to be gifted with a healthcare plan we are forced to
purchase, and fined if we don't, which purportedly covers at least 10
million more people, without adding a single new doctor, but provides
for 16,000 new IRS agents needed to oversee the program, written by a
committee whose chairman says he doesn't understand it, passed by a
congress that didn't read it but exempted themselves from it, and signed
by a president who smokes, with funding administered by a treasury
chief who didn't pay his taxes, for which we will be taxed for four years
before any benefits take effect, by a government which has already
bankrupted social security and Medicare, all to be overseen by a surgeon
general who is obese and by a country that's broke.*
– Dr. Barbara Bellar on the Affordable Care Act

The health industry is in perpetual crisis. Science in general is on a collision course with mercantilism that will lead society, and probably the whole world as connected as it is today, into another Dark Age of uncontrolled epidemics and technologies. Even mass murder is possible as states, acting despotically for the holistic interests of the powerful, use technologies to tyrannize the rest by undermining the rights and liberties of the individual mundane. More and more today we are seeing a medical police state where governments, and the medical establishment they protect, push vaccines and other drugs onto a naive public by using scientific disinformation carefully constructed to convey a rational, utilitarian purpose, while conning people into mass acceptance of these nefarious "health" programs. At the same time, federal and state governments conveniently hold licenses over the heads of physicians to require them to prescribe expensive drugs and other remedies in a make-work program for drug companies and research facilities.

Writes Heather Callaghan:[56]

> *A push for mandatory vaccination continues as SB277 makes its way through California's Capitol. It is a shining monument to Big Pharma's coffers and medical control as the bill removes religious and philosophical exemptions for student vaccination, leaving only medical exemptions signed by MDs. Since medical exemptions are rare, it forces parents to take their child into the doctor's [sic] for jabs or be removed from school - a violation of the right to attend public school.*

The Sacramento Bee found that 29 California lawmakers, nine of twenty members of the Assembly or Senate health committees, received donations from drug companies ranging from $33,100 to $95,150.[57] The author of the bill, Sen. Richard Pan (D-Sacramento), is a medical doctor. Pharmaceutical companies the likes of GlaxoSmithKline and Abbott Laboratories & Co, Inc. have spent millions more in direct lobbying payments pushing legislation favorable to the biotech and pharmaceutical companies at the expense of the health and financial well-being of the residents of California. Senate Bill 277 passed and was signed into law by Governor Jerry Brown. The law went into effect July of 2016.

America is not really a capitalist country. On average Americans pay 47% of their yearly incomes in taxes (e.g., property tax, income tax, sales tax). Wealthy people pay a higher percentage as they make more money and buy more luxurious property (e.g. boats, summer homes). Maybe the problem isn't capitalism but instead socialism. Healthcare has become expensive because it is monopolized by government regulations. You want antibiotics? Well, shell out $200 first for a doctor to write a mandatory prescription for an expensive, regulated, monopolized drug that you can't get over the counter. People wonder why healthcare is so expensive. And who wrote Obamacare? Surprise, surprise, the insurance and medical/pharmaceutical industries! It really is a race to the bottom for the rest of us.

The whole concept of prescription drugs is to keep the money flowing to Big Pharma and Big Medicine. It has little to do with "protecting" people. If you want a prescribed drug, you first must go to a physician to get the prescription; see how

---

[56] Callaghan, Heather. "Forced Vaccine Bill Author Se. Pan Wins Top Recipient of Big Pharma Cash." June 23, 2015. http://www.activistpost.com/2015/06/forced-vaccine-bill-author-sen-pan-was.html

[57]   Miller, Jim. "Drug Companies donated millions to California lawmakers before vaccine debate." Sacramento Bee (online), June 18, 2015.

that works? My wife and I took our daughter to the doctor for what we suspected to be pink eye. By the time we reached the examination room, our daughter's problem had already been diagnosed by both the woman at the reception desk and the nurse who checked our daughter's temperature and blood pressure. In a free society, we could have skipped the doctor visit, saving hundreds of dollars and time off from work, and drove to the pharmacy or department store to buy a special topical antibiotic off the shelf. Instead, we were forced to spend $200 for a doctor to tell us what we already knew. Most laws are made to protect the financial interests of lobbyists and one group or another they represent. When I have a headache, I drive to the store and buy some aspirin. But if I have an internal infection, I am first required to go to a doctor, spending hundreds of dollars for the office call, and possibly tests, to get a prescription for antibiotics. Because the antibiotics are strictly controlled, they are far more expensive than aspirin, although both are equally as dangerous if not utilized correctly.

Government regulations in this way have increased the cost of healthcare while making the medical system more and more dangerous.[58] In a well-researched analysis of literature reporting injuries and deaths caused by government-sanctioned medicine, Dr. Gary Null and colleagues found an appallingly high amount of mortality caused by the U.S. medical system. More patients died in the hands of healthcare workers than from heart attacks or cancer![29] In this study they found that nearly 800,000 patients died from conventional medical mistakes, while about 700,000 died from heart disease and 550,000 from cancer. The economic costs from these medical mistakes amount to over a quarter-trillion dollars, no less the human cost.

To add fuel to the fire, U.S. patients now must deal with the Affordable Care Act (ACA). Affectionately (or not) called "Obamacare" by the various proponents and opponents in the media, the ACA was voted into law in 2010 and signed by President Barrack Obama. Passed without a single vote from Republican representatives or senators, and 34 House Democrats voting against it, the ACA forces all American adults into the medical system by requiring them to purchase healthcare insurance or pay a fee (ruled a "tax" by the Supreme Court). Proponents of the ACA have argued that 40,000 people die every year from lack of affordable healthcare. So, while nearly a million people die every year from medical mistakes, proponents argue that too many people are dying for lack of medical care?

---

[58] Null, Gary, *et al.* 2004, "Death by Medicine," http://www.webdc.com/pdfs/deathbymedicine.pdf

After inception of the ACA, millions of people around the country began losing their medical plans or were forced to pay higher premiums to the health insurance companies. A few years into the ACA, it became clear that the health insurance companies, which lobbied Congress heavily for favorable legislation, were guaranteed extraordinary fiduciary gains as a result of their lobbying efforts.[59,60] Today we are discovering that the many "miracles" of science are really far more dangerous than the ancient remedies the modern despotic class outlawed decades ago. Other than some chemotherapeutic drugs for cancer and microbial infections, that actually remedy the disease, most drugs are designed to treat the symptoms. With the discovery of cholesterol-lowering drugs in the 1960s, a media blitz emerged in our society warning people of the dangers of cholesterol. Drugs were advertised on TV and in magazines. Doctors pushed the prescriptions, and everyone was promised would add years to their lives, protecting them from stroke and heart attack. The swine flu "epidemic" in the 1970s brought hundreds of millions in sales to shareholders of pharmaceuticals involved. This was an "epidemic flu" shot that sickened hundreds of people and killed twenty-five in the US alone.[61] Only one person died from the virus, but twenty-five died from the vaccine. That's a 25:1 ratio!

The fraudulent hype and commercialism foisted on society by these pharmaceutical charlatans make the term "snake-oil salesman" seem an innocent prank by comparison. Much of this is only coming to light, thankfully, since the Information Age of the Internet and the use of powerful computers for meta-analysis of a multitude of both demographic and biochemical data.

The pharmaceutical cartel

The 1930s began the establishment of a pharmaceutical cartel by the wealthiest of the oil industry.[62] Within a few generations, this cartel had overwhelming control of the health, pharmaceutical, even a good share of the food industries in the United States.

---

[59] Lenzer, Robert. 2013. "ObamaCare Enriches Only The Health Insurance Giants and Their Shareholders." Forbes. http://www.forbes.com/sites/robertlenzner/2013/10/01/obamacare-enriches-only-the-health-insurance-giants-and-their-shareholders/

[60] Salerno, Joeseph T. 2014. "What You Were Never Told About Obamacare." Mises Institture, January 14, 2014. http://mises.org/blog/what-you-were-never-told-about-obamacare

[61] "1976 Swine Flu Outbreak," http://en.wikipedia.org/wiki/1976_swine_flu_outbreak

[62] Fraser, Ivan and Beeston, Mark. "The Brotherhood. Part 9: The Pharmaceutical Racket." http://www.educate-yourself.org/nwo/brotherhoodpart9.shtml

In the early half of this century the petrochemical giants organised a coup on the medical research establishments, hospitals and universities. The Rockefellers did this by sponsoring research and donating monetary gifts to US universities and medical schools where research was drug based and further extended this policy to foreign medical establishments via their International Education Board. Those who were not drug based were refused funding and were soon dissolved in favour of the more lucrative pharmaceutical-based projects.

In 1939 the 'Drug Trust' alliance was formed by the Rockefeller Empire and I.G. Farben. After the war, I.G. Farben was dismantled but later emerged in the many guises of the companies with whom they had signed cartel agreements. These companies include: Imperial Chemical Industries (ICI), Borden, Carnation, General Mills, M.W. Kellogg Co., Nestle, Pet Milk, Squibb and Sons, Bristol Meyers, Whitehall laboratories, Procter and Gamble, Roche, Hoechst and Beyer and Co. (two extant pharmaceutical companies who initially employed convicted war criminals Friedrich Jaehne and Fritz ter Meer as board chairmen). The Rockefeller Empire – in tandem with the Chase Manhattan Bank now owns over half of the USA's pharmaceutical interests and is the largest drug manufacturing combine in the world. Since the war the drug industry has steadily netted an ever increasing profit from sales of drugs to become the second largest manufacturing industry in the world next to the arms industry (also owned by the self same Elite agencies).

Today, health care is a multi-billion pound industry world-wide with ever increasing expenditure by taxpayers into the system which funnels the majority of this staggering profit into the hands of the drug manufacturers who are, as we have seen, headed by the major Elite manipulators of this century. These companies now control the vast majority of health care and set the standards for the practice of medicine in all developed countries. Doctors are no longer free to choose the most reliable and safe forms of therapy available but are at the mercy of their financial reliance on sponsoring (frequently bribing) drug companies. Once out of drug-company (sic) sponsored medical school, doctors embark on a career of increasing workloads and have ever increasing amounts of new pharmaceutical products to use and understand. The sheer volume of literature which a GP will receive from drug sales reps has resulted in the present situation whereby GPs are poorly educated about the chemicals which they are giving to their patients and are essentially gleaning most of their post-graduate training from the salesmen of private business. The moral implications of this are staggering.

Cardiovascular Disease and the Decades-Old Cholesterol Scam

Obstetrician-gynecologist McGee has been in general practice in Ecuador and China as well as the U.S., and his overseas experience included epidemiology and health statistics in rural areas where people live on simple foods. The title of his book arises from his insistence that more than 80 percent of angiograms and heart bypass surgeries are unnecessary. He also argues that cholesterol isn't as major a factor in provoking heart attacks as it is made out to be, and that advertising and greed are among the main forces driving many drug companies and much of medical practice to say that it is. This isn't the ivory-tower spouting of a fanatic, for, whatever one may think of his satire and sarcasm, some of which is very clever, McGee knows the medical literature and thoroughly documents his points from the contents of reputable journals. He blasts some fresh air through modern medicine and blows away some of its profitable sacred cows.[63]

Possibly one of the worst of medical-scientific-industrial swindles for profit ever perpetuated in modern times is the cholesterol theory of heart disease, along with the proliferation (and profiteering) of statin drugs. For example, studies conducted in the past 20 years have shown that there is a lack of evidence for low-density lipoprotein (LDL, the "bad" cholesterol) treatment to target risk of cardiovascular events.[64] "For those with LDL cholesterol levels less than 3.36 mmol/L (<130 mg/dL), the authors found no clinical trial subgroup analyses or valid cohort or case-control analyses suggesting that the degree to which LDL cholesterol responds to a statin independently predicts the degree of cardiovascular risk reduction."

A striking report just published in the *New England Journal of Medicine* indicates the accumulation of calcium in coronary arteries, and not cholesterol, more accurately predicts a future heart attack or other heart trouble, far more than cholesterol or other standard risk factors.

This report gives evidence of a major misdirection by modern medicine – the creation of cholesterol phobia in the population at large. Prior studies show use of cholesterol-lowering drugs does not reduce mortality rates for coronary artery disease. This report follows a front-page report in *Business Week* magazine declaring cholesterol-lowering drugs to be of marginal value.

The traditional diet-heart hypothesis predicts that lowering serum cholesterol by diet replacement of animal fat with vegetable oil rich in linoleic acid will 1) reduce cholesterol deposition on arterial walls, 2) slow progression of atherosclerosis, 3) reduce heart events and 4) improve survival. Although a causal effect has been established that vegetable fat diets indeed lower cholesterol, no study has confirmed that reducing cholesterol definitively reduces cardiovascular disease. A recent study

---

[63] McGee, Charles T. *Heart Frauds: Uncovering the Biggest Health Scam in History.* (Piccadilly Books, Colorado Springs, 1993) ISBN-13: 978-0941599566

[64] Hayward, R.A., *et al.* (2006) "Narrative Review: Lack of Evidence for Recommended Low-Density Lipoprotein Treatment Targets: A Solvable Problem." Annals of Internal Medicine, 145(7):520-530. http://www.annals.org/cgi/reprint/145/7/520.pdf

in the British Medical Journal[65] of unpublished data from the Minnesota Coronary Experiment showed that although an intervention diet of vegetable fat substitution for animal fat significantly reduced serum cholesterol by 13.8 percent, "(t)here was a 22% higher risk of death for each 30 mg/dL (0.78 mmol/L) reduction in serum cholesterol in covariate adjusted Cox regression models..."!

Statins are the single-most profitable medication in magic pill-mills of Big Pharma. As Natural News editors reported, "A recent study found nearly 100% of men and 62% of women aged 66-75 should take a statin medication even if their cholesterol level is normal.

A number of bad effects from long-term statin use have come to light in recent years, including cognitive problems,[66,67] peripheral nerve damage,[68] possible liver and kidney toxicity, reduced steroid hormone synthesis,[69] and depletion of essential nutrients and metabolic factors. By lowering cholesterol, statins can have deleterious effect on human health by depletion of vitamin D, D_3 specifically, an essential vitamin in bone and teeth health as well as immune and cardiovascular support. Vitamin D is synthesized in the body from the sterol cholesterol. Reducing cholesterol concomitantly reduces Vitamin D synthesis.

Orchestrated Pandemic Hysteria

"Within my long lifetime, **its ruthless enforcement throughout Europe ended in two of the worst epidemics of smallpox in record**, our former more dreaded typhus and cholera epidemics having meanwhile been ended by sanitation. After that failure, the credit of vaccination was saved for a while by the introduction of isolation, which at once produced improved figures. At present, intelligent people do not have their children vaccinated, nor does the law now compel them to. The result is not, as the Jennerians prophesied, the extermination of the human race by smallpox; on the contrary more people are now killed by vaccination than by smallpox."---George Bernard Shaw (August 9, 1944, the *Irish Times*)[70]

[65] Ramsden, C.E. *et al.* (2016) "Re-evaluation of the traditional diet-heart hypothesis: analysis of recovered data from Minnesota ACoronary Experiment (1968-73)." 353:1-17.

[66] Graveline, Duane, MD, MPH, Low Cholesterol and Cognitive Problems. October 2011. http://www.spacedoc.com/articles/low-cholesterol-cognitive-effects

[67] Natural News Editors, "Statins cause brain dysfuntion." December 23, 2014. http://www.naturalnews.com/048087_statins_brain_dysfunction_cholesterol.html

[68] Statin Drugs. GreenMedInfo, http://www.greenmedinfo.com/toxic-ingredient/statin-drugs?ed=35335

[69] Metzler, David. *Biochemistry: The Chemical Reactions of Living Cells* (Academic Press, London, 1977).

Shaw was particularly adamant about his opposition to vaccination calling it "a peculiarly filthy piece of witchcraft".[71] Apparently, this has been going on for some time. In December of 1775, General George Washington sent John Hancock a letter in part with disturbing information Washington heard from an American sailor.[72] According to the sailor, a besieged British general, William Howe, was sending Boston civilians out of their city infected with the Smallpox virus, hoping the virus would spread through the American troops. The country would be plagued by smallpox, taking the lives of over 130,000 North Americans during the American war for independence.[73]

David Rockefeller, Chairman of The Rockefeller Group and one of the richest people in the world, has stated that infant mortality has decline by 60% from 40 years ago, and life expectancy has increased from 46 years old in the 1950s to 63 years old today. [74,75] Of course, these are old data. Life expectancy in the United Sates is close to 80 years old now at the turn of the 21st century. According to Rockefeller at that time world population will have risen geometrically to 8 billion by 2020. He was right about that. In 2015 the human population is about 7.3 billion. This is a problem for Rockefeller by virtue of his concern for depletion of resources, such as energy and water. He believes because of widespread industrialization there should be calls for international cooperation to combat the problem of over-population. "The UN can and should play an essential role in helping the world find a satisfactory way of stabilizing world population and stimulating economic development in a manner that is sensitive to religious and moral considerations." Ironically, some of the most invasive of ecocentric social engineering of modern mankind has come from the meddling billionaire corporatists and their well-funded foundations.   Further, comrade Rockefeller suggests that "without careful coordination, unrestrained economic growth poses further threat to our environment"

---

[70]   Shaw, George Bernard (August 9, 1944, the *Irish Times)*

[71]   Shaw, George Bernard Sixteen Self Sketches (Dodd, Mead, 1949).

46   Document for December 4th: Letter from General George Washington to John Hancock, President of Congress, 12/04/1775 http://www.archives.gov/historical-docs/todays-doc/index.html?dod-date=1204

47   Fenn, Elizabeth Anne. *Pox Americana: The Great Smallpox Epidemic of 1775-82.* (Hill and Wang, New York, 2001).

[74]   Cuddy, Dennis PhD. DIALECTICS, ROCKEFELLERS, AND POPULATION CONTROL November 27, 2006   http://www.newswithviews.com/Cuddy/dennis84.htm.

[75]   David   Rockefeller   talks   about   Population   Control.   March   8,   2008. http://www.liveleak.com/view?i=824_1205035963

Years ago, population control was the answer, although some countries such as the United States had seen some of the slowest growth since the Great Depression.[76] And as for the most populated country on Earth, China's horrendous policy of population control by abortion and infanticide has resulted in a shortage of labor pools for its exploding economic expansion! So now Rockefeller and other billionaires have turned to climate change, gun control and other media-concocted maladies of human existence Of course this is a job for intergovernmental policies, or better yet for them, a One World Government to tackle the crisis of the month, and best not be left alone to individuals and the magic hand of free markets to solve.

That was then. This is now. Every now and then a pathogenic virus, or bacterium, is unleashed that sickens thousands and sometimes millions before the right measures are taken to combat it. Most of the time the target hosts' immune system adjusts to protect the hosts. Sometimes the pathogen will evolve less resistance to cytokinesis to the detriment of itself. Wars too will be concocted to thin the herd.

Unfortunately, as usually is the case, government regulation and edicts end up doing the opposite of protecting the population. And, typically, governments use disease to control the population. It is really that simple. Government propaganda, filtered through its sycophantic national, corporate media, inadvertently contradict itself about health issues. One day, on two different stations, I first heard former vice president Al Gore inform us that as the earth's climate *changes*, which he believes will be in a warmer direction, or Global Warming, viral infectivity will radiate out from the equatorial populations to upper and lower hemispheric populations. Of course, this is ridiculous. Acute influenza outbreaks, for instance, become more prevalent in the winter months when populations are exposed to less sunlight and more intemperate conditions.

But even more entertaining than that was shortly after on ABC News that same morning, the network's blabbering Barbie doll tells us that viruses die off in summer months and is worse in the winter. Astonishingly, Barbie got it right! But didn't an expert theologian of Global Climate Change orthodoxy, Al Gore, tell us that as the earth warms up so will the viruses?

Medical advances and better health within the population makes a pandemic unlikely. But that doesn't mean the various governments will use the threat of

---

[76] "US population growth slowest since Great depression." The Economic Times, January 1, 2013. http://articles.economictimes.indiatimes.com/2013-01-01/news/36094128_1_population-growth-census-figures-census-bureau

infectious diseases to consolidate power.   Vaccines are generally mandated, especially for children, by governmental health agencies, despite the risks of serious side-effects and death. And with the help of mass media, governments have little resistance to herding the masses to the clinics for shots.

A number of untested vaccines, such as for anthrax and small pox, given to troops going off to fight the Persian Gulf War against Iraq had been thought to be the cause of the general malaise commonly known as Gulf War Syndrome, from which possibly as many as 200,000 military personnel from that era are known to be suffering, attributed to disease associated with these experimental vaccines, or possibly the anti-nerve agent drug they took. [77]

Vaccines, Autism[78] and the Great Vaccine Epidemic

Most people will tell you that we need government to protect people from force and fraud by the dark forces of our society. Now imagine a corruption and cover up within a government agency involving something so unimaginable that people everywhere would demand at the very least a congressional investigation into the allegations. Think there wouldn't be an immediate call for a relevant committee hearing into the charges? Think again.

Early in 2015, Dr. William Thompson, Senior Scientist for the Center for the Center for Disease Control, reported that a whistleblower came forward with allegations of a cover up at the CDC to hide data from a study showing that African-American boys younger than 36 months who received the MMR vaccine had a significantly higher risk for autism. The scientist Thompson relayed this whistleblower's story to Florida representative Bill Posey (R) who tried to move House leadership to hear testimony in a relevant committee session but had to settle for sharing the information on the House floor:[79]

> *I rise today on matters of scientific integrity and research. To begin*
> *with, I am absolutely, resolutely, pro-vaccine. Advancements in medical*
> *immunization have saved countless and greatly benefitted public*

[77]   Verger, Rob. "For Soldiers With Gulf War Illness, a Clue to the Mystery in Their Cells." Newsweek March 29, 2014.   http://www.newsweek.com/sick-soliders-gulf-war-illness-clue-mystery-their-cells-238850

[78]   Kirby, D.   "The Next Big Autism Bomb: Are 1 in 50 kids potentially at risk?" Huffington Post, March 26, 2008.   http://www.huffingtonpost.com/david-kirby/the-next-big-autism-bomb_b_93627.html

[79]   Adl-Tabatabai, Sean." CDD Say They Destroyed Documents that Prove Vaccines Cause Autism." Investment Watch, July 30, 2015 http://investmentwatchblog.com/cdc-say-they-destroyed-documents-that-prove-vaccines-cause-autism/

health. That being said, it's troubling to me that in a recent Senate hearing on childhood vaccinations, it was never mentioned that our government has paid out over $3 billion through a vaccine injury compensation program for children who have been injured by vaccinations.

Regardless of the subject matter, parents making decisions about their children's health deserve to have the best information available to them. They should be able to count on federal agencies to tell them the truth. For these reasons, I bring the following matter to the House floor.

In August 2014, Dr. William Thompson, a senior scientist at the Centers for Disease Control and Prevention, worked with a whistleblower attorney to provide my office with documents related to a 2004 CDC study that examined the possibility of a relationship between [the] mumps, measles, rubella vaccine and autism. In a statement released in August, 2014, Dr. Thompson stated, 'I regret that my co-authors and I omitted statistically significant information in our 2004 article published in the journal Pediatrics.

A re-examination of the vaccine-autism link, published in *Translational Neurodegeneration* (2014), revealed that African-American boys vaccinated for measles, mumps and rubella earlier than 36 months of age were at a significantly higher risk for developing autism.[80] An interesting study has emerged showing that populations of vaccine-free children have not experienced problems with autism[81]

In 2016, an explosive article by Kevin Galalae was published in Epidemiology open access that demonstrates the coordinated effort by the United Nations and industrial nations in the West to drastically reduce human populations in third-world countries of the African continent and elsewhere.[82,83]

All epidemics and pandemics of the past 30 years are fabrications of the UN system and its partners in crime at the national level for the purpose of lowering births below the magic line of replacement level fertility and, more recently, also for limiting life to an economically acceptable and environmentally sustainable age.

---

[80]   Hoooker, Brian S. 2014. "Measles-mumps-rubella vaccination timing and autism among young african american boys: a reanalysis of CDC data." *Translational Neurodegenration* 3(16):1-6.

[81]   Dan Olmstead."The Age of Autism:'A pretty big secret.'" United Press Iinternational, Consumer Health   Daily   .,   Dec.   7,   2005. http://www.upi.com/NewsTrack/Health/2005/12/07/the_age_of_autism_a_pretty_big_secret/6829

[82]   Galalae K (2016) "Turning Nature against Man: The Role of Pandemics, Vaccines and Genetics in the UN's Plan to Halt Population Growth." Epidemiology Open Access (Sunnyvale) 6: 232. doi:10.4172/2161-1165.1000232

[83] Frompovich, Kathryn, "There's A Plan for Human Population Control – Is it Vaccines?" Natural Blaze online, April 29, 2016. http://www.naturalblaze.com/2016/04/theres-a-plan-for-human-population-control-is-it-vaccines.html

Vaccines are big money for the pharmaceutical companies that patent and produce them. Because the government passively requires vaccines in children (before they enter the school system) Big Pharma stands to gain an endless market of vaccine recipients for their expensive drugs.   Adding to that, health insurance companies have given their insurance clients lucrative incentives to get as many vaccines as possible.   Extrapolating data from a study published in *Archives of Pediatric and Adolescent Medicine*,[84] "Blue Cross will give your pediatrician $400 per child that has received 100% of the 25 vaccines they recommend by the age of 2...Pediatric practices, according to this study, average 1,546 patients per doctor. This means that a 5-doctor pediatric practice, if they reach 100% compliance on vaccinations, will receive a bonus of just over $3,000,000."[85] As pediatrician Bob Zajac told Minnesota state legislators, "It's absolutely true that you make a ton of money off of vaccines .... I lose $700,000 a year because I don't make every kid vaccinate."[86]

A new vaccine against the human papillomavirus (HPV) that goes by the name GARDASIL has been recently fast-tracked by FDA. According to Dr. Kim Mulvihill,[87] "a federal reporting system has received more than 5, 000 reports of adverse events, a small percent of them serious, following GARDASIL vaccination.   However (of course), a report does not mean the vaccine caused the problem.

In a surprising confession at the 4th International Conference on Vaccination in Reston, Virginia, Dr. Diane Harper "a leading expert responsible for the Phase II and Phase III safety and effectiveness studies which secured the approval of the human papilloma virus (HPV) vaccines, Gardasil™ and Cervarix™," informed her audience that Gardasil provides little protection against cervical cancer, that "in the U.S. [it] is already extremely low and that vaccinations are unlikely to have any effect upon the rate of cervical cancer.[88]

Another vaccine that is getting the scrutiny it deserves is the new shingles vaccine given to the elderly to control *Herpes zoster*. In a letter[89] to American Family

---

[84] Bocian, A.B., *et. al,* "Size and age-sex distribution of pediatric practice: a study from Pediatric Research in Office Settings." Arch. Pediatr. Adolesc. Med. Jan:153(1):9-14.

[85] Vaccine money incentive quotes. http://www.whale.to/vaccine/quotes15.html

[86] Vid. https://www.facebook.com/wearevaxxed/videos/359946507685965/

[87] Mulvihill, K. "GARDASIL Vaccine Turns Girl into a Gimp?" The National Expositor, May 21, 2008, http://www.nationalexpositor.com/News/1239.html

[88]   The Daily Sheeple, January 6th, 2014. http://www.thedailysheeple.com/lead-developer-of-hpv-vaccines-comes-clean-warns-parents-young-girls-its-all-a-giant-deadly-scam_012014

Physician Journal, David Brownstein, MD, addressed a serious and confounding interpretation of the data reported in the study in a recent study of over 52,000 patients regarding the effectiveness of the vaccine in older adults.

> However, reading the section titled Practice Pointers presented a different picture. In this section, the author states that, over a median surveillance period of 3.12 years, with over 52,000 participants, there was a 51% relative risk reduction in confirmed cases of herpes zoster in those that received the vaccine. Furthermore, the author stated that among those aged 60-69, the number needed to treat to prevent one case of shingles was 50. Among those 70 years and older, the number needed to treat was 100.
>
> These numbers show that, in those aged 60-69, the shingles vaccine was ineffective for 98% (forty-nine out of fifty) of those studied. For those aged 70 and older, the vaccine was 99% ineffective, since 99 out of 100 received no benefit.
>
> I am incredulous that anyone looking at this data could proclaim that the shingles vaccine was effective. In fact, it wasn't. According to this data, the shingles vaccine was a 98-99% failure.

A study of more than 3,500 Group Health patients (ages 65 to 94), the largest case-control study to date, showed no significant protection from influenza vaccination to pneumonia, adding fuel to the controversy about how effective flu vaccine protects the elderly.[90]

Some people scoff at the charges of "Health Nazis" when rebuking coercion by the pharmaceutical and health industries' attempts to lobby politicians to enact laws that benefit the industries. They fall into the one shoe covers all feet argument when they insist that the polio vaccine "irradicated" a horrible childhood disease, therefore all vaccines should be utilized to control every pathogenic virus. Nothing could be more blatant and obvious than Merck's latest attempt to use government to force people to use its human papillomavirus   vaccine.

A study published in 1997 of mortality rates in England/Wales between 1838 and 1980 reveal a natural decline in five major infectious diseases before vaccines were introduced (Figure 2). Interestingly, when a more stringent smallpox vaccination law was passed in 1897, the rate of deaths per 100,000 people increased sharply three times over a span of about 22 years before falling at a similar rate the other diseases fell. An internal control, scarlet fever, for which there has never been a vaccine developed, dropped at about the same rate as the other diseases. Better knowledge of sanitation and better nutrition, along with natural immunity to disease, are thought

---

[89] Brownstein, David, "Should you get a shingles vaccine?" November 14, 2013. Dr, Brownstein's Holistic Medicine, http://blog.drbrownstein.com/should-you-get-a-shingles-vaccine/

[90] Flu Vaccine may not Protect Seniors Well. August 4, 2008. Science Daily,

to be the underlying solutions for a downward trend in mortality rates in England during these years. Notice that the pertusis and measles vaccines were developed and distributed at a time when the two diseases were nearly wiped out by natural immunity.

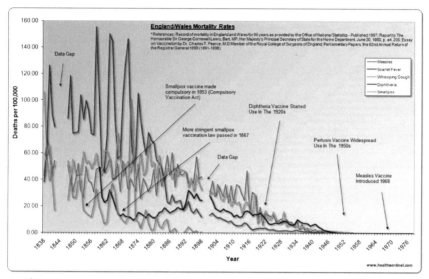

Figure 2

As with England, in the United States (Figure 3) between 1900 and 1965, diphtheria deaths per 100,000 after vaccinations declined coincidentally with the natural decline of typhoid deaths. And like England/Wales data, all disease deaths decline similarly with scarlet fever for which there was no vaccination.

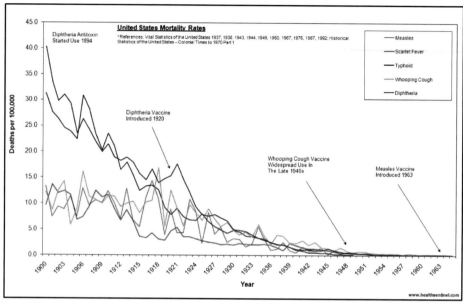

Figure 3

Caution: Chemotherapy May be Hazardous to Your Health

German scientists from Friedrich–Schiller University in Jena dropped a bombshell during the 27th San Antonio Breast Cancer Symposium when they reported that the gold standard of cancer drugs, taxol, may actually induce metastasis in patients who receive the drug.[91]

> Such a release of cancer cells would result in extensive metastasis months or even years later, long after the chemo would be suspected as the cause of the spread of the cancer. This little known horror of conventional cancer treatment needs to be spread far and wide, but it is not even listed in the side effects of taxol.

Writes author Tony Isaacs, for Natural News:[92]

---

[91]   27th Annual San Antonio Breast Cancer Symposium, (abstract 6014) "Conventional Cancer Treatments" alternativecancer.us/conventional.htm "Hiding the Truth about Losing the War on Cancer" http://tbyil.com/waroncancer.htm

[92]   Isaacs, Tony, "Chemo Does Not Cure: Often It Inflicts Damage and Spreads *Cancer*," NaturalNews.com,   September   15,   2009. http://www.naturalnews.com/027028_cancer_health_cancer_cells.html

> First of all, though survival rates are slightly higher for the first couple of years compared to those who opted out of chemo, after the third year the survival rate for those who opted out is greater than those who were treated with chemo and the gap widens significantly every year after that.

> Secondly, and perhaps most important of all, the survival rates compare all of those who either undergo chemotherapy or decide against it. That includes the very large number of people who do little or nothing to address their cancer naturally and merely forego chemo. If chemo survival rates were compared with those of people who not only opted out of chemo, but also chose a non-invasive natural protocol to eliminate the toxins and other causes of cancer, to boost their immune systems and to attack the cancer naturally without inflicting damage to the rest of the body, there would surely be no comparison.

Any bets this news was not circulated through the mainstream news networks and publications? Of course, news like this would send shockwaves not only throughout the news world but also the medical communities, as patients begin questioning the efficacy of these poisons in their bodies already wrecked by cancer. Billions of dollars a year are exchanged for the production and distribution of these highly toxic chemotherapeutic drugs, despite increasing evidence that these drugs do little to "cure" cancer, and many times do more harm and expedite the patients' demise.

Additionally, honest oncologists will tell you that cancer patients spend an inordinate, and unnecessary, amount of money during their terminal stages. I have been told the majority of money spent by patients and their insurance companies is during the final weeks to few months before their deaths. Fortunately for cancer patients, a new generation of anti-cancer drugs are coming to fruition that modulate the patient's immune system to attack the cancer without all the side effects of toxic chemotherapeutic drugs.

The Medical Industry's War on Herb

Turned-off cannabinoid receptor turns on colorectal tumor growth
Researchers find CB1 suppresses tumors, a new potential path for treatment, prevention
Raymond DuBois, M.D., Ph.D. Provost and Executive Vice President at. M. D. Anderson Cancer Center[93].

Cannabinoids Offer Novel Option For Treatment of Brain Cancer, Study Says. Busto Arsivo, Italy: Cannabinoids possess

---

[93] http://www.eurekalert.org/multimedia/pub/9366.php?from=118901http://www.eurekalert.org/multimedia/pub/9366.php?from=118901

anti-tumor activity in glioblastoma cell lines and may offer a new therapeutic option for the treatment of brain cancer, according to a *review* published in the January issue of the journal Expert Review of Neurotherapeutics.

Investigators at the University of Insurbia, Center of Neuroscience, wrote: "[C]annabinoids have been shown to exert antiproliferative effects on a wide spectrum of cells in culture. Of interest, cannabinoids have displayed a great potency in reducing glioma tumor growth either in vitro or in animal experimental models. ... Moreover, cannabinoids appear to be selective antitumoral agents as they kill glioma cells without affecting the viability of nontransformed counterparts."[94]

In 2006, investigators at Complutense University in Spain reported that the intracranial *administration of THC decreased recurrent GBM tumor growth in humans*.

Of course, the government-sanctioned remedies, that don't always work, don't necessarily stop persistent parents from finding a cure for their children.[95] In England doctors couldn't find a cure for Michelle's and Peter's young boy, Reuben, who suffered from a rare blood condition and in need of routine transfusions. The parents turned into investigators and eventually found a natural supplement to boast his blood and strengthen his immune system.

And, of course, this hasn't stopped the global establishment elite from waging an international war against dietary supplements, such as vitamin and herbal extracts. Bill Sardi, a health writer and dietary supplement advocate wrote,[96]

Europeans visiting America are shocked to see so many overweight Americans. Never do Americans realize, unlike other nations, they are being intentionally bred to overeat. The medical profession does little to stop this, treating all dietary-related diseases as if they are drug deficiencies.

Processed foods are adulterated with taste stimulants and other ingredients that create more hunger by raising insulin resistance. Insulin that can't enter cells to produce energy, disengages satiation. This is one way food producers increase their sales, by getting Americans to eat more food.

The government is complicit in spawning the "diabesity" epidemic by subsidizing the production of non-nutrient-dense foods and high-fructose corn syrup, and promoting a "food

---

[94] "Cannabinoids offer novel option for Brain Cancer Treatment, Study Say." NORML January 24, 2008. http://norml.org/news/2008/01/24/cannabinoids-offer-novel-option-for-brain-cancer-treatment-study-says

[95] "Parents find cure for son's 'untreatable' blood disorder." Telegraph, February 9, 2009 http://www.telegraph.co.uk/health/healthnews/4569991/Parents-find-cure-for-sons-untreatable-blood-disorder.html

[96] Sardi, B. "The Growing War Between Modern Medicine and the Public." http://www.lewrockwell.com/sardi/sardi99.html December 13, 2008.

pyramid" that suggests Americans consume more food, not less (17–23 servings a day), and many servings of meat, processed gains and dairy products which foster obesity.

The FDA Kills

Iplex, an experimental drug the FDA will not approve, may be the only thing that gives Joshua Thompson more time. Joshua has the debilitating disease amyotrophic lateral sclerosis, better known as Lou Gehrig's disease.[97] Anecdotal evidence from patients who were fortunate to obtain the drug, before it was lost to a patent dispute, showed the drug would slow the progression of the disease. Joshua's case is one of many cases where the menace of "unintended consequences" always rears its ugly head in defense of "responsible prohibition" and "keeping the public safe."

Any government powerful enough to prohibit drugs from the market is also powerful enough to force drugs on the public. We are living in a time when regulation of people's health is getting people killed. Regulations on supplements and alternative medicines are making people sick before their time.

By regulating the flow of new drugs into the market, the FDA also decides what companies succeed and which fail. For this purpose, pharmaceutical companies help finance studies for their drugs and recruit FDA officers into the government.[98] As a result, for example, the FDA seeks to ban pyridoxamine (vitamin B6) so a pharmaceutical company can make a profit from it.[99]

Since the discovery of cholesterol in 1769 by Francois Poulletier de la Salle, it has been the focus of interest through the nineteenth and twentieth centuries. By 2010, no less than 13 Nobel awards have been given to cholesterol researchers.

And since the discovery of cholesterol-lowering drugs (statins) in the 1960s,[100] our society has been inundated with an almost war-on-cholesterol mentality propaganda blitz by the health science community and their corporate darlings, the drug companies, to sell us these drugs. Then we are told that, well, maybe there is

---

[97]   Harmon, Amy, "Fighting for a Last Chance at Life." New York Times, May 16, 2009. http://www.nytimes.com/2009/05/17/health/policy/17untested.html?_r=2&ref=health

[98]   Saul, Andrew W. (omns@orthomolecular.org) :Rigged Drug Studies Favor| The Manufacture." Orthomolecular Medicine News Service, November 8, 2008. http://www.rense.com/general84/rig.htm

[99]   http://www.lef.org/magazine/mag2009/jul2009_FDA-Seeks-to-Ban-Pyridoxamine_01.htm

[100]   Fiket, Maja, "The Discovery of Cholesterol," May 24, 2010. http://www.livestrong.com/article/130231-discovery-cholesterol/

"bad" cholesterol and "good" cholesterol and the race was on to find cholesterol-lowering drugs with higher specificity to "bad" cholesterol. Whole industries in food and medicine were developed to sell us products that would promote "good" cholesterol and reduce the "bad" cholesterol. Today, statins are the most-sold drug in the world.

Well, now meta-analysis programs have revealed that cholesterol isn't the culprit giving people heart attacks and vascular disease, but inflammation caused by reactive C-protein.[101] A pioneer in functional medicine and author, Dr. Mark Hyman has reported that much of the hype surrounding cholesterol is probably not true. Many more variables play as much a role in fighting cardiovascular disease as just lowering cholesterol. In fact, as most health-conscience people know, high-density cholesterol is actually beneficial to one's health. Hyman noted that three quarters of the people who have heart attacks have normal cholesterol.

High Blood Pressure or Just a Pain in the Neck

A University of Chicago study showed that a simple neck adjusted by a qualified chiropractor could drop high blood pressure 14 points.[102] No adverse effects, no side effects, no problem were found by the study leader George Bakris, MD. "This procedure has the effect of not one, but two blood-pressure medications given in combination," he said. Of course, exercise and yoga to lower stress, a low-carb diet, low salt intake, and refraining from caffeine and sweetener substitutes can all be employed to control hypertension.

Cancer Treatment "encourages" Cancer

Just as advice to people to stay out of the sun to avoid cancer, new information coming out a New York research facility suggests a common treatment for prostate cancer may actually cause the cancer cells to proliferate.[103] Many chemotherapeutic

---

[101] Mark Hyman, MD, "Why Cholesterol May Not Be the Cause Of Heart Disease," http://www.huffingtonpost.com/dr-mark-hyman/why-cholesterol-may-not-b_b_290687.htmlSeptember 20, 2009

[102] DeNoon, Daniel J. "Chiropractic Cuts Blood Pressure." WebMD March 16, 2007. http://www.webmd.com/hypertension-high-blood-pressure/news/20070316/chiropractic-cuts-blood-pressure#1

[103] White, L. "Why a Common Treatment for Prostate Cancer Ultimately Fails." University of Rochester Mediacl Center http://www.urmc.rochester.edu/pr/news/story.cfm?id=2082, August 25, 2008.

drugs can cause the patient's immune system to weaken, attenuating its ability to fight the cancer.

New Diabetic Drug Kills Diabetics

Eli Lilly and Amylin Pharmaceuticals have reported a new drug, Byetta, developed to reduce blood sugar in diabetics is responsible for four new deaths by pancreatitis, inflammation of the pancreas, a serious and sometimes fatal condition.[104] According to the *AOL money and finance* article, "... diabetes patients are already three times more likely to develop pancreatitis compared with healthy patients." See the cognizant dissonance here? Why would a healthy person need to take this drug? It isn't like an aspirin, where the person would use it short-term to alleviate an acute headache. But give Byetta to a diabetic, someone already potentially inflicted with a fragile, chronic condition like pancreatitis, can increase that person's risk of dying 300 percent.

Fraudulent Studies

> "It is simply no longer possible to believe much of the clinical research that is published, or to rely on the judgment of trusted physicians or authoritative medical guidelines. I take no pleasure in this conclusion, which I reached slowly and reluctantly over my two decades as an editor of the New England Journal of Medicine." – Dr. Marcia Angell, a physician and longtime editor-in-chief of the New England Medical Journal (NEMJ)[105]

> "The case against science is straightforward: much of the scientific literature, perhaps half, may simply be untrue. Afflicted by studies with small sample sizes, tiny effects, invalid exploratory analyses, and flagrant conflicts of interest, together with an obsession for pursuing fashionable trends of dubious importance, science has taken a turn towards darkness." – Dr. Richard Horton, the current editor-in-chief of the Lancet – considered one of the most well respected, peer-reviewed medical journals in the world[106]

In a recent video[107] Dr. Peter Rost, MD, reveals the truth about the ties between the pharmaceutical and medical industries. Rost, a former vice president of the

---

[104] Perron, M. "Companies report 4 new deaths with diabetes drug." AOL money & finance http://money.aol.com/news/articles/_a/bbdp/companies-report-4-new-deaths-with/149533, August 27, 2008

[105] Marcovitch, Harvey, "Editors, Publishers, Impact Factors , and Reprint Income." PLoS Med.7(10):1-2 http://www.ncbi.nlm.nih.gov/pmc/articles/PMC2964337/ Oct 2010

[106] Horton, Richard, "Offline: What is medicine's 5 sigma?" The Lancet 385:1320, Apr 11, 2015

[107] Walia, Arjun, "Pfizer Vice President Blows the Whistle: Tells all about the Pharmaceutical Industry."

pharmaceutical giant Pfizer, and present whistleblower on the entire industry, shares the truth about the horrible Gardasil vaccine against the potentially deadly human papillomavirus... Author of *The Whistleblower, Confessions of a Healthcare Hitman*

> Baystate Medical Center in Springfield, Mass., has asked several anesthesiology journals to retract the studies, which appeared between 1996 and 2008, the WSJ reports. The hospital says its former chief of acute pain, Scott S. Reuben, faked data used in the studies.

In 2009, the Wall Street Journal reported[108] that a "former chief of acute pain, Scott S. Reuben, faked data used in 21 studies," asking "several anesthesiology journals to retract the studies."   Since this revelation both painkillers, Pfizer's Bextra and Merck's Vioxx, have been pulled from the market.

A Minnesota judge recently ruled that a 13-year old boy must be given chemotherapeutic drugs to treat the boy's Hodgkin's lymphoma.[109]

> For opting to explore alternative and natural remedies rather than chemotherapy for their son, the parents were accused of medical neglect and now face having their son taken away from them by Child Protective Services (CPS). They may also face prison time if they refuse to follow the judge's orders.

Any government that has the power to prohibit drug use has the power to force drug use. This is the underlying argument against the drug war that more and more people are beginning to understand as they see their own liberties slowly being crushed under the jackboot of paternalistic despotism.

> As the critical, life-saving importance of maintaining the best oral hygiene possible finally surfaces, it is natural that each of us would desire the best and most efficient tools available for ourselves and our families in order to combat potentially deadly oral bacteria. Brushing and flossing combined are the suggested daily routine for keeping bacteria under control. Unfortunately

Feb 2016   http://www.realfarmacy.com/pfizer-whistleblower/

[108]   Rubenstein, Sarah, "A New Low in Drug Research:21 Fabricated Studies." Wall Street Journal March 11, 2009.   http://blogs.wsj.com/health/2009/03/11/a-new-low-in-drug-research-21-fabricated-studies/

[109]   Adams, Mike. "Court orders parents to poison their 13-year old child chemotherapy ," NatualNews.com, May 15, 2009.   http://www.naturalnews.com/026283.html

[110]   Sparrowdancer, Mary, "New Dangers of Oral Bacteria." October 15, 2008. http://www.rense.com/general83/dendo.htm

for us all, however, the most promising flossing tool for combating periodontal disease, FlossRings and sterilized floss segments, remain largely or completely unavailable to us thanks to CNN, which deliberately and repeatedly maligned and destroyed these products on national TV. This irresponsible piece of CNN "news" eliminated the only serious competitor to the 100-year-old dental floss industry, an industry that has been predominantly presided over by Johnson&Johnson. Johnson&Johnson, said to be the largest pharmaceutical and medical devices company on earth, has been referred to by CNN as a "partner" in various joint undertakings.[110]

Writes Karen DeCostar:

The lack of a free market for organs has long been the cause of needless deaths. And now, because marijuana is not a corporatist state-approved drug (unlike the overpriced pills pushed by Big Pharma), patients waiting for organ transplants, who smoke pot to deal with the pain, are being turned down for transplants. Medical marijuana, approved in some states, is not approved by the Feds, and thus the heavy hand of federal authoritarianism comes down upon those who dare to be prescribed marijuana (legally), by a doctor, because they are in unbearable pain. However, patients are free to fill up on all of Big Pharma's powerful, prescription drugs that bring with them numerous health-destroying side effects. Marijuana, on the other hand, is a painkiller that doesn't come with all of the hazardous side effects.

The UCLA Medical Center requires that patients get off of pot for six months before they can get back on the transplant list. Medical marijuana patients are put in the same class as careless drug abusers when it comes to granting possibility of a transplant. The federal government, under the Controlled Substances Act, lists marijuana as a Schedule 1 drug, and still refuses to recognize the medical use for marijuana. Timothy Garon smoked some pot while he awaited a possible liver transplant. He was denied because of "drug use." He died.

To quote William F. Buckley on this: "The anti-marijuana campaign is a cancerous tissue of lies, undermining law enforcement, aggravating the drug problem, depriving the sick of needed help, and suckering well meaning conservatives and countless frightened parents.

Supreme Court Helps out Big Pharma

Well, no wonder. If the FDA approved the drug, then it must be safe, right? This is the incestuous relation of corporate-state fascism. Corporations have been doing this for decades. As stated above, the chemical companies petitioned Congress to outlaw hemp to make way for competition-free marketing for their newly discovered synthetic fibers. I've been telling people for years who think that the FDA is "there to protect us" that the FDA was established to protect Big Business from financial ruin. Now the Supreme Court will prove it.

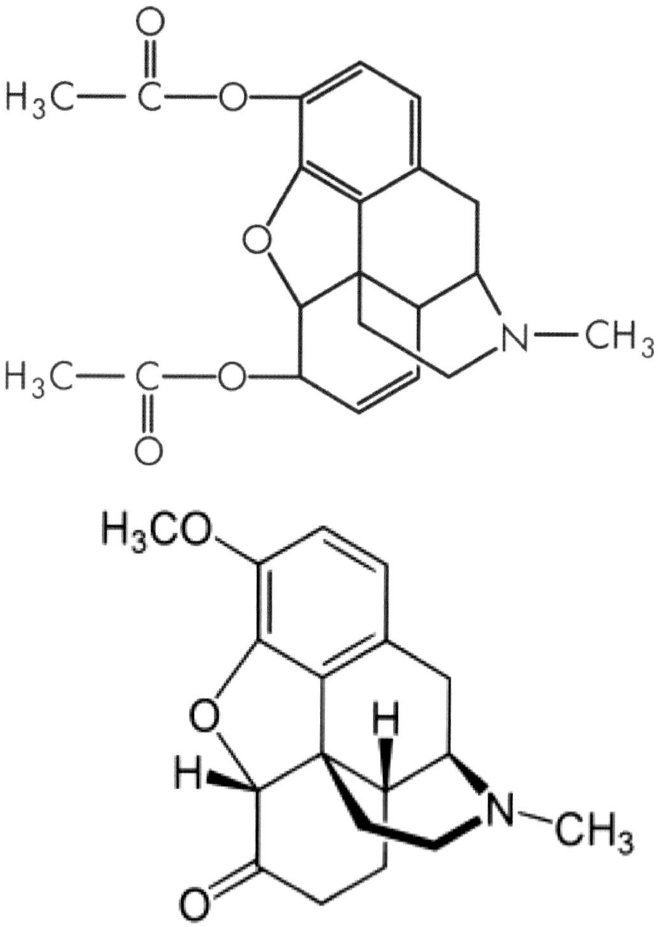

Figure 4

The two chemical structures above represent two highly addictive, regulated drugs (Figure 4). The top graphic is the chemical structure for heroin, and the bottom one is oxycodone. If someone sells the bottom drug with the right credentials, he can live in a nice house, in a nice neighborhood and make a good life for himself. But if someone sells the heroin drug, he could possibly live in a nice house, in a nice neighborhood, but could lose all his property to forfeiture if busted for drug trafficking. One drug is controlled and legal, the other is controlled and illegal.

When the Taliban took over in Afghanistan, it went about to destroy the opium crops in 2000. Within two years the 9/11 attacks happened, the U.S. invaded Afghanistan and restored opium production above the level that was destroyed by the Taliban. Fast-forward eleven years and the U.S. finds itself in the middle of an "opioid epidemic," coincidental with national legislation that cracked down on doctors for over-prescribing pain-killing drugs. Patients could no longer find medical relief for their pain, so they resorted to finding heroin on the streets.

"Obamacare" vs. "Maocare"
(China's Health Care During Mao's Time)

Trying hard to leave a better world for them. I can't imagine how European parents felt the first half of the 20th Century, the utter despair of watching their communities being destroyed by overburdensome states. The path to hell is sometimes paved with "good" intentions. Maybe Americans could afford health insurance if they weren't paying nearly half of their incomes for various local, state and federal taxes, from which many receive little to no benefit of services in return.

During the national debates over defunding the Affordable Care Act (ACA, or more affectionately known as "Obamacare"), before the ACA went into effect in 2013, critics compared the ACA to a "communist takeover" of the American healthcare system. But as blatant emotional nuances go, and in some respects "Maocare" was better than "Obamacare", they are correct in the comparison because the process of healthcare, with its diagnoses, prognoses, treatments and payments were to be dictated by government regulations.

According to the website ilookchina.net,[111] "After the Communists won China in 1949, health care improved. Prior to that, life expectancy for the Chinese people was thirty-five years. By Mao's death in 1976, **average life expectancy** had increased by

---

[111] China's Health Care During Mao's Time, February 17, 2010
http://ilookchina.net/2010/02/27/chinas-health-care-during-maos-time/

twenty years." This assessment is highly misleading. According to a 2010 United Nation report on global life expectancy since 1950, humans *worldwide* were living 45 percent longer into the beginning of the 21st century, from 47 years to 68 years. Much of this sharp increase occurred as the emergence of mass production of better antibiotics and other drugs improved medical outcomes. With the technological improvements in agricultural, people were receiving better nutrition.

There were three basic areas of medical care in Communist China. Free substandard medical care was provided to the proletarian working class, meaning workers and peasants. Mao started a program called '<u>bare-foot doctors</u>'. This program was the backbone of rural health care in China. This meant anyone could become a doctor. Mao told the people that if they wanted to be a doctor, they didn't need to go to medical school. All they had to do was have the motivation to provide medical care to needy people and the government would support them and provide limited training.

The second class of medical care went to people like teachers, clerks and secretaries, 'friends' of the working class, the proletariat. The only difference was that these 'friends' had to pay to get medical treatment. It was possible to face financial ruin from one hospital stay.

The third class was termed the enemy of the proletariat like former shop-owners, landlords and denounced intellectuals like liberal arts professors. These people were denied treatment altogether. Estimates of 50 to 100 million Chinese died under Mao's revolutionary holocaust, far more than Hitler's or even Stalin's. Most died from denial of health care, starvation or execution, the epidemy of Obamacare's so-called "death panels."

PRISON-INDUSTRIAL COMPLEX

"When you let people do whatever they want, you get Woodstock; when you let governments do whatever they want, you get Auschwitz." ~ <u>Doug Newman</u>

"The more laws and order are made prominent, the more thieves and robbers there will be." ~ Lao Tzu

"The more corrupt the state, the more numerous the laws." ~ Tacitus

"When a man wants to murder a tiger he calls it sport: when the tiger wants to murder him he calls it ferocity. The distinction between Crime and Justice is no greater." ~ George Bernard Shaw

Evidently, some Americans still can't distinguish between real crimes like murder, rape and theft that deny the natural right to life, liberty and the pursuit of happiness, and prohibitions that deny the same. ~ David Alva Personett

The Rise of the American Police State

In the statist's mind, denying others their rights and liberties is freedom for the statist, freedom from the actions of others that do not fit the statist's world view. They want to live in a country where they are free *from* the liberties of others. In the Bizarro World of statists, freedom *from* is far more important than freedom *to*, even though the statist will sometimes break his own rules (e.g., drug laws, drunk driving laws, speed limits, perjury, and tax evasion). Much of the time the restrictions on liberties are for the libertine or other uncustomary behaviors of others. Sometimes to deny the liberties of others is simply to protect them from themselves. Non-alcoholic recreational drug use, prostitution, environmentalism and home-schooling are examples of the many "issues" statists use to employ government force against others.

From the less obscene attempts by municipalities to fill their coffers with traffic fines[112] to "blue laws" banning certain activities on Sundays to attempts by politicians and bureaucrats to lie and murder as they wrestle for more power from their citizenry, the various governments within the boundaries of the United States have become less freedom-minded and more willing to ignore the constitutional restraints put on government power to protect the citizenry. Power is always predicated on the potential for people to trade liberty for security. Governments have a vested interest in relying on crime to justify its power over the citizenry. The more criminal acts the state can drum up, the more power it can consolidate for itself. Therefore, in recent decades governments have instituted tougher illicit drug laws, asset forfeitures, hate crimes, gun laws, environmental protection laws, and other non-violent, non-covetous "criminal" statutes to keep the Prison-Industrial Complex running smoothly and profitably for the sake of government bureaucrats, the courts and private prison contractors.

Prisons have become the 21st Century factory lines. Even mainstream media is beginning to understand the tragic state of America's prison-industrial complex. David Person recently reported in USA Today that "(s)tate contracts guarantee younger, healthier prisoners, who tend to be mostly minorities," making prisoners less costly to house.[113]

The war on drugs has been very lucrative to mercenary groups, such as Blackwater USA, [114] which had been "... 'tapped' by the Pentagon's Counter Narcoterrorism Technology Program Office to compete for a share of a five-year, $15 billion budget to 'fight terrorists with drug-trade ties.'" So instead of just legalizing or decriminalizing narcotics and marijuana, whereby making treatment and education that works, and is easier to obtain for addicts, these mercantilists made a fortune in interdiction that has been shown to have near zero effect on drug trade supply and demand.

---

[112]   "Red-Light Cameras Just Don't Work" RideLust.com   http://www.ridelust.com/red-light-cameras-just-dont-work/, August 18, 2008

[113]   Person, David. "Halt private prison quotas" USA Today (on line), March 18, 2014.

[114]   Scahill, Jeremy. "Blackwater's Private Spies. Information Clearing House, July 6, 2008. http://www.informationclearinghouse.info/article20054.htm

As the state becomes more totalitarian, the justice system becomes more malevolent towards the rights of the accused, all the while rubberstamping the authority of the state. One aspect of Adolf Hitler's reign of terror usually overlooked by historians was the criminal justice system, as most of the historical focus concentrated around the operations of concentration camps, especially as it victimized the Jewish population. This was pointed out by Nikolaus Wachsmann in his book *Hitler's Prisons: Legal Terror in Nazi Germany*.[115] Ordinary jails were turned into hellish purgatory chambers of racial attacks, torture and slave labor. Local jails became holding grounds for future deportation to slave labor camps or worse. And it was all "legal." Ordinary public officials were put to work in nefarious collaborations with the Third Reich. Chillingly similar to U.S. federal legislation since September 11th, 2001, local public policies were slowly swallowed up by Nazi centralized edicts that gave local authorities broader jurisdiction to punish enemies of the Third Reich. In the U.S., congressional legislation, such as the PATRIOT Act and National Defense Authorization Act, as well as numerous executive orders from the President, has loosened up citizen rights found in the Bill of Rights, all in the name of fighting the drug war and "domestic terrorism," in turn nationalizing local police with military gear left over from occupations in Iraq and Afghanistan, and gutting constraints on searches and arrests.

> A Summit County Common Pleas judge ordered the county medical examiner to delete any reference that Tasers contributed to the deaths of three Ohio men.
> All three men were in an 'agitated' state and 'on drugs' when police officers shot them with Tasers, and the judge ordered their deaths be ruled 'accidental' also that any reference to "homicide or "electrical pulse stimulation" should be deleted from death certificates and autopsy reports."
> Five sheriff's deputies had been indicted on charges related to the death of one of the men, who also had a history of mental illness. The judge further ordered that man's death be ruled as "undetermined" and to "delete any references to homicide and the death possibly being caused by asphyxia, beatings or other factors."[116]

Despite no known medical terminology for "excited delirium," an Ohio judge ruled in favor of excited delirium- induced death claim by Taser International, manufacturer of the stun gun, and against the medical examiners who claimed Taser

---

[115]   Wachsmann, Nikolaus *Hitler's Prisons: Legal Terror in Nazi Germany* (Yale University Press,   2004?) **ISBN**: 030010250X

[116]   Sweet, Diane. "Judge orders all references to 'Taser' stricken from medical examiner's reports." http://rawstory.com/news/2008/Judge_orders_all_references_to_Taser_0504.html, March 4, 2008. [Original story in the Cleveland Plain Dealer].

strikes contributed to the cause of death of several people in police custody, including those noted above. To date, the term "excited delirium" is not found in medical textbooks.

If anyone wants to know why politicians and government bureaucrats are viewed with little respect, this is a good example.

Dear ACLU Supporter,

Why is 7-year-old John Anderson from Minneapolis on the national Terrorist Watch List? He pushed Tommy too hard on the playground. His July 4th birthday means he distracts other Americans from celebrating their country. John didn't pick up the blocks during playtime.

The truth is that we don't know how he got on the Terrorist Watch List. Or if he can get off it. It took an Act of Congress to get Nelson Mandela, winner of the Nobel Peace Prize, off the list.

According to USA Today: John Anderson of Minneapolis, [now 7] was first stopped at Minneapolis-St. Paul International Airport in 2004, when his family took him for his first airplane ride to Disney World. "We checked in at the ticket counter, and the woman said in a stern voice, 'Who is John Anderson?'," says his mother, Christine Anderson. "I pointed to my stroller."

Her son is allowed to fly. But because his name is flagged, his family cannot print out a boarding pass for him online and he must check in at the ticket counter so an airline official can see that he's a child.[117]

When government suspends "rights" tyranny inevitably follows[118]

History proves that there is always advance warning when governments enter the final stages of transitioning from freedom to tyranny. The three most obvious warnings are sounded when government begins openly spying on people, publicly punishing opinions and raising up standing armies. The U.S. government and its state, county, municipal and corporate minions have legalized unwarranted surveillance, searches and seizures; those who speak and write in opposition to government policies are subject to punishments ranging from character assassination and harassment to prison sentences and sudden, suspicious deaths and; police at all levels

---

[117]   http://webmail.att.net/wmc/en-US/v/wm/48A6D97500017BCB0000355F22230703729B0A02D2089B9A019C04040A0DBF9B9B0A029F0E0B?cmd=Show&no=1197&uid=54070&sid=c0

[118]   Idaho Observer http://www.proliberty.com/observer/20080730.htm. July 2008.

are being militarized in dress, weaponry, demeanor and tactics. What Thomas Jefferson pointed out as historical fact over 200 years ago is supported in contemporary experience as described by Ron Paul.   The truth is plain to see: The U.S. government has become obsessed with surveillance and the enforcement of its increasingly unpopular policies with militarized police authority.

The excuse that militarizing police is necessary for making the homeland safe from terrorists is as ancient as tyranny itself. The U.S. government is committed in the direction of tyranny; it cannot and will not turn itself around. To turn an infamous quote from President Bush on its head, "You are either with us [the people] or you are with the terrorists [the U.S. government].

How the Drug War Leads to Other Bad Legislation

You can always tell what the state's agenda is by looking at what the corporate-state-controlled media talking points are. When Congress begins debating a budget for the drug war, for example, reports about teen drug use or crime-ridden communities will pepper the TV and print news shows.

Nearly the day after Barack Obama was inaugurated to the highest office in the land, TV and print media was beginning to direct national attention to the drug war in Mexico. The government there was seriously losing the war, and supposedly it was spilling over America's border. Interestingly, it turns out that much of the media attention was not about the concerns of the Mexicans, the violence and mayhem brought about by U.S. foreign drug policies, always the folly of prohibition that citizens and businesses have to endure. But instead the media discussed the "fact" that the drug cartels were getting most of their heavy firepower from across the border in the US. This was the real agenda of the corporate state.

If one ignores the anti-gun sentiment of Obama and his attorney general, Eric Holden; if you ignore the history of this kind of reporting that covertly builds support for federal legislation to "fix" the problem (for the state) the media obsessively and dutifully report; If you ignore the fact that you know the CIA and the NSA have a history of manipulating media to further an agenda at home and overseas, then you just may believe that *something* needed to be done to stop the shipment of guns into the hands of drug cartels.

a well-known history of running its own CIA-employed drug smuggling operation (see below),[119]

---

[119] Borjesson, Kristina, Ed. Into the Buzzsaw (Amherst, Prometheus Books, 2002), pp. 311-332.

No thanks to the Supreme Court and its perverted interpretation of the Commerce Clause of Article I, Section 8 of the U.S. Constitution, the federal government now has imperial powers to protect the free flow of goods amongst the several states (its original intent), it now can regulate every activity within every state on a whim. For example, in Gonzales v. Raich,[120] the Supremes, using the Commerce Clause, ruled that Congress' laws against medical pot superceded the states' authority to regulate even homegrown pot. Justice Thomas dissented stating,

> If the majority is to be taken seriously, the Federal Government may now regulate quilting bees, clothes drives, and potluck suppers throughout the 50 States. This makes a mockery of Madison's assurance to the people of New York that the "powers delegated" to the Federal Government are "few and defined", while those of the States are "numerous and indefinite," Respondent's local cultivation and consumption of marijuana is not "Commerce ... among the several States... Certainly no evidence from the founding suggests that "commerce" included the mere possession of a good or some personal activity that did not involve trade or exchange for value. In the early days of the Republic, it would have been unthinkable that Congress could prohibit the local cultivation, possession, and consumption of marijuana.

The "conservative" Scalia voted with the majority in Gonzalez v. Raich.

The "among the several states" clause was never intended to be interpreted the way it is now by the imperial federal government. Growing pot for personal use is not "commerce." The court did an end-around on that by stating that the individual uses fertilizer and other things for growing that could have crossed state lines. It's ridiculous!

Public Support for the War on Drugs has Dwindled to Nearly Nothing :

In July of 2001, Portugal did something bold and unusual for a Western nation-state: Portugal ended its drug war.[121] What has happened in the 15 years since is something of a vindication for the decades of libertarian thinking that surmises that drug wars actually do more harm to society than the drugs themselves. Drug-induced deaths decreased by 80 percent, while the number of heroin addicts dropped

---

[120] https://en.wikipedia.org/wiki/Gonzales_v._Raich

[121] What Happened (And What Didn't) When Portugal Decriminalized Drugs. Editorial, Foundation for Economic Education, July 6, 2015   http://fee.org/anythingpeaceful/detail/what-happened-and-what-didnt-when-portugal-decriminalized-drugs

by half over the same period. Intervention changed from criminalization of the offender to treatment and harm-reduction.

According to DrugWarFacts.org, compiled data from the U.S. Department of Justice, Bureau of Justice Statistics, 86% of all federal prison sentences are for victimless crimes, primarily for drug offenses. Some may rationalize that victims are involved with drug offenses. But alcohol consumption carries a measurable social impact as well, but to my knowledge distributors for Budweiser or Jim Beam have never had armed SWAT teams crash through their doors in the middle of the night!

Landslide At The Ballot Box: Election Day Voters Reject Bush War Doctrine
Millions of Americans nationwide voted on Election Day for marijuana law reform, approving nine out of ten ballot measures to liberalize penalties on cannabis use and possession. In Massachusetts, where 65 percent of voters decided to reduce marijuana possession penalties to a $100 fine, and Michigan, where 63 percent of voters approved legalizing the medical use of cannabis, supporters for pot law reform outnumbered supporters for President-Elect Barack Obama.[122]

H.R.5843 This measure, if passed, would strip the federal government of its authority to arrest responsible adult cannabis consumers. NORML founder and Legal Director Keith Stroup worked extensively with Frank's staff to write this important legislation, which represents the first cannabis decriminalization measure introduced in Congress in 24 years.[123]

How Heroin Became an Epidemic in the U.S.

By 1999, the Taliban in Afghanistan, presently called the Islamic Emirate of Afghanistan, had taken control of most of Afghanistan, and controlled nearly all of the Afghani poppy fields and opium production. In 2000, Taliban leader Mullah Mohammed Omar began a program of eradicating the poppy harvest and replacing farmers' losses with subsidized food crops.

---

[122]   Americans Reject Bush Drug War Doctrine -- Landslide At The Ballot Box: Voters Approve Nine Out Of Ten Marijuana Law Reform Measures. National Organization to Reform Marijuana Laws. November 5, 2008   *http://www.norml.org/index.cfm?Group_ID=7742*.

[123] Fisher, R.   House of Representatives to Consider Cannabis Decriminalization! National Organization to Reform Marijuana Laws   http://capwiz.com/norml2/issues/alert/?alertid=11280301

A month after the 9/11 attacks on the United States of America, Afghanistan was invaded by the U.S. for harboring Al Qaida leader Osama bin Laden and his mercenary army. At the time Afghanistan provided 75% of the world's opium supply with "an estimated 3276 tonnes of opium from cultivation on 82,171 hectares."[124] After Omar's decree, opium production dropped to 74 metric tonnes on 1,685 hectares. Surplus stock of opium was not destroyed, and the Taliban went on to sell off opium the following year in a bid for international recognition for entry into the United Nations. Without poppies, Afghanistan still survived on its trillion-dollar wealth of untouched minerals.

By the spring of 2002, Afghani farmers had lost their financial support from the Taliban and went back to growing poppies.[125] Ten years later, according to journalist Abbey Martin of Media Roots, "Afghanistan's opium trade isn't just sustaining, it's thriving more than ever before. According to a recent report from the UN Office on Drugs and Crime, 2013 saw opium production surge to record highs."[126]

Now 15 years later, we are seeing a manufactured "heroin epidemic" at a time when state and federal governments are cracking down on opioid prescriptions to people with serious chronic pain conditions. They are being driven to the streets in search of heroin while the tough-on-crime political parasites callously cash in on campaign contributions and votes. Those unlucky enough to find heroin cut with fentanyl are killed off quickly, creating the horrendous "heroin epidemic" people are reminded nearly daily on the network news. Like all war, the drug war is a racket.

The Department of Insane Bullies: The Myth of "Police Protection"

"Those who suppress freedom always do so in the name of law and order." – John V. Lindsay

To serve and protect. We see this motto every day on police cars everywhere, even in the movies. We are told by the media and politicians every time, usually before elections, that taxes need to be raised to increase law enforcement personnel and to fight crime. Yet in numerous cases where city police departments were sued because the police failed to respond to victims' pleas for help, court judges have

---

[124] Taliban, from Wikipedia. https://en.wikipedia.org/wiki/Taliban#Economy

[125] Muhawesh, Mnar, Us War in Afghanistan is Fueling Global Heroin Epidemic and Enabling the Drug Trade. Mint Press News. July 21, 2016. https://en.wikipedia.org/wiki/Taliban#Economy

[126] Martin, Abbey, "How Opium is Keeping US in Afghanistan: CIA's Shady History of Drug Trafficking." Media Roots. January 3, 2014. http://mediaroots.org/opium-what-afghanistan-is-really-about/

repeatedly ruled in favor of the government, noting that police do not have a *legal obligation* to protect the public.[127]

So why, you ask, do we spend billions every year throughout the country for various law enforcement agencies to catch drug users and sellers when they neither have the legal nor fiduciary responsibility "to protect" the public from drugs when the majority of the public wants to reform drug laws? Drug prohibition has never made any sense. Just as alcohol prohibition never stopped drinking and actually had a number of unintended consequences such as increasing alcoholism and corrupting politicians and judges.

Prohibition breeds corruption into cops, judges and politicians. It's why they push for it: to make even more money. Even a church secretary with over $28,000 of parishioners' donations[128] isn't immune from what's becoming a national epidemic of highway robbery by costumed criminals, the infamous "asset forfeiture." Murray Rothbard had it right: "For if the bulk of the public were really convinced of the illegitimacy of the State, if it were convinced that the State is nothing more nor less than a bandit gang writ large, then the State would soon collapse to take on no more status or breadth of existence than another Mafia gang." Like war is a racket, the drug war has become the domestic version of World War Two. Drug interdiction and asset forfeiture have become the moral equivalent of piracy on the high seas.

The answer is simple. Law enforcement was established to protect the powers-to-be, whether private or public, from the rest of the citizenry. Historically, law enforcement was established privately, bought by the wealthy for the protection of the wealthy. This is still true in gated communities, wealthier areas of a community, country clubs, banks and shopping malls. In fact, still today, 60 percent of uniformed security in the U.S. is still in the hands of private companies. But like education (see Chapter Six), agriculture, and other factions of our society, governments muscled more and more control of those security responsibilities, using the force of taxation to pay for it. After all, who better to pay for the security of the political class and its various parasitic associates than the taxpayers, from their point of view.

---

[127] Stevens, R.W. *Just Dial 911? The Myth of Police Protection.* Foundation for Economic Freedom, Vol 50(No. 4): on-line. http://www.fee.org/Publications/the-Freeman/article.asp?aid=1758

[128] Sabilla, Nick. 2014. *Cops Use Traffic Stops To Seize Millions From Drivers Never Charged With A Crime* http://www.forbes.com/sites/instituteforjustice/2014/03/12/cops-use-traffic-stops-to-seize-millions-from-drivers-never-charged-with-a-crime/

Government police, and even unconstitutionally national guardsmen and U.S. soldiers have been used to protect companies from strikers, even gunning them down. In 1932 Hoover ordered the 12th Infantry Regiment commanded by Douglas MacArthur and the 3rd Calvary Regiment, supported by six M1917 tanks commanded by Major George Patton to protect his administration from WWI veterans camped out at the White House and demonstrating for the benefits promised to them for signing up during the war. Eventually after a four-month standoff, the army, commanded by the future World War Two commanding officer of the Pacific campaign General Douglas MacArthur, went in to clear out the demonstration. Later that year, the Bonus Army incident was thought to be a contributing factor on Franklin Roosevelt's landslide victory over President Hoover. The incidental show of force by US military, clearly in violation of the Constitution, cost the lives of two unarmed veterans, injuring 55 more, as well as arresting 135 veterans before the violence was over July 28.[129] Because the incident occurred in Washington, D.C., the Posse Comitatus Act could not be used to prohibit military force to remove the veterans and other demonstrators from the all government property.

Terrorism is constantly in the news since September 11, 2001. We are constantly bombarded (pardon the pun) by reports of terrorists, terrorist plots, terrorist attacks, terrorist cells, terrorist camps, terrorist weapons, and terrorists caves. In the three years since 9-11, up to September 2004, approximately 2930 people around the world were killed by terrorists.[130] Of these deaths, over 1700 occurred in 2004, a year after the US invaded Iraq in March of 2003. Many of these deaths, of course, were of military targets in Iraq and Afghanistan. The government-media complex, including social media warriors on the Internet, called the Iraqi and Afghani combatants "terrorists" and not enemy combatants defending their homeland from invaders. The bean counters who keep track of these incidences consider roadside bombings of military targets to be terrorist attacks. "In the same span of time, 2003 to 2005, a little more than 2000 people were killed in the custody of American police officers.[131] Nearly as many people were killed by state agents within *one* country than by the horrible attacks of terrorists around the world. Possibly, Americans should rethink who the real threat is to their peace and well-being!

The Paramilitarization of the War on Drugs

---

[129] Bonus Army. Wikipedia: https://en.wikipedia.org/wiki/Bonus_Army

[130] Robert Rivas and Robert Windrem, Worldwide terrorism-related deaths on the rise, NBC News, September 2, 2004. http://www.msnbc.msn.com/id/5889435/

[131] Study: 2,002 died in police custody over 3 years. Associated Press, October 11, 2007. http://www.msnbc.msn.com/id/21255937/

President Richard Nixon is responsible for escalating the modern war on drugs. This was born out of the American military's victories leading up to the unconstitutional wars Korea and Viet Nam. So we had the various utopian war in the 1960s and 70s, such as the War on Poverty, War on Illiteracy and, of course, the Prohibition-esque, doomed for failure War on Drugs.

Many Americans believed the national fervor that all they had to do to fight the war on drugs is to kill or to cage all drug dealers and users, as they killed or imprisoned the Germans and Japanese, the problem would just go away. Americans like and glorified wars then, but after fighting the Communists in two wars that ended in stalemate, at best, Americans needed a war they believed they could win. Movies and the news media romanticized wars in a way that attracted new generations to accepting and participating in the bloodbaths throughout the last half of the Twentieth Century. In fact, all the federal government had to do is declare war on something and the people would give a Pavlovian response of support.

Slowly, all three branches of government did their part to federally militarized state and local law enforcement agencies with funding to pay for equipment and combat training. The drug war was the Trojan horse that stampeded over Posse Comitatus (sp) and bring violence on both sides into the streets. As the unintended consequence of sky rocketing homicides from gang turf wars growing out of the underground market for the illicit *hooch* during Prohibition, we now see gang shootings from a large percentage of inner city homicides today.

Prohibitions create governmental make-work programs. Raids, with military tactics utilizing armor, automatic weapons and various kinds of hand grenades have been estimated to be 40,000 per year in the U.S.[132] And the federal government alone spends over $40 billion a year in interdiction programs, drug courts and other police actions. Over 40 years of war against (some) drugs has had no significant effect on drug trafficking or use.

According to a 2008 FBI report, police arrest drug offenders every 18 seconds.[133]

The fact is that the drug war has done little to removing drugs from our streets and to "protect our children," the latter mantra purported *ad nauseum* by proponents of the anti-drug police state. But the drug war has had little effect in "protecting our

---

[132] Balko, R. "Overkill: The Rise of Paramilitary Police Raids in America." Cato Institute on-line, July 17, 2006. http://www.cato.org/pub_display.php?pub_id=6476

[133]   Federal Bureau of Investigation 2008 Crime in the United States, http://www.fbi.gov/ucr/cius2008/arrests/index.html

children." An international study[134] on governmental drug policies in three countries revealed that anti-marijuana laws have little effect on drug use amongst teenagers.

> **Bethesda, MD:** The enforcement of strict anti-cannabis laws is not associated with a reduction in the prevalence of adolescent marijuana use, according to international survey data to be published in the *International Journal of Drug Policy.*
>
> Investigators from the United States, Canada, and the Netherlands reviewed the self-reported use of marijuana and alcohol among nearly 5,000 10th graders in all three nations. Researchers reported that youth cannabis rates "did not differ across countries" despite widely disparate legal policies.

> In the United States, **33 percent** of 10th grade boys and **26 percent** of 10th grade girls reported using cannabis during the past year. In Canada, where marijuana is similarly prohibited but anti-pot laws are seldomly enforced, **32 percent** of boys and **31 percent** of girls said they'd used marijuana in the previous year. And in the Netherlands, where the sale of cannabis is legally regulated for those over 18 years of age, **29 percent** of 10th grade boy and just **20 percent** of girls said that they had used pot in the past year.

But, then, anyone who understands the consequences of prohibition knows that people don't use illicit drugs because the law forbids it; they use illicit drugs because they want to whether the drugs are legal or not, or whether the laws are enforced or not. The above study published in the IJDP supports this truism. As the article points out, "More importantly, the data are inconsistent with the contention that decriminalization policies encourage adolescent cannabis use." People are going to have to understand that other people will do things others refuse to obligate, and that NOT putting people in cages for non-violent "offences" is a moral imperative.

The war on drugs is purely economic. Like any war, there is big money in the drug war. People who think the war was created to keep people from harming themselves, and to protect society, don't understand society at all. People can harm themselves from a good number of "legal" sources, including junk food, poor driving habits, lack of exercise, war, caffeine, tobacco, ethanol and a myriad of other routes to poor health and death. We live in a society obsessed with controlling human nature, without thinking about the unintended consequences of poorly conceived, illogical solutions. As an example, let's take forcing people to exercise. How wonderful it would be to get people to exercise more often. Just imagine the healthcare costs that could be spared if we could just get people to exercise 30 to 90 minutes a day. If only we could microchip everybody with an app that could monitor a person's physical exertion, imagine the harm to society we could avoid. Do you think everyone would obey? Do you not think society would see an explosion in

---

[134]   Simons-Morton, Bruce, et al., *Cross-national comparison of adolescent drinking and cannabis use in the United States, Canada, and the Netherlands* International Journal of Drug Policy (In press, 2009).

judication and imprisonment? Somebody in power is making big money deciding who gets freedom and does not.

A recent revelation involving Senate Majority Leader Mitch McConnell emphasizes the futility of fighting a war on drugs that only benefit the mercantilists and politicians controlling the levers of governmental policies. Apparently, 90 pounds of cocaine was found on a cargo ship belonging to family business of McConnell's wife. This same family has donated millions to Senator McConnell's campaign since the 1980s. McConnell married his wife, Elaine Chao, in 1993.[135]

People need to understand what is going on here. Hundreds of billions of dollars are being made on the drug enforcement-prison-banking-industrial complex. The same private prisons and money-laundering schemes involved in this "enterprise" are providing millions to politicians like McConnell to recapitulate the mountains of money through tougher drug war laws, asset forfeitures, on and on. This serves multiple gains for all involved at the expense of our civil liberties and standard of living as taxpayers.

A Reasonable Solution to Police Abuse

From a blog at Liberty Crier Anarchyst chimes in with a list of requirements and punishments expected to discipline police and cause them to execute their duties without infringing on the rights of the mundanes:[136]

> 1. Eliminate both "qualified" and absolute" immunity for ALL public officials. This includes, police and firefighters, all court officials, code enforcement and "child protective service" personnel. Require all public officials and employees who deal with the public to purchase and maintain personal liability (malpractice) insurance at their own expense as a condition of employment. You can bet that insurance companies would be more efficient in rooting out the "bad apples". No insurance=no job. Make these "public officials" personally liable for their behavior.

---

[135] Vibes, John. "90 Pounds of Cocaine Found on Cargo Ship Owned by Anti-Drug Senator's Wife. November 8, 2014. http://thefreethoughtproject.com/90-pounds-cocaine-cargo-ship-owned-anti-drug-senators-family/#WbtuovSqQ3xcpTup.01

[136] WSB-TV, Atlanta, GA, "Okra mistaken for pot in man's garden," October 2, 2014 http://www.wsbtv.com/news/news/local/okra-mistaken-pot-mans-garden/nhbHW/ reported at
http://libertycrier.com/oops-cops-raid-georgia-mans-home-mistaking-okra-weed/ October 4, 2014

2. Require all public officials to maintain a video and audit trail when dealing with the public. Equipment malfunction would NOT be an excuse and would be grounds for immediate and permanent dismissal and loss of pension. Wearable personal equipment would be mandatory--along with dash cams.

3. Prosecutors must have NO immunity and should be subordinate to the grand jury. As it stands now, grand juries are "rubber stamps" for prosecutors. Grand juries should be able to indict without seeking a prosecutor's "permission".

4. Civilian police review boards should be comprised of citizens with NO police ties. Those with police officers as relatives would automatically be disqualified from serving on civilian police review boards.

5. Police agencies should be prohibited from investigating themselves. Outside disinterested agencies should investigate charges and accusations of police wrongdoing, preferably at the county sheriff or state police level.

6. "Asset forfeiture" should be abolished. It is nothing but a corrupting influence (and a good moneymaker). It is legalized robbery at its best.
These changes would do much to reign in abuses by all public officials

The "Privatization" of Prisons

The privatization of prisons and the war on terror and drugs are intimately connected, pretty much incestuously connected because the lineage traces back to one family: the government. The movers and shakers in the prison "industry" are for the most part connected to the Republican Party elite. This is primarily why the GOP lays it on so thick with the "law-and-order" crowd. There's money to be made in those Hells. Vice has always been with us. Why not create a multibillion-dollar industry for the "entrepreneurial" types in our society and create jobs, to boot?

Private prisons house nearly half of all immigrants detained by the federal government at a cost of detaining each of them at $166 per night.[137] Corrections Corporation of America reported that 43 percent of its total revenues come from

---

[137] Shen, Aviva "Private Prisons Spen $45 Million on Lobbying, Rake in $5.1 Billion for Immigration Detention Alone." Think Progress (on line), August 3, 2012. http://thinkprogress.org/justice/2012/08/03/627471/private-prisons-spend-45-million-on-lobbying-rake-in-51-billion-for-immigrant-detention-alone/

federal contracts, reaping $162 million net income in 2011. Another company, The GEO Group, saw its net income raise from 16.9 million to78.6 million since 2000. Money donated to political parties by prison industries, especially "law and order" Republicans is on the rise. The private prison industry spent $450,000 in campaign contributions to Republican congressional committee members. Democrats in key congressional positions received about one-half that amount. From 2000 to 2010, private prisons spent $45 million lobbying state and federal legislators, along with campaign contributions.[138] In 2011, private prisons spent millions on lobbying to put more people in jail through harsher penalties and longer sentences.

The drug war is essentially about churning out inmates for the prison mercantilists and augmenting those numbers with laws such Three-Strikes thus maximizing the number of inmates *per capita* and the number of those who are nonviolent drug offenders.

A case in point is the lurid case where Pennsylvania judges took millions in bribes to direct juvenile offenders to the state-approved "private" detention centers.[139, 140] Similar to the corruption manifested from alcohol prohibition in the 1920s, two judges were prosecuted for taking bribes to send kids who really did nothing more than idiotic pranks to privately run juvenile detention centers. Counties in Pennsylvania, like in so many other states, contract out detention of juvenile centers, paying them by the head. Some states do this with prisons, as well. In turn, politicians are bribed by the beneficiaries of these state contracts every election to stay "tough" on crime, and especially support tough drug laws that will bring in plenty of new "clientele." Of course, this is blatant *fascism,* when profits are "privatized" and cost are socialized! It is this kind of corruption that mangles the idea of *real* private enterprise and distorts further the principles of freedom and rights in so many ways.

Prosecutors say Luzerne County Judges Mark Ciavarella and Michael Conahan took $2.6 million in payoffs to put juvenile offenders in lockups run by PA Child Care LLC and a sister company, Western PA

[138] Kang, Lee and Reynolds, Francis, "What does Millions in Lobbying Money Buy? Five Cngresspeople in the Pockets of Private Prison Insustry." The Nation (on line), February 27, 2013.
http://www.thenation.com/article/173122/what-does-millions-lobbying-money-buy-five-congresspeople-pocket-private-prison-indus#

[139] The Associated Press "Pa. judges accused of jailing kids for cash :Judges allegedly took $2.6 million in payoffs to put juveniles in lockups " Februaryhttp://www.msnbc.msn.com/id/29142654/

[140] Stephen Chen , "Pennsylvania rocked by 'jailing kids for cash' scandal," CNN online, http://www.cnn.com/2009/CRIME/02/23/pennsylvania.corrupt.judges/index.html, February 23, 2009.

Child Care LLC. The judges were charged on Jan. 26 and removed from the bench by the Pennsylvania Supreme Court shortly afterward.

No company officials have been charged, but the investigation is still going on.
The high court, meanwhile, is looking into whether hundreds or even thousands of sentences should be overturned and the juveniles' records expunged.

Among the offenders were teenagers who were locked up for months for stealing loose change from cars, writing a prank note and possessing drug paraphernalia. Many had never been in trouble before. Some were imprisoned even after probation officers recommended against it.

Private prisons in the U.S. date back to the establishment of San Quenton prison in California.[141] After a number of scandals, The State of California took over control of the prison. With the burden of more criminals created as a result of the war on drugs and so-called "three-strikes law," the latter being something the judges hate because they lose judicial discretion of the mitigated circumstances of the individual.

The modern private prison-industrial complex first emerged, when Hamilton, Tennessee, contracted out its incarceration operations to Correction Corporation of America around 1984. By the year 2000, 153 private prisons were established for caging over 119 thousand prisoners.[142]

---

[141] Schmalleger, F., & Smykla, J., *Corrections in the 21st Century.* (New York: McGraw-Hill 2007).

[142] Charles W. Thomas, "Number of Private Facilities by Geographical Location," Private Corrections Project. (09/04/2001)

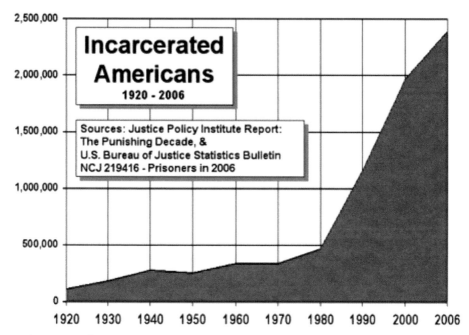

Figure 5

Notice the geometric climb in incarceration rate after 1980. This vector trend started about the same time as when the federal government began to "get tough" on illicit drugs and the drug war escalated by then-President Nixon and further escalated by then-President Reagan. By the mid-1980s the prison-industrial complex was in full gear with government-contracted prison companies coming online and with expanded police and judicial powers to attack the millions of non-violent drug offenders. Eventually, the Federal government even harassed medicinal marijuana dispensaries and users in a number of states whose state referenda decriminalized marijuana use with a doctor's prescription. The war on drugs was a full-blown war on the American people and their rights.

The Prison-Industrial Complex has taken its toll on young, black men especially (see graph below). It has taken 50 years for white men, ages 20-24 years, to reach the incarceration rate of black men.

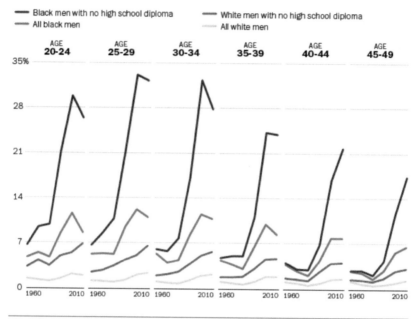

Figure 6

Some states, such as Illinois and New York have proposed bans on prison "privatization". Others, such as Louisiana, have imposed a moratorium on more private prisons.

A for instance: A recent local news broadcast, speaking on the issue of rapists, said around 70 percent of rapists claimed to have an alcohol or a drug habit. There are about 20 million people at any time using illicit drugs many factors more of people using alcohol), while there are 84 to 100 thousand rapes reported every year, between 1993 1n3 2005.[143] As you can see, the number of rapists is a fraction (~ 0.5%) of people using illicit drugs at any time. The vast majority of illicit drug

---

[143] Crime in the United States. FBI:UCR https://ucr.fbi.gov/crime-in-the-u.s/2012/crime-in-the-u.s.-2012/violent-crime/rape

users and alcohol consumers do not rape and murder people. Yet, the way the media present the numbers that drug addiction is a prerequisite for being a murderer and/or rapist.

Recent developments in the science of addiction have shed a new light on the origins of addiction.[144,145]

So, let's get to the heart of why we have a drug war and how it relates to how public opinion is being manipulated. It has now been almost forty years since Nixon modernized and escalated the prohibition of (some) drugs to declare a "war on drugs," borrowing from the left's various declarations of *wars* on America's many societal ills, many of which ironically were created by the federal government itself. The war on drugs was a convergence of late 1960's middleclass parental anxiety over white kids turning on to illicit drugs, and of a plan[146] by the political–financial class to consolidate more power into its hands through the force of government. Illicit drug use had exploded across the country, drugs like heroin and marijuana typically reserved for the subtle extermination of colored populations trapped in government-subsidized ghettos throughout the country.

As the war on drugs escalated throughout the next three decades (1970 -2000), spin-off industries, such as government-subsidized "private" prison industry, exploded, and our constitutional protection from government meddling and harassment, shrunk to meaningless words on a piece of paper. In the meantime, certain agencies within the federal government were making millions and eventually billions in available cash through covert drug running and money laundering operations around the world.

Privatizing Rendition (Torture) Centers

I've scanned the Constitution a few times looking for intent on a few issues. It seems to me that the Constitution describes an individual in two ways: as a *citizen* and as a *person* (or *people*). The only times it uses *citizen* is when it pertains to

---

[144]   Hari, Johann. 2015. "The Likely Cause of Addiction Has Been Discovered – It's Not What You Think." Wakeup-world.com May 26, 2015. http://wakeup-world.com/2015/05/26/the-likely-cause-of-addiction-has-been-discovered-its-not-what-you-think/

[145]   Hari, Johann, Chasing the Scream: The First and Last days of the War on Drugs (New York, Bloomsbury, USA, 2015).

[146]   Cook, Richard C. (former federal government analyst for the Reagan Administration). 2008. Is An International Crisis Driving World Crisis? http://www.richardccook.com http://www.rense.com/general81/deso.htm

something relative to the state within the strictures of government duties (controversies between states and *citizens*, or *citizens* and *citizens*, or a *citizen* must be such and such an age to hold such and such office). But as it pertains to protecting someone's rights, such as in the Bill of Rights, then it mentions the individual as a *person*. In other words, a human being, with no borders. A human right!

The Supreme Court was justified in its decision to give prisoners held at Gitmo their day in court, many of whom are there simply because they were kidnapped for the $25K bounty for turning in so-called terrorists. Justice Scalia outright lied in his dissent in *Boumdiene v. Bush*:[147,148]

> To bolster his argument that the Guantanamo detainees should be denied the right to prove their innocence in federal courts, Justice Antonin Scalia wrote in his dissent in *Boumediene v. Bush*: "At least 30 of those prisoners hitherto released from Guantanamo have returned to the battlefield." It turns out that statement is false.

> According to a **new report** by Seton Hall Law Center for Policy and Research, "The statistic was endorsed by a Senate Minority Report issued June 26, 2007, which cites a media outlet, CNN. CNN, in turn, named the DoD as its source. The '30' number, however, was corrected in a DoD press release issued in July 2007, and a DoD document submitted to the House Foreign Relations Committee on May 20, 2008 abandons the claim entirely.

Comic Books Lead to Drug Abuse

When I started realizing why I was in school to learn to read, I went through a phase, about 10 years old or older, when, especially in the summer with more free time, I got into reading comic books. These included the Marvel and DC series, and when I got a little older, Mad Magazine and eventually Zap and other adult comics in my later teens. Comic books gave wonderful lessons in morality and ethics to a young kid. Good *vs* Evil. Right *vs.* Wrong. Aggression vs. Civility. What was Success and what was a fundamental failure? These were excellent lessons for a child as he was soon going into a world with more freedom and a heightened curiosity.

---

[147] Hart, Len. *The Un-American Lies of Antonin Scalia.* The Existential Cowboy, June 25, 2008. http://existentialistcowboy.blogspot.com/2008/06/un-american-lies-of-antonin-scalia.html

[148] Cohn, Marjorie. *Scalia Cites False Information in Habeas Corpus Dissent.* Huffington Post, June 2, 2008. http://www.huffingtonpost.com/marjorie-cohn/scalia-cites-false-inform_b_108682.html

But there were elements in our society,[149] the busy bodies, who had the same contempt for comic books as they did for pool halls and taverns. Comic books were a waste of time, super heroes dressed in homoerotic costumes "polluting" the minds of our children. Good kids should be reading those certified to sit on the shelves of churches and government schools.

Writes Jamie Coville for an Integrated Arts website, "Dr. Fredric Werthham was the scariest thing to ever happen to comic books. He was a highly distinguished psychologist who thought comic books were bad for kids, and his efforts to have them censored had a horrible and lasting impact that still affect comic books to this day." In psychologist Werthham's mind, "Their crude blacks and reds spoils [sic] a child's natural sense of colour; their hypodermic injection of sex and murder make the child impatient with better, though quieter, stories." Possibly before the 1960s, a time when I read comics fervently, they had taken the adult content out of them. Or possibly social pressures succeeded in cleaning up content, where outright government intervention would have simply created an underground market for this literature. But that didn't stop federal to local busy bodies from trying to outlaw comics. Writes Coville, "the Cincinnati Parents Committee began rating almost all comic books published on their own criteria of art, writing, printing, and objectional content." Possibly, a comic book with a low art rating wouldn't have sold many copies anyway.

Canada to this day has this code on its federal books:

> *163. (1) Every one commits an offense who...*
> *(b) makes, prints, publishes, distributes, sells or has in his possession*
> *for the purposes of publication, distribution or circulation a crime comic.*
>
> *(7) In this section, "crime comic" means a magazine, periodical or book*
> *that exclusively or substantially comprises matter depicting pictorially*
> *(a) the commission or crimes, real or fictitious; or*
> *(b) events connected with the commission or crimes, real or fictitious,*

---

[149] Coville, J. *Seduction of the Innocents and the Attack on Comic Books:* The Comic Book Villain, Dr. Fredric Wertham, M.D. http://www.psu.edu/dept/inart10_110/inart10/cmbk4cca.html

whether occurring before or after the commission of the crime.
(1949)

Apparently, the content of such magazines causes some kids, a tiny minority, to copy the crimes committed in the stories.   One has to wonder if some kids neglect to finish their job painting a fence after reading Huck Finn, or pitching stones at taller men as David did in the Bible.

In a libertarian society the actions of the individual are the responsibility of the individual, not the fault of the gun, drug, or comic book.   Only in the realm of an authoritarian state, could the actions of an inanimate object be blamed for the potential actions of irresponsible and morally challenged individuals.

Current drugs laws exist under three major premises: 1) Health issues[150] that lead to disease and manifest criminal behavior, such as theft to support one's habit, 2) an underground economy and exchange not regulated properly and taxed, and 3) illicit drugs fund other criminal activity, such as terrorism.

Drugs are unhealthy, and highly regulated, yet the state and municipalities regulate approving frightfully incredible levels of toxins and infectious disease in the water we drink
Halogens (e.g., chlorine, fluorine) have been introduced into public water systems around the world for decades. Evolutionary selection has allowed the creation of halogen-resistant microbes such as algae and microcysts. Lead pipes were used for years. Now, recently, reports of other people's meds they throw out are found in the water we drink

Lethal Laws

Writes Jay Simkin, "Military rifles are society's "life preservers." Without them gun control can ultimately lead to mass murder."[151]

> The Down-Side of Gun Control
>
> Advocates cannot see any harm in gun control, but it has a
> nasty

---

[150] How dangerous is your tap water?http://www.aquasanastore.com/water-you_b02.html

[151] Simkin, Jay, *et al.*   Lethal Laws: Gun Control is the Key to Genocide (Jews for the Preservation of Firearms Ownership, July 1994).

downside. Its victims number in the tens of millions. Its downside is

genocide: the mass-murder of civilians on account of religion,

language, or political views. Since 1900, at least seven major genocides have occurred worldwide involving 50-60 million victims.

MAJOR 20th CENTURY GENOCIDES -- THE COST OF GUN-CONTROL

Date of Perpetrator Gov.	Date	Target	# Murdered (Estimated)	Gun-Ctrl Law	Source Document
Ottoman Turky	1915-17	Armenians	1-1.5 Mil.	1866	Art. 166, Penal Code
Soviet Union	1929-53	Anti-Comm. Anti-Stal.	20 Million	1929	Art. 128, Penal Code
Nazi Germany & occupied Europe March 18	1933-45	Jews, Anti-Nazis, Gypsies	13 Million	1928	Law on Fire-arms & Ammun. April 12, Weapons Law,
China Communists 1966- 1976	1948-52 Pro-Reform Group	Anti-	20 Million Penal Code.	1935	Arts. 186 & 7
Guatemala Indians	1960-81	Mayan 1964	100,000 Decree #283	1871	Decree #36
Uganda Politica Rivals	1971-79	Christians, 1970	300,000 Firearms Act	1955	Firearms Ord.
Cambodia Persons	1975-79	Educated	1 Million Penal Code	1956	Arts. 322-328,

TOTAL VICTIMS: 55.9 MILLION

TOTAL WAR-INDUSTRIAL COMPLEX

People do not make wars; governments do. ~ Ronald Reagan

Every gun that is made, every warship launched, every rocket fired signifies, in the final sense, a theft from those who hunger and are not fed, those who are cold and are not clothed. This world in arms is not spending money alone. It is spending the sweat of its laborers, the genius of its scientists, the hopes of its children.... Under the cloud of threatening war, it is humanity hanging from a cross of iron. ~ Dwight Eisenhower on military spending

Our government has kept us in a perpetual state of fear – kept us in a continuous stampede of patriotic fervor – with the cry of grave national emergency. Always there has been some terrible evil at home or some monstrous foreign power that was going to gobble us up if we did not blindly rally behind it by furnishing the exorbitant funds demanded. Yet, in retrospect, these disasters seem never to have happened, seem never to have been quite real.[152]

T he US military's political wing, the Department of Defense, is the largest employer in the world, employing 3.2 million people.[153] The U.S. spent more on defense in 2012 than did countries with the next 10 highest defense budgets combined. The U.S has outspent China, the next highest military spender, by six to one. At the least, 50% of all federal research and development "investments," as the

---

[152] In 1957. As quoted in Merchants of Fear: Why They Want Us to Be Afraid, Christopher Catherwood, Joseph DiVanna, Globe Pequot (Lyons Press, Guilford, 2008), p. 131

[153] "Which is the world's biggest employer? - BBC". 2012-20-03. http://www.bbc.co.uk/news/magazine-17429786. Retrieved 2012-20-03.

politicians like to call them, go to military research. Government-funded research dollars have picked up the past 15 years, but it is nothing compared to what the military spends (Figure 1).[154]

Nowhere has a country spent so much money to preserve its sociopolitical and economic machine as has the United States federal government. As Lew Rockwell notes:[155]

> Who has benefited from the American warfare state? Who, that is, apart from those with political connections or government jobs? The question answers itself. Everyone else has suffered from the trillions of dollars looted from them so the Pentagon might have the power to obliterate every conceivable enemy city a dozen times over. We have suffered from increased indebtedness, and – because capital formation is undermined by the squandering of resources in war and in massive diversion of resources to the military sector – lower real wages than we would otherwise have enjoyed. We've suffered from the civilian research and development that never occurred because the brains behind it were siphoned into military research. The costs go on and on.

---

[154]   Dooley, J.J.   U.S Federal Investments in Energy R&D: 961-2008. U.S. Department of Energy. PNNL-17952 http://www.wired.com/images_blogs/wiredscience/2009/08/federal-investment-in-energy-rd-2008.pdf,

October 2008.

[155] Rockwell, Lewellyn H. "Who are the Champions of the Common Man?" September 19, 2013 https://www.lewrockwell.com/2013/09/lew-rockwell/who-are-the-champions-of-the-common-man/

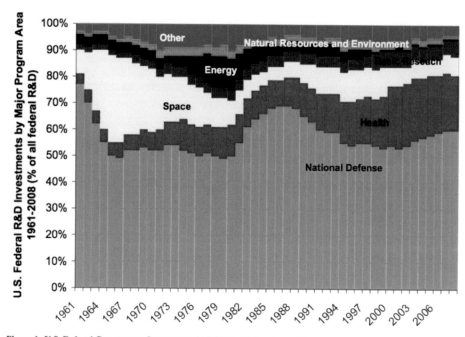

Figure 1: U.S. Federal Government Investments in R&D by Major Area of Focus

Figure 7

Writes Kathryn Muratore:[156]

> We always hear how important it is to strengthen science and promote innovation through federal funding of R&D. (This is of course nonsense as true economic and technological advances come most efficiently from a free market, not from a centrally-planned science program.) But, I wonder how many proponents of science funding realize what an overwhelming role the military plays, especially in the post-Manhattan Project age.

World War Two was the last major war between nation-states. It was the last war that the US and its allies won definitively. Since then, the U.S. has fought a number of proxy wars (see the table below), primarily against civilian militias in civil wars, predicated on the notion that ideologies and problems can be fought as a war with giant bureaucracies and bloated budgets. The civil wars in

---

[156]   Muratore, K. 2009 "More Proof Of The Military-Industrial-Congressional Complex" http://www.lewrockwell.com/blog/lewrw/archives/34006.html, August 25, 2009

Korea and Vietnam were realistically global proxy wars between the communists in China and the former Soviet Union, and the crony capitalists in the West. In the minds of many Americans, through the 1950s and 1960s, there was a need to contain the communists in Eurasia.   Even anti-state Ayn Rand believed that volunteering to join forces to fight tyranny was an honorable endeavor. Mao Zedong murdered over 50 million of his Chinese countrymen in a culture war against anyone who clung to the more bourgeois accomplishments of society. Although the wars were sold in the West on the basis that communism threatened American freedom and way of life (a legitimate argument at the time), it took infringements of our rights, and on our way of life, through implementation of the draft and increased taxes and debt to   fight   the   wars.

1950-1953 Korean War

Communist North Korea, supported by China, invades non-communist South Korea. UN forces, principally made up of U.S. troops, fight to protect South Korea. The Korean War is the first armed conflict in the global struggle between democracy and communism, called the Cold War.

1961 Cuba

The U.S. orchestrates the ill-fated Bay of Pigs invasion, an unsuccessful attempt by Cuban exiles to overthrow Fidel Castro's communist regime in Cuba.

1961-1973 Vietnam War

In 1955, communist North Vietnam invades non-communist South Vietnam in an attempt to unify the country and impose communist rule. The United States joins the war on the side of South Vietnam in 1961, but withdraws combat troops in 1973. In 1975 North Vietnam succeeds in taking control of South Vietnam. The Vietnam War is the longest conflict the U.S. ever fought and the first war it lost.

1965 Dominican Republic

U.S. president Lyndon Johnson sends marines and troops to quash a leftist uprising; he fears the Dominican Republic might follow in the footsteps of Cuba and turn communist.

1982 Lebanon

U.S. troops form part of a multinational peacekeeping force to help the fragile Lebanese government maintain power in the politically volatile country. In 1983 241 U.S. Marines and 60 French soldiers are killed by a truck bomb. The multinational force withdraws in 1984.

1983 Grenada

U.S. President Ronald Reagan invades the Caribbean island nation of Grenada to overthrow its socialist government, which has close ties with Cuba. A U.S. peace-keeping force remains until 1985.

1989 Panama

U.S. President George H. W. Bush invades Panama and overthrows Panamanian dictator and drug-smuggler Manuel Noriega. Noriega is later tried and convicted on a number of charges, and is imprisoned in the United States.

1991 Gulf War (Kuwait and Iraq)

Iraq invades the country of Kuwait. The Gulf War begins and ends swiftly when a U.S.-led multinational force comes to Kuwait's aid and expels dictator Saddam Hussein's forces.

1993 Somalia

A U.S.-led multinational force attempts to restore order to war-torn Somalia so that food can be delivered and distributed within the famine-stricken country.

1994 Haiti

After Haiti's democratically elected president Jean-Bertrand Aristide is ousted in a coup in 1991, a U.S. invasion three years later restores him to power.

1994-1995 Bosnia

During the Bosnian civil war, which begins shortly after the country declares independence in 1992, the U.S. launches air strikes on Bosnia to prevent ethnic cleansing. It becomes a part of NATO's peacekeeping force in the region.

1999 Kosovo

Yugoslavia's province of Kosovo erupts in war in the spring of 1999. A U.S.-led NATO force intervenes with air strikes after Slobodan Milosevic's Serbian forces uproot the population and embark on a plan of ethnic cleansing of Kosovo's ethnic Albanian population.

2001—2014 Afghanistan

The Taliban government harbored Osama bin Laden and the al-Qaeda terrorist group, responsible for the Sept. 11, 2001, attacks on the United States. After Afghanistan refused to turn over Bin Laden, the U.S. and UN coalition forces invaded. The Taliban government was ousted and many terrorist camps in Afghanistan were destroyed. Thereafter, the Taliban begin regrouping. By 2005, the Taliban and coalition troops are [sic] it was engaged in ongoing clashes with coaltition [sic] troops. The year 2006 was the deadliest year for U.S. soldiers in Afghanistan since 2001.

On May 2, 2011 (May 1 in the U.S.), U.S. troops and CIA operatives shot and killed Osama bin Laden in Abbottabad, Pakistan.

May 1, 2012, President Obama and President Karzai signed the *Enduring Strategic Partnership Agreement between the Islamic Republic of Afghanistan and the United States of America*. The Agreement provides for the possibility of U.S. forces in Afghanistan after 2014, for the purposes of training Afghan Forces and targeting the remnants of al-Qaeda. Afghanistan will be a "Major Non-NATO Ally" and as such, the U.S. will support the training, equipping, advising and sustaining of Afghan National Security Forces, and social and economic assistance.

2003—2010 Iraq War

The U.S. and Great Britain invade Iraq and topple the government of dictator Saddam Hussein. The U.S. engagement in Iraq continues for the next several years amid that country's escalating violence and fragile political stability.

On Aug. 31, President Obama announces the end of U.S. combat missions in Iraq. Effective September 1, 2010, the military operations in Iraq acquired a new official designation: "Operation New Dawn"; the U.S. is still committed to providing support to Iraq for further development in the areas of defense and security; education and culture; energy; human rights; services and trade.[157]

---

[157]   Major   Military   Operations   Since   World   WarII
http://www.infoplease.com/timelines/militaryoperations.html#ixzz3P03h9zh

The U.S. now has created wars on "problems," such as the war on poverty (1960s), drugs (1970s and escalated in the 1980s) and terrorism (2001-?). These fights are still ongoing and packaged and sold as "wars" to rally public support, ignoring the fact that most of these social problems can be traced to meddling governmental economic and foreign policies in the first place. Trillions of dollars have been spent on these "wars," with the so-called War on Drugs raking in over a trillion (with a T) dollars taken out of the economy the past four decades alone.[158]

In Figure 8 (next page) from the U.S. Office of Management and Budget, and reprinted by The Heritage Foundation in 2014, a comparison of outlays paid by U.S. taxpayers (or borrowed) for 2003 and 2013 is shown. Only a few outlays, such as the Postal Service budget, have declined. Military budgets along with social programs for the elderly and poor have exploded in the past decade. When the Left tells you that the Right wants to cut social program budgets, or the Right tells you that the Left wants to cut military spending, they are lying. The cuts they are really talking about are cuts to the level of increase to spending. Of course, real spending cuts rarely happen.

By the mid-1970s socialism had semantically transformed from *government ownership of the means of production* to *"government-enforced redistribution of income through the welfare state and progressive income tax,"* as Dr. Thomas DiLorenzo described in his article *The Problem With Socialism*.[159] The usual suspects are given to justify such exorbitant budgets for "running the country," an authoritarian term used to desensitize public perception of what is in reality a true totalitarian state. Despite the aggressive warmongering nature of American foreign policy that includes the unprovoked attack of more than five countries, and the covert meddling in many more, the past 15 years, the military is still referred to as the "Defense" Department. The negative economic impact on the poor by the insane U.S. foreign policy is realized by an ever-increasing "need" for social programs. The cycle of war and poverty is self-perpetuating.

---

[158] "Wasted Tax Dollars" Drug Policy Alliance. http://www.drugpolicy.org/wasted-tax-dollars

[159] DiLorenzo,Thomas, "The Problem With Socialism," July 18, 2006. https://www.lewrockwell.com/2016/07/thomas-dilorenzo/criminal-rip-off-called-socialism/

Where Does All the Money Go?

OUTLAYS, IN MILLIONS OF 2013 INFLATION-ADJUSTED DOLLARS	2003	2013	% Change	Share of 2013 Spending
650 Social Security	594,481	813,551	36.85%	23.55%
050 National Defense	506,880	633,385	24.96%	18.33%
600 Income Security	419,087	536,511	28.02%	15.53%
570 Medicare	312,385	497,826	59.36%	14.41%
550 Health	274,949	358,315	30.32%	10.37%
900 Net Interest	191,706	220,885	15.22%	6.39%
700 Veterans Benefits and Services	71,366	138,938	94.68%	4.02%
400 Transportation	83,996	91,673	9.14%	2.65%
500 Education, Training, Social Services	103,430	72,808	-29.61%	2.11%
Other (371, 373, 376)	7,384	-81,360	-1201.84%	-2.36%
750 Administration of Justice	44,259	52,601	18.85%	1.52%
150 International Affairs	26,549	46,418	74.84%	1.34%
300 Natural Resources and Environment	37,154	38,145	2.67%	1.10%
250 General Science, Space, Technology	26,088	28,908	10.81%	0.84%
800 General Government	29,010	27,755	-4.33%	0.80%
450 Community, Regional Development	23,607	32,336	36.97%	0.94%
350 Agriculture	28,174	29,492	4.68%	0.85%
270 Energy	-908	11,042	-1316%	0.32%
372 Postal service	-6,474	-1,839	-71.59%	-0.05%
950 Undistributed Offsetting Receipts	-68,107	-92,785	36.23%	-2.69%
Total Outlays	**2,705,019**	**3,454,605**	**27.71%**	

Source: U.S. Office of Management and Budget, *Budget of the United States Government, Fiscal Year 2015: Historical Tables*, 2014, pp. 156–157, Table 8.4, http://www.whitehouse.gov/omb/budget/Historicals/ (accessed September 17, 2014).

Federal Spending by the Numbers 2014 ☎ heritage.org

Figure 8

The War on Poverty in the 1960s was initiated at a time when poverty in America was actually declining, especially amongst minorities. As President Lyndon Johnson pushed for his War on Poverty, the poverty level in unadjusted numbers was in decline from 22.4% in 1959 to 19% in 1964, the year Johnson announced his plan to not only end poverty but prevent it from happening (see Figure 9 (4)). During the 1970s prosperity flat lined from inflation caused by growing government spending for new social programs and pay down for the war in Viet Nam. "The War on Poverty was not a failure. It was a catastrophe!" says Louis Woodhill:[160]

---

[160] Woodhill, Louis. "The War on Poverty Wasn't a Failure. It was a Catastrophe." Forbes (online), March 19, 2014. http://www.forbes.com/sites/louiswoodhill/2014/03/19/the-war-on-poverty-wasnt-a-failure-it-was-a-catastrophe/

Shortly after the War on Poverty got rolling (1967), about 27% of Americans lived in poverty. In 2012, the last year for which data is available, the number was about 29%

...

The adaptation of the working-age poor to the War on Poverty's expanded welfare state was immediately evident in the growth of various social pathologies, especially unwed childbearing. The adaptation of the middle class to the new system took longer to manifest, but it was no less significant.

Even people with incomes far above the thresholds for welfare state programs were forced to adapt to the welfare state. As crime rates (driven by rising numbers of fatherless boys) rose in the cities, and urban schools systems became dangerous and dysfunctional, the middle class (of all races) was forced to flee to the suburbs.

The War on Poverty accomplished a necessary role for the Military-Industrial Complex, that was to provide young, poor, desperate boys (and now girls) with the military.

Figure 4.
Number in Poverty and Poverty Rate: 1959 to 2011

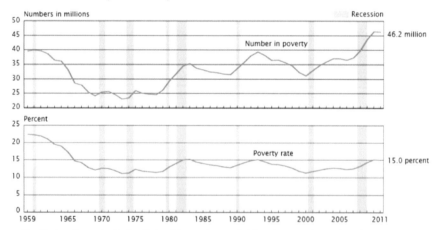

Note: The data points are placed at the midpoints of the respective years. For information on recessions, see Appendix A.
Source: U.S. Census Bureau, Current Population Survey, 1960 to 2012 Annual Social and Economic Supplements.

Figure 9

During the 2014 Republican primary for U.S. Representative, 4th District, the incumbent Ander Crenshaw, in his campaign ad, stated that the number one responsibility of the federal government is to protect the American people. This is a fallacy. Nowhere in the U.S. Constitution does it mandate federal protection with a standing army, other than a Navy to protect sea lanes and state militias to put down insurrection and defend against foreign invaders.   The Founding Fathers were terribly troubled with the prospect of assembling a permanent army, especially on American soil. This tradition of military avoidance dates back to the Roman republic, where it would be considered an act of treason and war to bring the Roman army across the Rubicon onto the Roman homeland.

The ironies of our society are infinite. During the time when eastern African shores were plagued by Somalian pirates, when unemployed and desperate Somalis and other indigents raided merchant vessels in the West Indian Ocean, the U.S. and other Western nations were invading North African and Middle Eastern countries with impunity. It was almost laughable (watching American generals and admirals lamenting about defending the world from these thugs, and uttering the word *pirate,* conjuring images of the then-president Thomas Jefferson ordering the fledgling U.S. Navy to the Mediterranean to destroy the pirates congregating on Barbary Coast of North Africa. For the last eight years, prior to this latest "crisis," we had been listening to the constant drone of *terrorism, terrorism, terrorism.* Terrorists this, terrorist that, but now pirates were a problem that demands the attention of our military and a war effort of our patriotic citizens. Now is the time to crush the problem of pirates. What's next: stagecoach robbers?   Of course, problems with pirates, or terrorists for that matter, could easily be resolved if Congress would just invoke a *letter of marque and reprisal* which could give shipping businesses, for example, the authority to go after and capture pirates (and terrorists) plaguing the African shipping lanes.

The War on Terror

Compiled from the FBI's own data,[161] the most terror attacks committed on U.S. soil between 1980 and 2005, were carried out by Latino groups (42%), and followed by extreme left wing groups (24%). Jewish extremist and Islamic extremists committed about equal numbers of attacks respectively at seven percent and six percent, and slightly more than communists groups (5%). But to believe U.S. news media, the overwhelming number attacks, and the worst problem for American security were the Muslims. It took the 9/11 attacks to sell it.

---

[161] " The Federal Bureau of Investigation, "Terrorism 2002-2005"U.S Department of Justice
https://www.fbi.gov/stats-services/publications/terrorism-2002-2005/terror02_05#terror_05sum

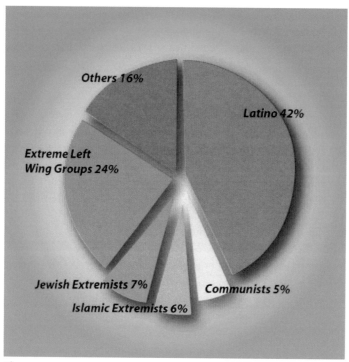

Figure 10

Chronological Summary of Terrorist Incidents in the United States 1980-2005

Date	Location	Incident Type	Perpetrator	Killed	Injured
1/7/1980	San Juan, PR	Pipe Bombing	Anti-Communist Alliance		
1/13/1980	New York, NY	Bombing	Omega 7		4
1/13/1980	Miami, FL	Bombing	Omega 7		
1/19/1980	San Juan, PR	Bombing	Omega 7		
3/12/1980	Hato Rey, PR	Armed Assault	Ejercito Popular Boricua Macheteros		
3/15/1980	Chicago, IL	Hostile Takeovers (2)	Armed Forces of National Liberation		
3/17/1980	New York, NY	Bombing	Croatian Freedom Fighters		3
3/25/1980	New York, NY	Attempted Bombing	Omega 7		
4/19/1980	Chattanooga, TN	Shooting	Justice Knights of the Ku Klux Klan		4
4/30/1980	New York,	Assault	Revolutionary		

Date	Location	Attack	Group		
	NY		Communist Party		
6/3/1980	Washington, DC	Bombing	Croatian Freedom Fighters		
6/3/1980	New York, NY	Bombing	Croatian Freedom Fighters		
7/14/1980	Dorato, PR	Multiple Bombings (2)	Organization of Volunteers for the		
	San Juan, PR		Puerto Rico Revolution		
7/14/1980	Ponce, PR	Multiple Arsons (2)	Organization of Volunteers for the		
	Mayaguez, PR		Puerto Rico Revolution		
7/22/1980	Hato Rey, PR	Multiple Bombings (4)	Revolutionary Commandos of the People,		
	Santurce, PR		Ready and at War		
	Rio Piedras, PR				
8/20/1980	Berkeley, CA	Pipe Bombing	Iranian Free Army		2
9/11/1980	New York, NY	Shooting	Omega 7	1	
10/7/1980	New York, NY	Attempted Bombing	International Committee Against Nazism		
10/12/1980	New York, NY	Bombing	Justice Commandos of the Armenian Genocide		4
10/12/1980	Hollywood, CA	Bombing	Justice Commandos of the Armenian Genocide		1
10/14/1980	Fort Collins, CO	Shooting	Libyan Revolutionary Committee		1
12/21/1980	New York, NY	Pipe Bombing	Armed Forces of Popular Resistance		
12/30/1980	Hialeah, FL	Attempted Bombing	Omega 7		
1/8/1981	Santurce, PR	Multiple IncendiaryBombings (3)	People's Revolutionary Commandos		
	Ponce, PR				
	Rio Piedras, PR				
1/12/1981	San Juan, PR	Bombing	Ejercito Popular Boricua Macheteros		
1/23/1981	New York City, NY	Bombing	Croatian Freedom Fighters		
1/26/1981	San Francisco, CA	Bombing	Jewish Defense League/American		

2/2/1981	Los Angeles, CA	Attempted Bombing	Revenge Committee 3-Oct
2/9/1981	Eugene, OR	Assault	Revolutionary Communist Youth Brigade
2/22/1981	Hollywood, CA	Bombing	Armenian Secret Army for the Liberation of Armenia
3/15/1981	San Juan, PR	Attempted Bombing	Armed Forces of Popular Resistance
4/21/1981	Santurce, PR	Robbery	Ejercito Popular Boricua Macheteros
4/27/1981	Washington, DC	Incendiary Bombing	Iranian Patriotic Army
5/16-18/81	New York City, NY	Multiple Bombings (5)	Puerto Rican Armed Resistance
6/25/1981	Torrance, CA	Incendiary Bombing	Jewish Defenders
6/26/1981	Los Angeles, CA	Bombing	June 9 Organization
7/30/1981	New York City, NY	Hostile Takeover	Libyan Students
8/7/1981	Washington, DC	Hostile Takeover	People's Mujahedin Organization of Iran
8/20/1981	Washington, DC	Arson	Black Brigade
8/20/1981	Los Angeles, CA	Bombing	June 9 Organization
8/27/1981	Carolina, PR	Bombing	Grupo Estrella
8/31/1981	New York City, NY	Hostile Takeover	Jewish Defense League
9/3-4/81	New York City, NY	Multiple Bombings (2)	Jewish Defense League
9/9/1981	Washington, DC	Assault	Concerned Sierra Leone Nationals
9/11/1981	Miami, FL	Multiple Bombings (2)	Omega 7
9/12/1981	New York City, NY	Bombing	Omega 7
9/22/1981	Schenectady, NY	Bombing	Communist Workers Party
9/24/1981	Miami, FL	Attempted Bombing	Omega 7
10/1/1981	Hollywood, CA	Bombing	Armenian Secret Army for the Liberation of Armenia
10/25/1981	New York City, NY	Incendiary Bombing	Jewish Defense League
11/11/1981	Santurce, PR	Bombing	Ejercito Popular Boricua Macheteros

Date	Location	Type	Group		
11/14/1981	Glen Cove, NY	Shooting	Unaffiliated Extremists		
11/20/1981	Los Angeles, CA	Bombing	Justice Commandos of the Armenian Genocide		
11/27/1981	Fort Buchanan, PR	Shooting	National Liberation Movement	1	
11/27/1981	Santurce, PR Condado, PR	Multiple Bombings (2)	Ejercito Popular Boricua Macheteros		
12/24/1981	New York City, NY	Attempted Pipe Bombing	Jewish Defense League		
1/28/1982	Los Angeles, CA	Shooting	Justice Commandos of the Armenian Genocide	1	
2/19/1982	Miami, FL	Multiple Bombings (2)	Omega 7		
2/19/1982	Washington, DC	Bombing	Jewish Defense League		
2/21/1982	Rio Piedras, PR	Pipe Bombing	Antonia Martinez Student Commandos		
2/28/1982	New York City, NY	Multiple Bombings (4)	Armed Forces of National Liberation		
3/22/1982	Cambridge, MA	Bombing	Justice Commandos of the Armenian Genocide		
4/5/1982	Brooklyn, NY	Arson	Jewish Defense League	1	7
4/28/1982	New York City, NY	Multiple Bombings (2)	Jewish Defense League		
4/29/1982	San Juan, PR Bayamon, PR	Multiple Bombings (2)	Provisional Coordinating Committee of the Labor Self-Defense Group		
4/29/1982	San Juan, PR	Shooting	Provisional Coordinating Committee of the Labor Self-Defense Group		
5/4/1982	Somerville, MA	Shooting	Justice Commandos of the Armenian Genocide	1	
5/16/1982	San Juan, PR	Shooting	Ejercito Popular Boricua Macheteros/ Group for the Liberation of Vieques	1	3
5/17/1982	Union City, NJ	Incendiary Bombing	Omega 7		

Date	Location	Type	Group		
5/19/1982	Villa Sin Miedo, PR	Shooting	Ejercito Popular Boricua Macheteros	1	12
5/20/1982	San Juan, PR	Attempted Bombing	Ejercito Popular Boricua Macheteros		
5/25/1982	San German, PR	Kidnapping	Grupo Estrella		1
5/30/1982	Van Nuys, CA	Attempted Bombing	Armenian Secret Army for the Liberation of Armenia		
6/10/1982	Carolina, PR	Multiple Bombings (3)	Armed Forces of Popular Resistance		
7/4/1982	New York City, NY	Multiple Pipe Bombings (2)	Croatian Freedom Fighters		
	Astoria, NY				
7/5/1982	New York City, NY	Multiple Pipe Bombings (2)	Jewish Defense League		
8/20/1982	Old San Juan, PR	Bombing	Armed Forces of National Liberation		
9/1/1982	Naranjito, PR	Attempted Bombing	Ejercito Popular Boricua Macheteros		
9/2/1982	Miami, FL	Bombing	Omega 7		
9/8/1982	Chicago, IL	Bombing	Omega 7		
9/20/1982	New York City, NY	Bombing	Armed Forces of National Liberation		
9/25/1982	Miami, FL	Attempted Bombing	Omega 7		
10/15/1982	Washington, DC	Hostile Takeover	Islamic Extremists		
10/22/1982	Philadelphia, PA	Attempted Bombing	Justice Commandos of the Armenian Genocide		
11/4/1982	New York City, NY	Smoke Bombing	Jewish Defense League		
11/16/1982	Carolina, PR	Multiple Robberies (2)	Ejercito Popular Boricua Macheteros	1	
12/8/1982	Washington, DC	Attempted Bombing	Norman David Mayer	1	
12/16/1982	Elmont, NY	Multiple Bombings (2)	United Freedom Front		
12/21/1982	New York City, NY	Attempted Pipe Bombing	Jewish Defense League		
12/22/1982	McLean, VA	Hostile Takeover	People of Omar		
12/31/1982	New York City, NY	Multiple Bombings (5)	Armed Forces of National Liberation		3
1/11-12/83	Miami, FL	Multiple Bombings (3)	Omega 7		
1/28/1983	New York City, NY	Bombing	Revolutionary Fighting Group		

Date	Location	Type	Group		
2/13/1983	Medina, ND	Shooting	Sheriff's Posse Comitatus	2	4
2/15/1983	Killeen, TX	Hijacking	Hossein Olya		
2/19/1983	Washington, DC	Pipe Bombing	Jewish Defense League		
3/20/1983	San Antonio, TX	Bombing	Republic of Revolutionary		
4/26/1983	Washington, DC	Bombing	Armed Resistance Unit		
4/27/1983	Miami, FL (4)	Attempted Bombings	Haitian Extremists		
4/29/1983	Rio Piedras, PR	Hostile Takeover	Ejercito Popluar Boricua Macheteros		
5/12/1983	Uniondale, NY	Bombing	United Freedom Front		
5/13/1983	New York City, NY	Bombing	United Freedom Front		
5/27/1983	Miami, FL	Bombing	Omega 7		
7/8/1983	Miami, FL	Kidnapping	Ejercito Revolucionario Del Pueblo		
7/15/1983	Rio Piedras, PR	Robbery	Ejercito Popular Boricua Macheteros	1	
8/8/1983	Detroit, MI	Attempted Incendiary Bombing	Fuqra		
8/8/1983	Detroit, MI	Shooting	Fuqra	1	
8/9/1983	Detroit, MI	Arson	Fuqra	2	
8/16/1983	Los Angeles, CA	Hostile Takeover	Carlos Martinez		
8/18/1983	Washington, DC	Bombing	Armed Resistance Unit		
8/21/1983	New York City, NY	Bombing	United Freedom Front		
8/27/1983	Washington, DC	Incendiary Bombing	Unknown		
10/12/1983	Miami, FL	Pipe Bombing	Omega 7		
10/30/1983	Hato Rey, PR	Rocket Attack	Ejercito Popular Boricua Macheteros		
11/7/1983	Washington, DC	Bombing	Armed Resistance Unit		
12/13-14/83	East Meadow, NY New York City, NY	Multiple Bombings (2)	United Freedom Front		
1/29/1984	New York City, NY	Bombing	United Freedom Front		
2/23/1984	New York City, NY	Bombing	Jewish Direct Action		
3/19/1984	Harrison, NY	Bombing	United Freedom		

Date	Location	Attack	Organization		
			Front		
4/5/1984	New York City, NY	Bombing	Red Guerrilla Resistance		
4/20/1984	Washington, DC	Bombing	Red Guerrilla Resistance		
5/9/1984	New York City, NY	Attempted Assassination	Bashir Baesho		
8/22/1984	Melville, NY	Bombing	United Freedom Front		
9/26/1984	New York City, NY	Bombing	Red Guerrilla Resistance		
9/26/1984	Mount Pleasant, NY	Bombing	United Freedom Front		
12/10/1984	Levittown, PR	Multiple Bombings (5)	Organization of Volunteers for the		
	Rio Piedras, PR		Puerto Rican Revolution		
	Ponce, PR				
	Mayaguez, PR				
	Cayey, PR				
1/25/1985	Old San Juan, PR	Rocket Attack	Ejercito Popular Boricua Macheteros/Organization of Volunteers for the Puerto Rican Revolution		
2/23/1985	New York City, NY	Bombing	Red Guerrilla Resistance		
5/15/1985	Northridge, CA	Pipe Bombing	Jewish Defense League		
8/15/1985	Paterson, NJ	Bombing	Jewish Defense League	1	1
9/6/1985	Brentwood, NY	Bombing	Jewish Defense League		1
10/11/1985	Santa Ana, CA	Bombing	Jewish Defense League	1	7
11/6/1985	Bayamon, PR	Shooting	Organization of Volunteers for the Puerto Rican Revolution		1
1/6/1986	Cidra, PR	Multiple Bombings (4)	Ejercito Revolucionario Clandestino/ National Revolutionary Front of Puerto Rico		
	Toa Baja, PR				
	Guanica, PR				
	Santurce, PR				
3/17/1986	Ponce, PR	Attempted Bombing	Commando Rojo		
4/14/1986	Rio Piedras, PR	Bombing	Organization of Volunteers for the Puerto Rican Revolution		

4/29/1986	San Juan, PR	Shooting	Organization of Volunteers for the Puerto Rican Revolution	1	1
5/14/1986	Phoenix, AZ	Sabotage	Earth First Organization		
9/2/1986	New York City, NY	Tear Gas Bombing	Jewish Defense League		17
9/15/1986	Coeur d'Alene, ID	Pipe Bombing	Aryan Nations		
9/29/1986	Coeur d'Alene, ID	Multiple Bombings (4)	Aryan Nations		
10/20/1986	New York City, NY	Incendiary Bombing	Jewish Defense League		
10/28/1986	Bayamon, PR	Multiple Bombings (7)	Ejercito Popular Boricua Macheteros		1
	Fajardo, PR				
	Mayaguez, PR				
	Aguadilla, PR				
	Santurce, PR				
	Fort Buchanan, PR				
11/4/1986	Puerta De Tierra, PR	Attempted Bombing	Ejercito Popular Boricua Macheteros		
12/28/1986	Yauco, PR	Multiple Bombings (2)	Ejercito Popular Boricua Macheteros		
	Guayama, PR				
4/16/1987	Davis, CA	Arson	Animal Liberation Front		
5/25/1987	Caguas, PR	Multiple Bombings (7)	Guerrilla Forces of Liberation		
	Carolina, PR				
	Mayaguez, PR				
	Cidra, PR				
	Aibonita, PR				
	Ponce, PR				
11/9/1987	Flagstaff, AZ	Sabotage	Evan Mecham Eco-Terrorist International Conspiracy		
1/12/1988	Rio Piedras, PR	Multiple Incendiary Bombings (2)	Pedro Albizu Campos Revolutionary Forces		
5/26/1988	Coral Gables, FL	Bombing	Organization Alliance of Cuban Intransigence		

95

Date	Location	Type	Group
7/22/1988	Caguas, PR	Pipe Bombing	Ejercito Popular Boricua Macheteros
9/19/1988	Los Angeles, CA	Bombing	Up the IRS, Inc.
9/25/1988	Grand Canyon, AZ	Sabotage	Evan Mecham Eco-Terrorist International Conspiracy
10/25/1988	Flagstaff, AZ	Sabotage	Evan Mecham Eco-Terrorist International Conspiracy
11/1/1988	Rio Piedras, PR	Multiple Bombings (2)	Pedro Albizu Campos Revolutionary Forces
4/3/1989	Tucson, AZ	Arson	Animal Liberation Front
6/19/1989	Bayamon, PR	Multiple Bombings (2)	Ejercito Popular Boricua Macheteros
7/3-4/89	Lubbock, TX	Malicious Destruction of Property	Animal Liberation Front
1/12/1990	Santurce, PR Carolina, PR	Multiple Pipe Bombings (2)	Eugenio Maria de Hostos International Brigade of the Pedro Albizu Campos Revolutionary Forces
2/22/1990	Los Angeles, CA	Bombing	Up the IRS, Inc.
4/22/1990	Santa Cruz County, CA	Malicious Destruction of Property	Earth Night Action Group
5/27/1990	Mayaguez, PR	Arson	Unknown Puerto Rican Group
9/17/1990	Arecibo, PR Vega Baja, PR	Multiple Bombings (2)	Pedro Albizu Group Revolutionary Forces
2/3/1991	Mayaguez, PR	Arson	Popular Liberation Army
2/18/1991	Sabana Grande, PR	Arson	Popular Liberation Army
3/17/1991	Carolina, PR	Arson	Unknown Puerto Rican Group
4/1/1991	Fresno, CA	Bombing	Popular Liberation Army
7/6/1991	Punta Borinquen, PR	Bombing	Popular Liberation Army
4/5/1992	New York, NY	Hostile Takeover	Mujahedin-E-Khalq
11/19/1992	Urbana, IL	Attempted Firebombing	Mexican Revolutionary Movement
12/10/1992	Chicago, IL	Car Fire and	Boricua

Date	Location	Attack	Perpetrator	Killed	Injured
		Attempted Firebombing (2)	Revolutionary Front		
2/26/1993	New York, NY	Car Bombing	International Islamist Extremists	6	1042
7/20-22/93	Tacoma, WA	Multiple Bombings (2)	American Front Skinheads		
11/27-28/93	Chicago, IL	Firebombings (9)	Animal Liberation Front		
3/1/1994	New York, NY	Shooting	Rashid Najib Baz	1	3
4/19/1995	Oklahoma City, OK	Truck Bombing	Timothy McVeigh and Terry Nichols	168	754
			(Michael Fortier found guilty of failing to alert authorities of plot)		
4/1/1996	Spokane, WA	Pipe Bombing/Bank Robbery	Spokane Bank Robbers		
7/12/1996	Spokane, WA	Pipe Bombing/Bank Robbery	Spokane Bank Robbers		
7/27/1996	Atlanta, GA	Pipe Bombing	Eric Robert Rudolph	2	112
1/2/1997	Washington, DC	Letter Bombing	Unknown		
	Leavenworth, KS	(Counted as 1 incident)			
1/16/1997	Atlanta, GA	Bombing of Abortion Clinic	Eric Robert Rudolph		8
2/21/1997	Atlanta, GA	Bombing of Alternative Lifestyle Nightclub	Eric Robert Rudolph		5
1/29/1998	Birmingham, AL	Bombing of Reproductive Services Clinic	Eric Robert Rudolph	1	1
3/31/1998	Arecibo, PR	Bombing of Superaqueduct Construction Project	Ejercito Popular Boricua Macheteros		
6/9/1998	Rio Piedras, PR	Bombing of Bank Branch Office	Ejercito Popular Boricua Macheteros		
6/25/1998	Santa Isabel, PR	Bombing of Bank Branch Office	Ejercito Popular Boricua Macheteros suspected		1
6/27/1998	Espanola, NM	Arson	Raymond Anthony Sandoval		
10/19/1998	Vail, CO	Arson Fire at Ski Resort	Earth Liberation Front		
3/19/1999	Santa Fe, NM	Attempted Bombing	Raymond Anthony Sandoval		
3/27/1999	Franklin Township, NJ	Bombing of Circus Vehicles	Animal Liberation Front		

4/5/1999	Minneapolis -St. Paul, MN	Malicious Destruction and Theft	Animal Liberation Front		
5/9/1999	Eugene, OR	Bombing	Animal Liberation Front		
7/2-4/99	Chicago, IL	Multiple Shootings	Benjamin Nathaniel Smith	2	8
	Skokie, IL				
	Northbrook, IL				
	Bloomington, IN				
8/10/1999	Granada Hills, CA	Multiple Shootings	Buford O'Neal Furrow	1	5
8/28-29/99	Orange, CA	Malicious Destruction and Theft	Animal Liberation Front		
10/24/1999	Bellingham, WA	Malicious Destruction and Theft	Animal Liberation Front		
11/20/1999	Puyallup, WA	Malicious Destruction	Animal Liberation Front		
12/25/1999	Monmouth, OR	Arson	Earth Liberation Front		
12/31/1999	East Lansing, MI	Arson	Earth Liberation Front		
1/3/2000	Petaluma, CA	Incendiary Attack	Animal Liberation Front		
1/15/2000	Petaluma, CA	Incendiary Attack	Animal Liberation Front		
1/22/2000	Bloomington, IN	Arson	Earth Liberation Front		
5/7/2000	Olympia, WA	Arson	Revenge of the Trees		
7/2/2000	North Vernon, IN	Arson	Animal Liberation Front		
7/20/2000	Rhinelander, WI	Vandalism	Earth Liberation Front		
12/1/2000	Phoenix, AZ	Multiple Arsons	Mark Warren Sands		
12/9-30/00	Suffolk County, Long Island, NY	Multiple Arsons	Earth Liberation Front		
1/2/2001	Glendale, OR	Arson	Earth Liberation Front		
2/20/2001	Visalia, CA	Arson	Earth Liberation Front		
3/9/2001	Culpeper, VA	Tree Spiking	Earth Liberation Front		
3/30/2001	Eugene, OR	Arson	Earth Liberation Front		
4/15/2001	Portland, OR	Arson	Earth Liberation Front		

Date	Location	Crime	Perpetrator		
5/17/2001	Harrisburg, PA	Bank Robbery	Clayton Lee Waagner		
5/21/2001	Seattle, WA	Arson	Earth Liberation Front		
5/21/2001	Clatskanie, OR	Arson	Earth Liberation Front		
7/24/2001	Stateline, NV	Destruction of Property	Earth Liberation Front		
9/9/2001	Morgantown, WV	Bank Robbery	Clayton Lee Waagner		
9/11/2001	New York, NY Washington, DC New Cumberland, PA	Aircraft Attack	Al-Qa'ida	2972	est. 12000
9/01–11/01	New York, NY Washington, DC Lantana, FL	Bacillus anthracis Mailings	Unknown	5	17
10/14/2001	Litchfield, CA	Arson	Earth Liberation Front		
11/12/2001	San Diego, CA	Burglary and Vandalism	Animal Liberation Front		
3/18/2002	Erie, PA	Vandalism	Earth Liberation Front		
3/24/2002	Erie, PA	Arson	Earth Liberation Front		
5/11–12/02	Harborcreek, PA	Vandalism/Destruction of Property	Earth Liberation Front/ Animal Liberation Front		
7/4/2002	Los Angeles, CA	Shooting	Hesham Mohamed Ali Hedayat	2	
8/02–10/02	Henrico and Goochland Counties, VA	Vandalism and Destruction of Property	Earth Liberation Front		
8/11/2002	Warren, PA	Arson	Earth Liberation Front		
9/15–16/02	Harborcreek, PA	Vandalism/Destruction of Property	Earth Liberation Front/ Animal Liberation Front		
11/26/2002	Harborcreek, PA	Arson	Earth Liberation Front/ Animal Liberation Front		
1/1/2003	Girard, PA	Arson	Earth Liberation Front		
3/3/2003	Chico, CA	Vandalism	Animal Liberation Front		

Date	Location	Crime	Group
8/03–9/03	San Diego, CA	Arson	Earth Liberation Front
8/22/2003	West Covina, CA	Vandalism and Destruction of Property	Earth Liberation Front
8/28/2003	Emeryville, CA	Bombing	Daniel Andreas San Diego Suspected
9/26/2003	Pleasanton, CA	Bombing	Daniel Andreas San Diego Suspected
1/19/2004	Henrico County, VA	Arson	Earth Liberation Front Suspected
4/1/2004	Oklahoma City, OK	Arson	Sean Michael Gillespie/Aryan Nations
4/20/2004	Redmond, WA	Vandalism and Arson	Earth Liberation Front
5/04–7/04	Provo, UT	Vandalism and Arson	Animal Liberation Front
12/27/2004	Lincoln, CA	Attempted Arson	Earth Liberation Front
1/05–2/05	Auburn, CA	Attempted Arson and Arson	Earth Liberation Front
	Sutter Creek, CA		
4/13/2005	Sammanish, WA	Arson	Earth Liberation Front
7/7/2005	Los Angeles, CA	Attempted Arson	Animal rights extremists Suspected
9/16/2005	Los Angeles, CA	Attempted Arson	Animal Liberation Front
11/20/2005	Hagerstown, MD	Arson	Earth Liberation Front

Table 1

Now, of course, one could argue that Muslims have killed more people on American soil, but the reason for this is blowback, a CIA term for retaliation for invading and occupying a foreign land and its population. People get angry when foreign powers take over their countries. They fight back with terrorism, because that is the only way possible without the vast resources of a nation-state such as the United States. Europe and the United States have been meddling in the Middle East since at least the 1920s.

Think of the war on terror as two neighbors with a weed problem. Neighbor Smith is annoyed because Neighbor Jones won't control his weeds (i.e., the terrorists, for those who haven't caught on). One spring the problem got so bad in Smith's yard that he took it upon himself to bomb the $%!^ out of Neighbor Jones' yard with the antifoliant Agent Orange. Yes, it eliminated the weeds, along with Jones' grass, shrubs and trees. In fact, there was so much depleted antifoliate on Jones' yard, the whole family was displaced and neighboring families' yards were deteriorating, as well. The whole neighborhood became unstable, and tensions escalated amongst the neighbors.

Of course, this would be unacceptable behavior for Smith to do within community standards. Yet, the U.S. has been behaving for decades just as Smith behaved, bankrupting the country with debt and government-brought non-productivity the whole way. Now, a weed problem to the actions of murdering terrorists shouldn't be misconstrued to justification for killing thousands of innocent Muslims who have no more control of the actions of terrorist and their murderous governments as we Americans have control of the authorities we are subjected on a daily basis.

April 20, 2008
The US of Militarism
Posted by Lew Rockwell at April 20, 2008 08:29 AM
One might say, duh, but the NY Times shows that TV's "military analysts" are shills for the military-industrial complex, planted by the Pentagon. Virtually all the "terrorism experts" on TV are similarly agents, as are many of the "journalists."

Just to show the hypocrisy of state control and how brainwashed people are, a church up the street from my house requests a cop stop by around 12:30 PM Sundays to help stop traffic so parishioners can get out of the parking lot. One exit is regulated by this cop and the other exit is open for those turning right and not having to cross traffic. Well, one Sunday I found myself getting into this traffic situation. Everyone dutifully stopped and waited for a number of cars to leave the parking lot. After going again I noticed the other exit was accumulating cars waiting to leave, so being the nice guy I am, I slowed and motioned to them take off. Well, the people behind me got a little perturbed and tooted their horns. In other words, it was perfectly OK for an agent of the state, carrying a gun and wearing the official state costume, to hold up traffic, but out of simple courtesy, an ordinary citizen might get a traffic ticket to the delight of other drivers for obstructing the flow of traffic.

March 14, 2007
Poor Chiquita Banana
Posted by Lew Rockwell at 01:45 PM
The company has been fined $25 million by the US government for paying taxes. That is, the banana grower paid off a guerrilla group in Columbia for protection, and unlike payments to governments, actually got the protection. This is illegal, of course, and the US's business, since the US claims galactic jurisdiction, and can't stand competition. By the way, for this money, the company will get...exactly nothing.

Eisenhower, although having admonished the military complex, did little to stop it.   In fact, he promoted it by establishing the Federal Interstate System, thus expanding federal power with a new perversion of the already much-maligned "interstate commerce clause," while providing a standing army with an internal network to bypass Posse Comitatus. The United States did little after World War II to heed Eisenhower's words.   The central banks and military industries exploded during those times.

The "Privatization" of War

First of all, it's not really "private".[162]   This is not revenue acquired by the market.   It is revenue confiscated by government from hard-working taxpayers and transferred to private companies, many of which undercut prices, in turn driving legitimately "private" companies out of business. As of 2007, the U.S. had 100,000 contractors in the occupation of Iraq, of which about 48,000 were "private" soldiers (mercenaries). Privatization was sold as an inexpensive approach to fighting 21st Century wars, but many of the contractors in Iraq received 1,000 dollars-a-day compensation to fight the war, protect dignitaries and do construction projects. According to reporter Jeremy Scahill, "These soldiers have operated with almost no oversight or effective legal constraints and are an undeclared expansion of the scope of the occupation." If they are killed, they do not count as official casualties.

Generally, these companies provide security, communication and construction support. Few are actually guns-in-hands mercenaries as stereotyped in the movies and books.

> Brendan Conway is charmed by Philip Gold's notion that every American male "should spend some time in uniform as a normal part of life and of citizenship" ("Selective service," Feb. 6). I'm not so charmed.
> Society remains primitive insofar as individuals are regarded as agents to butcher for - and to be butchered for - the collective.
>
> "Society progresses only as the depraved romance of the collective gives way to respect for the individual - the individual whose life and property are never regarded as being at the disposal of the state."
>
> Sincerely,

---

[162] Scahill, Jeremy. "Blackwater, Inc. and the Privatizaarion of the Bush War Machine." Urunet.info http://www.uruknet.de/?p=m30280&hd=&size=1&l=e

Donald J. Boudreaux
Chairman, Department of Economics
George Mason University

Table 2 (below) reflects the number of contractors shifted to Afghanistan from Iraq in the early "change" then-President Obama promised during the Spring of 2009, in preparation to alleged hints that American presence in Iraq would be drastically reduced over the following couple of years.   Despite Obama's call for removal of American presence during his presidential campaign to appease the antiwar Left, Obama quickly shifted focus to the "Good War" as parroted by columnists on the Left, particularly. In preparation for fighting the "Good War" contracts were re-negotiated and many contractors were moved from Iraq to Afghanistan ahead of the troops to build camps, runways, communication lines, for example, and protect the opium fields that were re-established in 2002 after the Taliban destroyed them before the 9/11 attacks.

American "Assets"	Iraq	Afghanistan
Contractors	132,610	68,197
Troops	141,300	52,300
Ratio	0.94 / 1	1.3 / 1

Table 2 Number of   total contractors vs.   military troops as of March 2009; Moshe Schwartz, Defense Acquisition Policy Analyst, Congressional Research Service.

Within six months of the time Table 1 had reported data, the number of contractors in the Central Asian theater rose to 280,000, according to Moshe Schwartz of Congressional Research Service. Schwartz said on C-SPAN that of the more than quarter million contractors, about 50,000 of them are American. The rest come prominently from indigenous sources (70% in Afghanistan and 25% in Iraq) or companies from American allies such as Israel (15,000 in Iraq and 5,000 in Iraq), and those in Europe and Asia. This theater is possibly the greatest make-work program ever developed by a conglomeration of neo-socialist states in the history of mankind.

Saying war is Big Business is an understatement. Granted, Americans have always used contractors to fight their wars, going all the way back to the 18th Century Revolutionary War for secession from imperial England, here in the 21st Century, wars have become a major source of income for the international banksters and other politically-connected parasites. We now know it is no "conspiracy theory" to say cabals of policy makers, think tanks, central banks and industrialists have been running things for a long time. It has been said that history doesn't happen by accident.[163]

The reasons for "private" contractors, of course, is to avoid manpower shortages needed to execute the logistics of these police actions and to avoid conscription, which is not politically palatable enough to reinstitute with these unpopular "wars." Despite the high disapproval ratings from disgruntled Americans, the District of Catastrophe continues to squander blood and treasure in wars for geo-strategic resources. When private contractors are maimed or killed, their demise is not considered as a casualty and reported to the American people. This helps the politicians and other shills continue to promote the war and show that we are "winning."

War Made Easy

"While we are making refrigerators, our enemies are building bombs." In 1940, FDR was clamoring for war in the European theater. His arrogant hubris for an argument was flawed on many levels. His leftist ideology gave him the allusion that industries were making refrigerators for him and his nation. Actually, FDR was producing nothing! But socialists, like FDR, never think of worker identity that isn't beholden to the whims of the state. For Roosevelt, bombs would have a better purpose for furthering his agenda than building cars and refrigerators, and stay out of the war.

To understand why oil (and its endless residuals of oil products) is so expensive, one only need look to the wars in the Central Asia. In 2004, besides subsidizing schools, and other infrastructure in Iraq and Afghanistan, the US military blew through 144 million barrels of oil that year,[164] 40 million barrels more than during peacetime, serving two occupations to where no indigents other than a few wealthy and corrupt crony capitalists want them there. That is nearly 400 thousand barrels a day. People use to call it a "war tax," but now it's just tacked on the cost of "doing business" with the world, much of it borrowed money.

Despite the Left's mythology that the Bush-Cheney administration attacked Iraq to steal the oil for their energy cronies' benefit; better yet, they sacked Iraq to disrupt the output and drive up the cost of reserves and future stores. That became evident[165,166] shortly after the invasion (see graph below). The spigot to the second

---

[163]   Attributed to both Franklin Delano Roosevelt or Winston Churchill.

[164] Karbuz, Sohbet. The US military oil consumption. http://www.resilience.org/stories/2006-02-26/us-military-oil-consumption

largest oil reserve in the world had been shut off and never recovered to pre-occupation levels (2003) until 2008, five years later. Coincidentally, into the last year of George W. Bush's second term, oil production had finally recovered again to pre-occupation levels.[167] Iraqi oil production has never recovered to levels before the Gulf War in 1990.   Notice that after the beginning of every war in Iraq (Iran-Iraq war (1980), First Iraq War (1990) and the Second Invasion of Iraq (2003)), oil production drops to zero, in turn driving oil prices up globally.

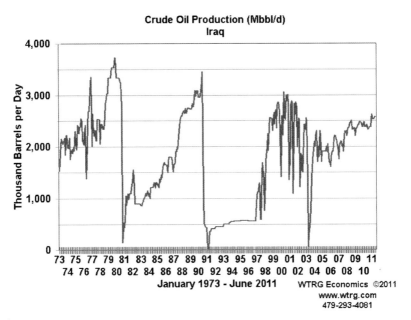

Figure 11

In another graphic[168] below shows oil production in nine other countries not plagued with the occupation of more than 130,000 foreign forces and a military police-state existence.

[165] Iraq: Oil and Economy 2002   http://usgovinfo.about.com/library/weekly/aairaqioil.htm

[166]   http://www.wtrg.com/oil_graphs/PAPRPIQ.gif

[167]   Fletcher, M and Pagnamenta, R. 2008 Iraq's revival boosted as oil production rises to 2.4m barrels a day. Times online, February 1, 2008. http://www.timesonline.co.uk/tol/news/world/iraq/article3285580.ece

[168]   Wednesday, May 03, 2006 http://donkeypath.blogspot.com/2006/05/graph-shows-iraqs-oil-production.html

Importance of Iraqi Oil to the U.S.
During December 2002, the United States imported 11.3 million barrels of oil from Iraq. In comparison, imports from other major OPEC oil-producing countries during December 2002 included:
(**Sands of Iraq hold world's 2nd largest oil reserve (2002)**)

Saudi Arabia - 56.2 million barrels
Venezuela 20.2 million barrels
Nigeria 19.3 million barrels
Kuwait - 5.9 million barrels
Algeria - 1.2 million barrels
Leading imports from non-OPEC countries during December 2002 included:
Canada 46.2 million barrels
Mexico 53.8 million barrels
United Kingdom 11.7 million barrels
Norway 4.5 million barrels

Most of Iraq's oil production since the American occupation has gone to Iraq's national budget, about $18 B. In other words, the political class is enjoying the work done by the citizenry. The workers couldn't have had a better slave master in deposed Saddam Hussein.

The propaganda blitz in 2007 was in full swing to milk the public out of more money for the war in Iraq. In November, the CNN website broadcast breaking news of the day regarding another suspect video of Osama bin Laden, condemning America's occupation in Iraq and Afghanistan. A few minutes later, on the same website the president George W. Bush announced he would ask Congress for $87 billion supplement money for the wars. This coincidence had CIA psychological operations (psy-ops) written all over it. It was no secret the CIA infiltrated corporate media and Hollywood for decades with the intent to channel and filter news for public consumption (see Chapter 8, Information–Media Industrial Complex). The CIA was in overdrive during the 1960's war in Vietnam.

The CIA does not work for these United States, pointed out so well in the 2009 movie *The International*. The CIA operates for the benefit of European and American central banks. Operatives, along with the help of the Israeli Mossad and British MI6, do their mischief around the world , wherever it suits their employers. They rig elections, assassinate political leaders, destabilize their governments, create civil wars and wars across boundaries, all in the interest of the bankers financing the warring, cash-strapped countries. Wars are big business. And as Franklin Delano Roosevelt said, "In politics, nothing happens by accident. If it happens, you can bet it was planned that way."

In 2009, and Italian court convicted 23 CIA agents for kidnapping and torture crimes.[169] Twenty-two were immediately sentenced to five years in jail. Milan CIA station chief Robert Seldon Lady was given eight years in the hoosegow. He was quoted in court saying, "I am not guilty. I am only responsible for following an order I received from my superiors,"

In 1986, President George HW Bush went to the Saudis and pleaded with them to cut production and increase the price because US oil companies (Bush's pals) weren't making any money.[170,171] In 1998, Bush went back to the Saudis and convinced them to cut oil production, sending oil prices up over 225%, sending oil company profits up over 33,000%, ahead of the 2000 election between his son, George W. Bush, and Democratic candidate Al Gore, Jr.[172]

Nixon's Crazy Price Controls

> The rapid increase in crude prices from 1973 to 1981 would have been much less were it not for United States energy policy during the post Embargo period. The US imposed price controls on domestically produced oil in an attempt to lessen the impact of the 1973-74 price increase. The obvious result of the price controls was that U.S. consumers of crude oil paid about 50 percent more for imports than domestic production and U.S producers received less than world market price. In effect, the domestic petroleum industry was subsidizing the U.s. consumer.[173]

The US military, The Department of Defense, is the largest employer in the world, employing 3.2 million people[174] Of particular interest are the missions of U.S. Special Operations Command (SOCOM). Since the terrorist attacks of 9/11, Special

---

[169] Alberici, Emma, *CIA agents jailed over cleric kidnap.* American Broadcasting Company, November 4, 2009. http://www.abc.net.au/news/stories/2009/11/05/2733681.htm

[170] Hershey, Robert D. Bush to Seek Saudis' Assistance in Stabilizing Plunging Oil Prices. The New York Times April 2, 1986.

[171] Bowen, Russell S. The Immaculate Deception (Carson City, American West Publishers, 1991), p.150.

[172] Moderate Independent, Did Former President George H.W. Bush Create an Oil Crisis in to get His Son Elected? January 2, 2004 http://www.moderateindependent.com/v1i18hwbush.htm

[173] Williams, J.L. **2007** WTRG Economics http://www.wtrg.com/prices.htm

[174] "Which is the world's biggest employer? - BBC". 2012-20-03. http://www.bbc.co.uk/news/magazine-17429786. Retrieved 2012-20-03.

Ops has grown in 12 years from 33,000 personnel to 72,000, in which about half are "badge operators," and rest are support personnel.[175],[176]

The ironies of our society are infinite. During the time when eastern African shores were plagued by Somalian pirates, unemployed and desperate Somalis and other indigents raiding merchant vessels in the west Indian Ocean. It was almost laughable watching American generals and admirals lamenting on about defending the world from these thugs, and uttering the word *pirate,* conjuring images of the then-president Thomas Jefferson ordering the fledgling U.S. Navy to the Mediterranean to destroy the pirates congregating on Barbary Coast of North Africa. For the last eight years, prior to this latest "crisis," we had been listening to the constant drone of *terrorism, terrorism, terrorism.* This terrorist this. This terrorist that. Now pirates were a problem that demand the attention of our military the war effort of or patriotic citizens. Now is time to crush the problem of pirates. What's next? Stagecoach robbers?

Think of the war on terror as two neighbors with a weed problem. Neighbor Smith is annoyed because Neighbor Jones won't control his weeds (i.e., the terrorists, for those who haven't caught on). One spring the problem got so bad in Smith's yard that he took it upon himself to bomb the $%!^ out of Neighbor Jones' yard with the antifoliant Agent Orange. Yes, it eliminated the weeds, along with Jones' grass, shrubs and trees. In fact, there was so much depleted antifoliate on Jones' yard, the whole family was displaced and neighboring families' yards were deteriorating, as well. The whole region became unstable.

Of course, this would be unacceptable behavior for Smith to do within community standards. Yet, the US has been behaving for decades just as Smith behaved, bankrupting the country with debt and government-induced non-productivity the whole way. Now, a weed problem to the actions of murdering terrorists shouldn't be misconstrued to justification for killing thousands of innocent Muslims who have no more control of the actions of terrorist and their murderous governments as we Americans have control of the authorities we are subjected on a daily basis.

---

[175]   McLeary, Paul. Life After Wartime: SOCOM Focuses on Global Parterships, Troop Mobilityhttp://www.defensenews.com/article/20131008/DEFREG02/31008001

[176]   Turse, Nick   Special Ops Goes Global. TomDispatch.com, January 7, 2014.http://www.tomdispatch.com/post/175790/tomgram%3A_nick_turse%2C_special_ops_goes_global/#more

To show the hypocrisy of state control and how brainwashed people are .... A church up the street from my house requests a cop stop by around 12:30 PM Sundays to help stop traffic so parishes can get out of the parking lot. One exit is regulated by this cop and the other exit is open for those turning right and not having to cross traffic. Well, one Sunday I found myself getting into this traffic situation. Everyone dutifully stopped and waited for a number of cars to leave the parking lot. After going again I noticed the other exit was accumulating cars waiting to leave, so being the nice guy I am. I slowed and motioned to them take off. Well, the people behind me got a little perturbed and tooted their horns. In other words, It is perfectly OK for an agent of the state, carrying a gun and wearing the official state costume, to hold up traffic, but out of simple courtesy, an ordinary citizen might get a traffic ticket to the delight of other drivers for obstructing the flow of traffic.

The U.S. military spends more money than the next seven militaries of other nations combined.[177] At the least, 50% of all federal R&D "investments," as the politicians like to call them, go to military research. Government-funded research dollars have picked up the past 15 years, but it is nothing compared to what the military spends (Figure 1).[178] Writes Kathryn Muratore:[179]

> We always hear how important it is to strengthen science and promote innovation through federal funding of R&D. (This is of course nonsense as true economic and technological advances come most efficiently from a free market, not from a centrally-planned science program.)
>
> But, I wonder how many proponents of science funding realize what an overwhelming role the military plays, especially in the post-Manhattan Project age.

The CIA, NSA and Other Cogs of the U.S. Security State

Americans have been programmed for many decades to believe that agents of the Central Intelligence Agency (CIA) in fact operate like the heroes in movies such as the James Bond series. Founding Father John Adams warned us about looking for

---

177   Does the U.S. Spend More on Its Military Than the Next 10 Countries Combined? Committee for a Responsible Federal Budget, November 11, 2015.

178   Dooley, J.J. U.S Federal Invetments in Energy R&D: 961-2008. U.S. Department of Energy. PNNL-17952 http://www.wired.com/images_blogs/wiredscience/2009/08/federal-investment-in-energy-rd-2008.pdf, October 2008.

179   Muratore, K. 2009 "More Proof Of The Military-Industrial-Congressional Complex" http://www.lewrockwell.com/blog/lewrw/archives/34006.html, August 25, 2009

monsters to destroy overseas. More to the truth is that these clandestine agencies operate for the benefit of those who enrich themselves from wars, rebellions, and civil wars.

Sitting in a restaurant booth finishing up a lunch, I couldn't help listening to an early drinker at the bar and an Army man in his desert kakis discuss the many benefits of being stationed over in Germany.   The old, possibly retired military drinker reminisced about travel through Europe and for the soldier to make sure he visited one of our many camps in Italy, a half-hour drive from the beach, some of the most expensive property in Italy. Apparently, we're still stationed in Italy to protect Italians from sharks.   And as for occupying Germany, you never know when the barbaric hoards from Russia will pour across Poland. Again. Anyway, It's great to see we are paying people to spread our fiat currency around the planet, while the Holy Homeland goes broke.

As I was listening to this I thought of their idol, the libertine and provokingly dense Commander-in-Chief George W. Bush, who believes he is more than just the Commander-in-Chief of the military but Commander-in-Chief of the whole planet. Which being worse, the worse excuse of a politician to walk into the White House or the nauseating hyper-nationalism we are witnessing in the US today, one can only reconcile that it is a tie in a race to the bottom. What the US has become the past generation is phenomenally pathetic.

When I hear the argument that we have to fight the war on (fill in the blank) at all costs, I have to think, "Well, I'm a molecular biologist.   Why not give me what I need to help find cure for diseases such as cancer or Alzheimer's?" If this does not sound bizarre to them then they are probably beyond reconciling the fact that *at all cost* will eventually bankrupt the country. Alas, a constitutional republic was probably as bad as an empire.

POLITICAL-INDUSTRIAL COMPLEX

If voting changed anything, they'd make it illegal. ~Emma Goldman

"That's not the way the world really works anymore. ...
We're an empire now, and when we act, we create our own
reality. And while you're studying that reality—judiciously, as
you will—we'll act again, creating other new realities, which
you can study too, and that's how things will sort out. We're
history's actors ... and you, all of you, will be left to just study
what we do."   ~ Karl Rove

Big Government isn't the savior. It's the devil, wearing a chicken suit. ~ Jim Babka

[41] When the ten other disciples heard what James and John had
asked, they were indignant. [42] So Jesus called them together and said,
"You know that the rulers in this world lord it over their people, and
officials flaunt their authority over those under them. [43] But among
you it will be different. Whoever wants to be a leader among you must
be your servant, [44] and whoever wants to be first among you must be
the slave of everyone else. [45] For even the Son of Man came not to be
served but to serve others and to give his life as a ransom for many." ~
Mark 10:41-45, The Holy Bible

The realm of politics has become big business. Billions of dollars exchange hands into the coffers of political action committees (PACs) and other collectives that push legislators in one direction or another to suit their "business" interests while rendering other businesses less competitive. Much of the time large corporations will support costly governmental regulations that corporations can absorb but that smaller, local businesses cannot. Examples would be environmental regulations, minimum wage and the Affordable Care Act, commonly called "Obamacare." These governmental interventions really have little to do with saving the environment or promoting prosperity or becoming more affordable.   They are job programs to keep millions of people employed by manipulating the way money comes and goes through society. Tax laws create accountants. Many such laws eventually have a negative effect by costing too much and/or stifling businesses, causing them to lay off workers or to seek better business environments in other states or countries.

A government should never be run like a business. That is a formula for disaster. The objective of any business is to grow and make more money. This governmental paradigm should give any freedom-loving soul pause. A government's objective should never be to grow and make more money. Businesses' employment tactics are designed to find the best talent. Governments should never take the best and the brightest from our society, where talents are focused on improving governmental programs that for the most part should not even exist in the first place. So, what we have today in this state-business model is self-important people with special interests creating more and more revenue by force to support their own selfish interests. It is always easy to be idealistic and compassionate with another person's money.

Thankfully, most of what we do in a day is anarchistic by virtue of our very nature. No authority has to tell us when we can go to the bathroom, or where we buy our food, or what car to buy or where we can live or do business (well, if you disregard zoning laws). But don't authorities try their best to direct and micromanage our lives? Much of what we consider to be "free," or a right, has many hidden restrictions that control people's behavior or perception without them even knowing it. Christians think they are free because they can attend the church of their choice without harassment, but are oblivious to the fact that their church is probably regulated by a federal 501(c)(3) restriction on political speech or other activities.[180,181,182] Most people think we have a choice of vehicle we can drive, but there are few choices due to the number of restrictions on the mechanical, material and aerodynamic designs mandated by both federal and state regulations. Possibly one of the most damaging restrictions on vehicles is the requirement to add ethanol in fuel mixtures

---

[180] Hallowell, Billy. "IRS suspends 'politiced' church tax audits until new regulations are finalized." The Blaze on line, October 22, 2012. http://www.theblaze.com/stories/2012/10/22/irs-suspends-politicized-church-tax-audits-until-new-regulations-are-finalized/#

[181] Johnson Amendment, http://en.wikipedia.org/wiki/Johnson_Amendment

[182] Hammar,, Richard R. "State regulation of psychologists and counselors." Church Law&Tax 1(4):4-10.

that ultimately destroys vehicle engines and skews commodity markets (the ethanol is primarily made from corn).

If corporations are outsourcing jobs, become an importer/exporter.   If machines are taking your jobs, learn how to build and run the machines.   The market is based on the Law of Nature.   Natural Law will never change.   Most politicians think they can defy Natural Law. That is the deceit and vanity of people who seek power. If politicians could, they would outlaw gravity if their constituents complained enough about not being able to fly.

Sad as it is, 90% of the adult American public is politically, historically and economically clueless. Henry Louis Mencken called them *Boobus americanus*.   For decades the government school system has made sure of that.   If you doubt this just watch a few Q&A shows, such as the Tonight Show with Jay Leno, where the host goes into the audience, or onto the streets, asking questions about anything from the Constitution to who is the president of the Senate to what year did the War of 1812 begin?   Using ballot-access laws and gerrymandering to keep the gentle tide of a Republican-Democrat duopoly moving uncontested, the political class has become the "best and the brightest" of our society's shysters.   In fact, many of the electoral laws, established by the two major parties, of course, look frighteningly similar to laws the communists used in the former Soviet Union.[183]

It is not the business of government institutions like public education or public libraries to inform the public systematically.   Government is in the business of promoting government. We are far better off educating and informing ourselves then let state institutions tell us what reality is.   Historically, home schooling and private schools have done a far-greater job educating children than the state.   Alternatively, privately educated students have higher GPAs, do far-better on college entrance exams, and require less remediation courses in college. This is discussed further in Chapter VI, *The Education-Industrial Complex.*

The left, which has become virtually all Democrats AND Republicans, has always pushed for more government with the argument that government can help the poor, educate the people, secure our borders, and pave our roads more efficiently and fairly than the private sector.   This is what is dangerous about those who promote the idea of running the government as a business by politicians who want to be perceived as fiscally responsible.   But do we really want governments run like a business model? Businesses work to accumulate more money and expand their

---

[183] Schmidt, A.J. ed. The Impact of Perestroika on Soviet Law. Martinus Nijhoff. 1990 , pp.39-40.

territories. Do we really want governments accumulating more money and expanding their territories? This is counter to liberty. In fact, a free country would want to minimize the role of government in society to make as little money as possible.

The state cannot possibly exist for very long in a capitalistic economy, the voluntary exchange of currencies and goods. And capitalism cannot exist for very long in a state economy. The Left uses public education to undermine the principles of liberty and capitalism. The Left attacks capitalism, blaming it for the tragic downturns in the economy and for the lower and middle class economic suffering. But how can capitalism accept blame for American strife, when capitalism barely exists? Small businesses that make up a large part of business in America have been crushed with regulations for decades, while corporations flourish with the help of federal and state subsidies. On an average about forty-seven percent of one's earnings (income) is taken in taxes by the various governments, local, state and national. Think about that for a moment. Nearly half of one's earnings (income) go to the various governments. How could capitalism possibly survive when nearly fifty percent of the currency is involuntarily vacuumed up by the politicians and bureaucrats to be spent on inefficient and usually ineffective social programs, and foreign interventionism. Governments are like Godzilla. History has shown that the larger and more central governments wreak more havoc on society. You've just been explained how they do it.

There is no more evidence of partisan entrenchment than in academia. Most people in academics are left wing partisans. They were educated in government universities. They work in government universities and they promote government programs and solutions to social problems.

Rarely does a politician legislate for the sake of the constituency. Politicians live for power and usually their own fiduciary self-interest. All people are greedy to an extent. No one wants a pay cut, for instance. But with the exception of a few politicians, such as Rep. Ron Paul (R-TX), rarely do politicians do something simply for the sake of liberty for even those who voted for them. Tax cuts rarely do not come with a price, not because precious government programs could be cut, but because, these days, spending is rarely cut. As a result, at least at the federal level, tax cuts are always paid for by borrowing and printing money. This would happen at the state and local levels if cities, counties and states could print fiat money, as well. But they cannot, fortunately, and legally to an extent must maintain balanced budgets.

In an episode of *Gunsmoke,* saloon owner Kitty Russell (played by Amanda Blake) is losing business to an uppity saloon owner from out of town, and who has his eye for Kitty's affection. Kitty is going broke as the smitten competitor is undercutting Kitty's prices, so she pleas with Marshall Mat Dillion to use his official capacity to bring the competitor in.[184] This is how mercantilists do their business, who use the guns of government to further their own business interests.

Before the 2004 election for president, George W Bush, a so-called "conservative" Republican pushed a massive drug give-away bill through congress. This bill was sold to the American public as only costing a few hundred billion (with a B) over many years. Barely after the program started, handing out billions of dollars of free prescription drug to millions of retired citizens, the program nearly went broke, and turned out to be projected to cost nearly a trillion (with a "t") dollars in a relatively short period of time, nearly ten-fold the cost sold to the gullible American public by the Bush administration. Curiously, during a debate and propaganda blitz toward passing this handout legislation, not a peep from the media about the fact that Bush family members and their associates owned tens of millions of dollars of stock in some of the biggest pharmaceutical companies in the world.[185,186,187]

The American people particularly resemble the cartoon character Charlie Brown, and their politicians are like Charlie's friend, Lucy. Lucy always tells Charlie that she will hold the football, so Charlie can kick it. And every time Charlie runs up to the ball and just before he kicks it, Lucy pulls the ball out and Charlie ends up falling on his back. If only we could have a thousand dollars for every time a pundit, newscaster or politician told us that this election is the most important election in 20, 50 or even a hundred years. The government and its crony "capitalists" have messed things up so badly that it takes a better, you guessed it, GOVERNMENT to fix the problems the prior government had gotten itself into. Well, the government once again fails its constituency, so it will take another monumental election to get us out of another mess!

---

[184] Gunsmoke, Series No. 335, Season 9, Episode 30, 1964.

[185] Bowen, Russell *The Immaculate Deception: Bush Crime Family (American West Publishers, Carson City, NV, 1991), p. 103*

[186] Gordon, G. and Donohue, A. *Members of Congress Face Conflict of Interest When It Comes to Drug Companies.* McClatchy Newspapers. September 29, 2000 http://www.americanchiropractic.net/general_%20interest/Conflict%20of%20Interest.pdf

[187] Eli Lilly Controversies. *Eli Lilly and the Bush Family.* Posted at http://en.wikipedia.org/wiki/Eli_Lilly_controversies#Eli_Lilly_and_the_Bush_Family

The reason the United States painfully revisits recessions, and depressions, is because most of the political class, politicians, lobbyists and regulators, are lawyers. So, the US has accumulated a plethora of laws, corporate giveaways and regulations. Few politicians are economists. And when they do have an economics background, such as a college professor or corporate leader would have, they are ignored by the media, especially if their economic positions conflict with the Establishment's collectivist agenda.

The Hunter-Gathers vs. the State

No movie in history has characterized the inherent evil of centralized government and religion as Mel Gibson' 2006 movie *Apocalypto*. It is a story about a rural hunter-gatherer tribe in Central America centuries ago. They are simple, good-natured, family-oriented people with values that balance nature, needs and liberties with personal responsibility. Despite their primitive ways, they personify freedom better than any population in modern, so-called "civilized" societies.

Their world is shattered one morning, when mercenaries from a wicked, centralized population of urban dwellers sack the tribe and haul their captives away hog-tied to large tree branches to be taken back to the population center where the rural hostages are painted up for sacrifice at the top of the hierarchy's' pyramidal temple. One can easily compare this urban exploitation of rural populations with the sacrifices endured by people miles away from the modern-day centralized states such as China and the United States. People today are dragged into the exploits of collectivist busybodies and strangers.

The Phony Left-Right Paradigm

> "If you want government to intervene domestically, you're a liberal. If you want government to intervene overseas, you're a conservative. If you want government to intervene everywhere, you're a moderate. If you don't want government to intervene anywhere, you're an extremist." — Joe Sobran (1946–2010)

Politically, registered independents outnumber either Republicans or Democrats in the United States, according to the Gallup polling company.[188]

---

[188] Jones, Jeffrey, M. "Record-High 42% of Americans identify as Independents." Politics, January 8, 2014.

Party Identification, Yearly Averages, 1988-2013

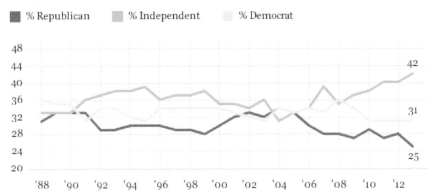

Based on multiple day polls conducted by telephone

GALLUP

Figure 12

Today, Americans are ruled by the politicians and bureaucrats of thousands of local governments, 50 state governments and especially an omnipotent federal government, a centralized leviathan that now rules unconstitutionally over all other governments in not only these United States but around the world. The overwhelming, economy-busting force and management of all these political playgrounds will eventually overtake the incomes, profits and pensions of all private sector jobs and industries of the country.

Nowhere has the state advanced more than under the phony, media-manipulated battle between the so-called Left and the so-called Right. Republican presidents Abraham Lincoln, Richard Nixon and George W. Bush have proven more than any that they can grow government as fast, if not faster than, any big-spending, big-government Democrat on the Left.

Now, the Right feeds off the anti-market socialism of the Left to its ends and the Left feeds off the police-state socialism of the Right. Possibly one of the best examples of how the Left and their entrenched bureaucracies betray the poor they espouse to represent is the changing tax laws to include waiter/waitress tips as income and therefore taxed.

Bottom line is more and more people are waking up to realize that the left–right paradigm of government politics is an illusion and the true struggle is freedom-believing people versus the state.

Anarcho-capitalism vs. anarcho-communism

America is an idea about freedom, self–governance and limited government. The flag represents this idea, like a book represents an idea. The flag is not the corrupt and evil Leviathan the state has become. Burning the flag is like burning books. You become the oppressor.

The flag is a source of inspiration and unity for a lot of people. A book is a bound collection of paper. No different than what you wrote. Lowes sells flags stamped with "Made in USA". I have no problem with someone burning the flag if it's his property, any more than if he wants to burn his own books. But inciting deep emotions and turning away people who may genuinely agree with you about other issues sets us all back.

Burning the flag is like throwing a Molotov cocktail at a public road. Nobody is hurt, you made your point, but nothing changes, except maybe pissing some people off. The victims here are the ones who don't understand that freedom is synonymous with anarchy.

So, what does this have to do about anarcho-communism and -capitalism? Communism relates to personal property – that is, property necessary to exist, such as clothing and food – whereas capitalism goes further to include private property accumulation that you wouldn't necessarily use, such as a business, rental property, other than to raise capital. This requires no central authority, other than to litigate and protect the rights of the individuals, which can be done through voluntary associations similar to law or law or medical associations. Anarcho-communism, on the other hand, would require a central authority to prohibit the possession of privatization and distribute "personal property" according to arbitrary standards set by committees within a central authority. In this way, anarcho-communism cannot be achieved or maintained.

Patriotism vs. Nationalism

Patriotism is the dedication to one's freedom, family and community as it relates to a national, ideologically unified identity. Whereas nationalism holds that the attributes of patriotism, individualism, family and community take a backseat to national unity.

"Racism is an ugly form of collectivism" ~ Ron Paul

As opposed to the demonized "me-first" myth perpetuated by the left about those who adhere to the principles of property rights and a free market, democracy is a collective "me-first" society that will never work. It is the demands of a perceived majority, a majority created by coercion and regulation, that fuels the legitimization and expansion of the state. Politicians love it, as they are always obliged to spend more of someone else's money on a trillion-dollar shopping spree for their constituents. Fortunately for the politicians, there is no accountability because the vastly large number of their constituency has no concern for losing other constituents' money. And some know that most of the federal income tax revenue is extracted from the very rich. So, in their minds, there is no liability. And it's easy to be charitable and feel others' pain with someone else's money. The politicians' argument is always *we were just doing what our taxpaying constituents wanted*. But the vast number of taxpaying constituents collectively pay a far less percentage of their incomes than the very rich. Such is a gamed system. Well, historically, in these freedom-loving United States, most taxpaying constituents want their stolen property back. The rich pay the most taxes, providing the most for infrastructure needed to do business, and therefore the politicians regulate society for the benefit of Big Business, and to the detriment of those who naively believe the majority rules. The colonists rebelled over a three percent tax. Americans pay roughly half their income in taxes, not including the hidden costs of regulation.

Don't think for a moment that the rise of a Marxist like Barack Obama could have happened by his own initiative. The political elite know the dynamics of race is changing the face of their empire. A President Obama would appear to be a sign from heaven, a Messiah to the many increasing non-white populations around the country, especially in the South. The elites know an economic calamity the size of the 2007-2008 crash would leave many who rely on government for their prosperity (government employees, those on welfare, senior citizens) would gravitate to one of their own who understands what it is like to be something other than white upper class. Today, during the recession as this book was being written, it is a rarity to government employees losing their jobs. The number of jobs in the government sector now overshadow those in the private sector.[189] Jobs are only being lost in the private sector.

---

[189] North, Gary, "Pink Slip Nation." https://www.lewrockwell.com/2009/08/gary-north/pink-slip-

The politicians want you to believe that liberty comes from government with the blessing of government. Of course, during special holidays, deifying wars and militarism, you should appreciate this "freedom" with service and sacrifice. And, of course, in grand Orwellian fashion, during wartime, which is usually all the time, we must sacrifice to preserve freedom (i.e., the government) for the benefit of government, ahem, freedom. Your rights are derived from the Constitution which, as Thomas Jefferson put it, chains the government to enumerated powers specified in the Constitution. But even Woodrow Wilson, who turned out to be a huge impediment to liberty as the President, understood that "Liberty has never come from the government. Liberty has always come from the subjects of government. The history of liberty is the history of resistance. The history of liberty is a history of the limitation of governmental power, not the increase of it."[190]

The American people wanted a balanced budget, so Bill Clinton allegedly gave them one. The fact that he raised taxes and borrowed more money from Social Security taxes to get the job done seems to be all but unbeknownst to the corporate media.[191] Special effects artist and news site owner, Michael Rivero, had to blog about Americans' sad gullibility, and their dependency on collective pipedreams:[192]

> Here is the problem. Starting back in the 1980s, our Social Security Taxes were raised to build up a lump of cash to cover the expected increase in costs as the Baby Boomers retired, and we all went along with that tax increase because many of us ARE Baby Boomers. But the problem is that Presidents, especially Clinton, looted the Social Security trust fund to balance the Federal Government's books. In Clinton's case, it was the Social Security money that allowed him to declare that his budget had a surplus. The problem is that now the Baby Boomers are starting to retire, and the Social Security Trust Fund (along with the Native American trust fund, the Federal Employees Retirement trust fund) are empty, filled with government IOUs. We The People are already taxed more than we can pay, as is evidenced by the flood of TV commercials for "Tax Resolution" services. Clinton "borrowed" his cash from the Social Security fund at a time when it was claimed the economy was booming. Obviously, if one has to borrow when the economy is good, there will never be a time when repayment is possible, and with the economy tanking now, certainly the government has to choose between denying the benefits we already paid for, or trying to tax us all a second time for those benefits.

nation

[190] Woodrow Wilson, 28th US President, speech 1912
[191] US braces for baby boom retirement wave
[192] www.whatreallyhappened.com/archives/cat_economy.html, (12-26-07)

Guess which they will choose.

So Much for Social Contracts

> *"It will be of little avail to the people that the laws be made by men of their own choice, if the laws be so voluminous that they cannot be read, or so incoherent that they cannot be understood."* [193] ~ *James Madison*

The U.S. Constitution was written to regulate the government, not to regulate us. I am not a big fan "social contracts" because I do not believe they will ever be enforced by those given the responsibility to own up to social contracts. Human nature is such that people will inevitably cut corners, ignore laws and use force to ensure survivability at the expense of others. The only way this can be sanely and safely done is through the open and peaceful channels of a free market environment.

Laws that only can be understood by lawyers will always be too complicated to enforce with inevitable results that undermine the liberties of the people. The ultimate "social contract" in America is the U.S. Constitution, written with the understanding and sole purpose to regulate the actions of the federal government. The specific design was to give limited authority, "enumerated powers", to the government and reserved everything else to the people and the states.

For many years, the political class has moved the country in a direction detrimental to people's earnings, savings and retirement. They use their various government guns to slowly rob workers and those in retirement by inflation, taxes, fees and financial/economic "bubbles". I never took much credence in retirement funds, knowing that, eventually, the powers-to-be would manage to rob the baby boomers by busting the stock market, as they did in 2008. The financial and housing market bubble of the mid-2000s were an obvious result of government programs, such as The Ownership Society program pushed by then-president George W. Bush. The political class knows there are billions of dollars in the private domain held in the hands of millions of retirees and their financial handlers. Every day new laws are passed to passively redistribute millions of pensions, IRAs and the like into the hands of political class and its "financial handlers" on Wall Street, including the health and insurance industries. Since Obamacare, for instance, health insurers are

---

T[193]   James Madison, "Father of the Constitution", *Independent Journal,* Federalist 62:   The   Senate,   Wednesday,   February   27,   1788. http://www.constitution.org/fed/federa62.htm

raising deductibles and out-of-pocket payouts to pay for the extra services the federal government requires of hospitals clinics.

Table 3 (next page) shows the debt-to-GDP changes incurred by the federal government as a function of the presidential terms from 1945 to 2009:

U.S. president	Party	Term years	Start debt/GDP	End debt/GDP	Increase debt ($T)	Increase debt/GDP
Roosevelt/Truman	D	1945-1948	117.5%	93.2%	0.05	-24.3%
Truman Harry Truman	D	1949-1953	93.2%	71.3%	0.01	-21.9%
Eisenhower1 Dwight Eisenhower	R	1953-1959	71.3%	60.5%	0.01	-10.8%
Eisenhower2 Dwight Eisenhower	R	1957-1961	61.5%	55.1%	0.02	-5.4%
Kennedy/Johnson	D	1961-1965	55.1%	46.9%	0.03	-8.2%
Johnson Lyndon Johnson	D	1965-1969	46.9%	38.6%	0.05	-8.3%
Nixon1 Richard Nixon	R	1969-1973	38.6%	35.7%	0.07	-2.9%
Nixon2 Nixon/Ford	R	1973-1977	35.7%	35.8%	0.19	+0.1%
Carter Jimmy Carter	D	1977-1979	35.8%	32.6%	0.18	-3.2%
Reagan1 Ronald Reagan	R	1981-1985	32.6%	43.9%	0.65	+11.3%
Reagan2 Ronald Reagan	R	1985-1989	43.9%	53.1%	1.04	+9.2%
Bush George H.W. Bush	R	1989-1993	53.1%	66.2%	1.40	+13.1%
Clinton1 Bill Clinton	D	1993-1997	66.2%	65.6%	1.12	-0.6%
Clinton2 Bill Clinton	D	1997-2001	65.6%	57.4%	0.42	-8.2%

Bush GW1 George W. Bush	R	2001-2005	57.4%	64.3%	1.88	+6.9%
Bush GW2 George W. Bush	R	2005-2009	64.3%	75.5%	3.02	+11 %

Table 3 shows debt-to-GDP changes the federal government incurred by presidential terms

How the Political Class Controls the Wars

Since World War Two, Americans, having won the war and having the only intact industrial infrastructure after the war, evolved a more and more malignant militaristic approach to its industrial and political culture which metastasized into the catastrophic economical wasteland we see in the country today. Americans became so war-happy that to sell another government solution to the public meant simply to declare war on the problem. Hence over the years, we were challenged by eager, power-hungry politicians to fight a war on poverty, a war on drugs, a war on illiteracy and now a war on terrorism. Yet, despite after more than thirty years engaged in the first three "wars on ...", poverty, drug trafficking and use and illiteracy hasn't significantly changed, other than more consolidation of political and bureaucratic power, at the expense of our rights and liberties, to fight those wars.

The myth the political class and its sycophantic media whores want us to believe is that people such as Ronald Reagan "won" the Cold War. The country won this 50-year excuse for government growth because our country had a relatively freer economy than the Soviets. By the 1980s the Soviet economy was in shambles so badly it barely had the money and resources to put a battle fleet out the sea. Yet, Americans were told by the Reagan administration that we needed to escalate military spending by an order of magnitude to meet the Soviet threat. By the end of the decade the Soviet empire had collapse and its satellite regimes were liberated

The Viet Nam war started with removing a foreign colony from Vietnamese soil .When the French could no longer *hold* the peninsula, The US stepped in to secure the interests of the West. A state-run economy can stimulate creativity, motivation and invention in some of the worst ways. In the Gulf of Tonkin in 1964, a sinister plot developed to generate public support for escalation in Viet Nam. While LBJ was growing the size and scope of the country from the numerous war on (fill in the blank), the military had plans to escalate the war in Vietnam.

Before the first Persian Gulf war, the Bush (41) administration along with a cheerleading media were pushing for a war in the Middle East. As Iraq became bogged down in a war with Iran, the United States soon found itself looking for a military foothold in the Middle East to counter the Soviet occupation of Afghanistan. Through his diplomat April Glaspie, President Bush assured Saddam Hussein of Iraq that the U.S. would not interfere with the Iraqi invasion of Kuwait (Kuwait has been cross-drilling into Iraqi territory). Bush then put the military on alert and began transporting thousands of troops and equipment onto Saudi Arabian soil to push the aggressor Saddam Hussein out of Kuwait!

In principle, economic support for Blackwater's mercenary protection service and what it provides should not be subsidized by the American taxpayers. I just think the oil companies should pay for Blackwater's services and not the US taxpayers. The oil companies in turn would add the cost of protection to their products and Americans would have less an inefficient, expensively bloated federal government. The 2008 presidential candidate Ron Paul had the best idea in 2002 when he wrote a bill to use the Article I, section 8 of the constitution for Letter of Marque to go after the terrorists as then-President Thomas Jefferson did in the early part of the 19th Century.

A crisis is generally good for the state. Ever notice whenever a Democrat is in the White House, domestic terrorism is crisis of the week. When the president is a Republican, the threat usually comes from outsiders (e.g., North Koreans, Arabs), as if either of those two countries' gun boats are steaming up the Potomac to sack Washington.

But the real question one should be asking is why the coincidence occurs. Why is domestic unrest a problem for Democrats and usually never a problem for Republicans? And, most importantly, why are the attacks structured that way? During the Clinton administration, several domestic incidents occurred that took the lives of hundreds of people. The only attack from foreigners experienced on American soil was the first Twin Tower bombing shortly after Clinton took office. Other than that all other attacks occurred overseas, and Clinton never did much more to retaliate than order a few missiles lobbed at some country his "experts" told him the attackers lived. Yet, over 70 separatists outside of Waco, TX, were incinerated for having the audacity to want to be just left alone.

During either Bush's term, it was as if the militias never existed. The most logical explanation for this was that the Bushes, and the Republicans, for that matter, were softer on gun control than Democrats.   But Republicans, and America's first gun control lobby, the National Rifle Association, will choose power over liberties nearly all the time. Gun restrictions benefit the Republicans as much as the Democrats. The duopolistic political parties know they cannot be outgunned by an angry mob armed to teeth. Heaven forbid! Who would be serving whom then?

Most Democrats and other leftists despise property ownership, especially when that property is protected by armed self-defense. Anything that gets in between socialist democrats and other people's properties is like ants under the skin. Of course, things are unfair. Nothing is fair and it never will be. Even if by monetary fiat the president ordered that every family was given a million dollars, those who had tens or hundreds of millions would still be envied by those with only a million.

Governments are by nature evil and corrupt because they are run by people with selfish and ulterior motives.   Human nature is corrupted enough, so that we should never collectively pull together numerous, flawed human characters to run our lives. Freedom seems to be the only unavoidable solution.   Governments break the Ten Commands. Governments murder.   Governments steal and cheat.   Governments and their willing enablers in the political class put the power of the state above the power of Nature's God, economics and the natural will of humans to be free. We, as people, like freedom.   We aspire to get more of it. Unfortunately, the left, especially, believe the freedom can be obtained through governmental fiat and some kind of collective justice. But only individual can have justice for whatever wrong uniquely perpetrated on them, their families and property.

Governments become everything Satan espoused when it tempted Christ in the desert, where He was fasting and meditating. Jesus was shown *all the kingdoms of the World* and told to only succumb to the greed and power Satan offered Him. Except for a few exceptional individuals in the District of Catastrophe, such as Texas Congressman Dr. Ron Paul,   most politicians leave their principles, if they had any to leave, at the door when they're elected. But there are principles that transcend national borders. Libertarians know what these principles are.   Most people aspire to become national treasures or heroes of their country.   Few have spanned national boarders to become champions of humanity.

People are beginning to understand that politics is no longer Republican *vs.* Democrat, liberal *vs.* conservative, or left *vs.* right. It has really become liberty *vs.* socialism. The state cannot give us freedom, not freedom Nature has given us in the first place. The state cannot even secure our freedom with taking some away from us. The state can only take what we already have or had.

Understanding that left-right paradigm in politics that was developed decades ago to give the perception within in two major voting bases that voters actually have a *choice*, is one big step to evolving into a higher anarchist model to thinking. Washington, D.C. and its various state subordinates are controlled by the special interests (sometimes called the powers-to-be). These "dot-orgs" control how media report the news and just bat issues back and forth for the benefit of those collectives of taxation and state power.

Terrorists have no more control of their respective governments, than their innocent victims in Europe or America have control of their governments. Oh, democracy is thought to have a role in controlling governments. But democratic governments are no more accountable to, representative of, their constituents then the populations within dictatorships. Democracies can be manipulated and therefore corrupted and bought maybe only slightly more difficult than in despotism. But freedom is spreading across boarders. When the populations of Asia, Africa, the Middle East and the Americas begin to understand that the problems they suffer nearly always (less natural disasters) originate with their governments. Terrorists attack us because our government will not leave the Middle East, and continue to corrupt and bribe their governments. But we have no more control over our government than they have over their governments. Unfortunately, as long as we continue to exact "collateral damage" on Middle Easterners, we will continue to target us citizens.

People think they can *change* things by just voting bad politicians out of office. That is extremely difficult to do. Going into the 2008 election, Congress had a 8 to 15 percent approval rating, depending on who and where the pollsters ask, yet incumbents, the congressmen and women with only about a 10% approval were voted back for another term. Ninety five percent of the incumbents who nine out of ten of the voters didn't like! Either voters disapprove of everyone else's representative and senator, or the ballot counting process is corrupted.

When politicians talk about a just economy what they are talking about is socialism. But there is nothing just about taking property from one individual or group and giving it to another individual or group. That is only theft. Most people act like they never left their parents' house. They want free health care, free utilities and food so cheap they don't have to consider it in their monthly budgets. But, of course, most politicians will oblige their constituents with as long a *wish list* they can afford. And what they can't afford they can always borrow the money from foreign banks.

We live in a fascist state. In fact, most of the world's most powerful governments are fascist now. Fascism is not brown shirts wearing swastika arm bands goose-stepping down the street and persecuting Jews. Fascism is an economic system where profits are privatized and costs are socialized. As communism is government taking over the property rights of businesses and other property holders, fascism is businesses (usually a select few) taking over government to their own advantage. Usually the military and energy industries are the primary beneficiaries of fascism, being the motor and means of war.

The GOP is fundamentally over. This is because Republicans are of two kinds. Those in the minority who adhere to the basic principles of freedom (e.g., individual liberty, limited government and free trade). then there are Republicans who are solely in the Party for power and greed. The latter are the mercantilists, for example, the Yankee Republicans, who have carried on, since its inception, a semblance of the Whig Party before it. Modern Republicans such as Geo. W. Bush pushed through his prescription drug benefit program worth trillions of dollars to the pharmaceutical companies and government coffers. Little was said in the corporate media about the fact that the Bush family invested millions in a variety of drug companies going back to 1980s and 90s.[194]

Republicans do not really hate big government. If you want to see Republicans cry, vote Libertarians or Constitutionalists into the majority. Republicans love power and the ability to turn a buck at the expense of taxpayers. Republicans only hate big government when the Democrats are in charge. In fact, this is the only time when Republicans as a party acts as principled politicians and make sense.

The Party of Lincoln and George W. Bush met at critical mass in the early part of the first 21st Century decade. Bush and a Republican congress gave us the biggest government, actually empire, the world had ever known. Fortunately, we have term limits and sensible enough electorate to make a change, even if it was to the Democrats.

Who is this "They"?

Recently, an article in BusinessWeek[195] showed that jobs created in the government more than doubled that of the private sector. This was during a decade-

---

[194] Bowen, Russell, Ibid.

[195]Mandel,   Michael,   A   Lost   Decade   for   Jobs,

span of time of a so-call conservative Republican leadership of George W. Bush and a Republican government. Worse yet, in the economic downturn since the infamous crash of 2008, private sector jobs have plummeted while government jobs have made gains.[196] In fact since December 2007, 5.7 million jobs were lost, 1.2 million of those jobs were manufacturing jobs since September 2008. In the same timeframe government jobs increased, further worsening the government debt and the chance of a recovery happening quickly.

The political class loves this, of course. As Daughty notes, the political class especially loves the fact that many of the government managers and other potentates of their special class receive salaries of more than double those of their "employers," the taxpayers in the private sector. The fact that government employees pay taxes as well is irrelevant. Might they be more conducive to raising taxes? To say the government is taking over is an understatement. The downturns in private-sector job growth are intimately linked to downturns in the national economy, usually created when government-fueled bubbles contract.[197] Since just before the infamous 911 attacks that 'changed everything forever," job growth vanished almost completely as the country geared up for perpetual war against terrorists in the Middle East and Africa. As Isaac Morehouse notes, "Government projects do 'create jobs.'" [198]

Slave Labor Overseas and Cheap Goods Here

The leftist organization Worker Rights Consortium cries about slave labor overseas while pushing for more taxes here in America. It rails on about Americans wanting cheap products here and not thinking about those suffering overseas to bring those products to American stores. But Consortium doesn't tell you is that Americans on an average turn over nearly one half of their incomes to the various local, state and federal governments for the "privilege" of living in this country and enjoying the "blessings" of freedom and government services. Leftists never understand the undercurrent of their economic policies they inflict on society.

---

http://www.businessweek.com/the_thread/economicsunbound/archives/2009/06/a_lost_decade_f.html June 23, 2009.

[196] Daughty, Richard, BLS (Bureau of Labor Statistics) Has One Letter Too Many. http://lewrockwell.com/daughty/mogambo11.html May, 20, 2009.

[197] Woods, Thomas. Meltdown: A Free-Market Look at Why the Stock Market Collapsed, the Economic Tanked and Government Bailouts Will MakeThings Worse. (2009)

[198] Morehouse, Isaac M. Government Projects do not "Create Jobs". The Mises Daily, Ludwig von Mises Institute http://mises.org/story/3058, August 19, 2008.

The State glorifying the state

When it comes to the state fallacy of self-importance, nothing is more flagrant than state funerals for fallen "heroes," the first responders. While these jobs can be dangerous, they are not nearly as dangerous as the 15 or more most dangerous occupations Americans can have per 100,000 workers:[199]

1. Fisherman, 129
2. Logger, 116
3. Airline Pilot, 72
4. Structural Iron and Steel Worker, 46
5. Farmer/Rancher: 40
6. Sanitation Worker, 36
7. Roofer, 34
8. Power Line Installer, 30
9. Oil and Gas Driller, 24
10. Merchant Mariner, 23
11. Coal Miner, 22
12. Truck Driver, 22
13. Taxi and Limousine Driver, 21
14. Police Officer, 19
15. Grounds Maintenance Worker, 17
16. Construction Laborer, 16
17. Construction Equipment Operator, 16
18. Cement Manufacturer, 13
19. Miller, 12
20. Athlete, Coach, Umpire and Referee, 10
21. Security Guard, 8
22. Firefighter, 7
23. Animal Slaughterer, 2

Obviously, there are other private sector jobs that are dangerous, and combat soldiers could be difficult to determine as it is inherently dangerous and casualty prone, but as you can see neither police officer and fire fighter is even in the top ten most dangerous employments. So as millions of dollars are spent for state funerals for fallen police, firefighters, or politicians for that matter, other worker casualties are barely mentioned in the papers and TV news broadcasts.

Israel, AIPAC and the Central Banks (Religion and Politics)

> *The two Internationals of Finance and Revolution*
> *work with ardour, they are the two fronts of the*

---

[199] Ranker, 2018 https://www.ranker.com/list/the-most-dangerous-jobs-in-america/american-jobs and http://www.thedailybeast.com/blogs-and-stories/2010-04-08/the-20-most-dangerous-jobs, April 4, 2010

Jewish Internationale. There is a Jewish conspiracy against all nations. --Rene Groos, 'Le Nouveau Mercure, Paris, May, 1927

If we don't believe in freedom of expression for people we despise, we don't believe in it at all. -- Noam Chomsky

Israel may have the right to put others on trial, but certainly no one has the right to put the Jewish people and the State of Israel on trial. -- Ariel Sharon

Every time we do something you tell me America will do this and will do that . . . I want to tell you something very clear: Don't worry about American pressure on Israel. We, the Jewish people, control America, and the Americans know it. -- Israeli Prime Minister, Ariel Sharon, October 3, 2001

Our race is the Master Race. We Jews are divine gods on this planet. We are as different from the inferior races as they are from insects. In fact, compared to our race, other races are beasts and animals, cattle at best. Other races are considered as human excrement. Our destiny is to rule over the inferior races. Our earthly kingdom will be ruled by our leader with a rod of iron. The masses will lick our feet and serve us as our slaves. -- Menachem Begin, Israeli Prime Minister to New Statesman magazine on June 25, 1982

Key elements of information in the United States and other states of the West are controlled by Jews loyal to Israel. Besides the Federal Reserve and the largest banks being controlled by Jews, the largest newspapers in the country as well a number of TV networks and production agencies in Hollywood are controlled by Jews loyal to Israel. Therefore, any news relating to how Israel operates in the world is skewed toward Israeli interests.

Grace Halsell, who's harrowing journal through life as a journalist to get the "news" about Israel's brutal treatment and occupation of Palestinians and their land, has exposed the horrid truth about what is really happening in that part of the world.

> My research led to a book entitled "Journey to Jerusalem." My journey not only was enlightening to me as regards Israel, but also I came to a deeper, and sadder, understanding of my own country. I say sadder understanding because I began to see that, in Middle East politics, we the people are not making the decisions, but rather that supporters of Israel are doing so. And typical of most Americans, I tended to think the U.S. media was "free" to print news impartially.

> It shouldn't be published. It's anti-Israel.

> In the late 1970s, when I first went to Jerusalem, I was unaware that editors could and would classify "news" depending on who was doing what to whom. On my initial visit to Israel-Palestine, I had interviewed dozens of young Palestinian men. About one in four related stories of torture.

> Israeli police had come in the night, dragged them from their beds and placed hoods over their heads. Then in jails the Israelis had kept them in isolation, besieged them with loud, incessant noises, hung them upside down and had sadistically mutilated their genitals. I had not read such stories in the U.S. media. Wasn't it news? Obviously, I naively thought, U.S. editors simply didn't know it was happening.

In order to get elected to the President of the United States (POTUS) in modern times, one must simply pass three criteria:

1. Put the interests of Israel above the interests of the United States

2. Have utter distain for the Constitution of the United States (and you must cross your fingers behind your back when swearing to the oath of office).

3. Have no problem murdering thousands, even millions of people living in Third World countries that refuse to do your bidding.

As it is, when it comes to the siren call for power, Jewish interests are no different than the interests of Catholics, communist, Republicans or the NAACP. As Dick Eastman wrote about the Jewish quest for power: "They are not exceptional; they are typical."

(1) If you noticed early in the primary elections of 2007-2008, all the presidential candidates of both parties, those blessed by their party and promoted by the corporate media, all of them, took a trip to Israel and to the most powerful banking families in the world, the Rothchildes, to be interviewed for the job of POTUS

(2) anti-Constitution: It is no secret to anyone who follows the principles of liberty that rarely any POTUS followed the Constitution when developing agendas for his administration.

A. Geo W Bush and his "g.d. piece of paper" quote about the Constitution

B. No one bound to the Constitution but the politicians and other parasites of govt who must take an oath of office to serve.

(3) Militarism: How many people at work or socializing in a restaurant, scarfing down the birthday cake heard the term "death by chocolate"? This subsection is about death by government. We learn about the delicious morsels devoured by mass murders with appetites of all political persuasions that disrespect human liberty and prosperity. In his fourth book in a series on genocide and government mass murder, R.J Rummel tallies the millions upon millions murdered by war and conquest.[200]

Total killed - military killed = civilian collateral

WWI 15 million[201]

Civilian (average estimate) about one-half, estimates of 6.0 - 9.0 million casualties

WWI 55 million (military 22 million)

Civilian (average estimate) more than one-half (~60 %), estimates of 6.0 - 9.0 million casualties

Best estimates are that Zionist-created Bolshevism accounted for the deaths of over 50 million humans in the 20th century. Vladimir Lenin was born Vladimir

---

[200]   Rummel, R.J. *Death by Government* (New Brunswick, N.J.: Transaction Publishers, 1994). http://www.hawaii.edu/powerkills/NOTE1.HTM

[201]   http://users.erols.com/mwhite28/warstat1.htm

Ilyich Ulyanov, whose mother ascended from the Jewish Blank family some of whom converted to Orthodox Christianity, including his maternal grandfather Alexander Blank. Lenin used the anti-Semitic sentiment of the early 20th Century to attack capitalism, including wealthy Jews

Not to be outdone, Mao Zedong, leader of the People's Party of China, murdered more of his countrymen than socialists Stalin and Hitler combined, estimated to be between 50 and 100 million Chinese, many of them by starvation. His hatred for intellectuals and scholars resulted in the deaths of hundreds of his particular enemies by burying them alive.[202]

If the 20th Century taught us anything, it is that socialism which puts humans in charge to decide life and death does not work. Governments of atheistic societies, such as communism, have murdered more people and destroyed more lives than any other authority in the 20th Century. Perhaps a moral conscience is better anchored to a humble soul.

The refutation that Israel does not significantly influence American foreign policy is soundly supported by the facts. It has been known for years that Israel has in its possession a number of nuclear weapons developed in an underground facilities in Israel. Yet, under the Symington amendment to the 1961 Foreign Relations Bill,[203]

A reminder that under the Symington amendment t the 1961 Foreign Appropriations Bill, it is illegal for the US Government to send foreign aid to any nation developing nuclear weapons that is not a signer of the Nuclear Non-Proliferation Treaty.

Folks, after you listen to this women trying to convince you to hate Israel's enemy enough to throw the life of your own child away, please remember the following facts.

Those were not Muslims who attacked a US-flagged ship, captured US citizens, and murdered a 19-year old American from New York last May.

Those were not Muslims high-fiving each other and celebrating while the World Trade Towers collapsed.

Muslims did not attack and try to sink the USS Liberty and blame Egypt for it.

---

[202]   http://en.wikipedia.org/wiki/Mao

[203]   Bryant, J. *US Army Confirms Israel has Nukes.* Military.com, March 18, 2009.http://www.military.com/news/article/March-2009/us-army-confirms-israeli-nukes.html?ESRC=dod.nl

Muslims did not steal weapons-grade uranium from the United States in the 1960s and build bombs with it.

Muslims did not build a clandestine weapons lab underneath Dimona.

Muslims did to get caught trying to sell a nuclear weapon to Apartheid South Africa.

Muslims did not lie this nation into attacking Iraq.

Muslims did not corrupt the US Congress. ~ Michael Rivero 083110

> *Watch money. Money is the barometer of a society's virtue.*
> *When you see that trading is done, not by consent, but by compulsion -*
> *when you see that in order to produce, you need to obtain permission*
> *from men who produce nothing - when you see that money is flowing*
> *to those who deal, not in goods, but in favors - when you see that men*
> *get richer by graft and by pull than by work, and your laws don't protect*
> *you against them, but protect them against you - when you see*
> *corruption being rewarded and honesty becoming a self-sacrifice - you*
> *may know that your society is doomed. – Ayn Rand*

If corporations are outsourcing jobs, become an exporter. If machines are taking our jobs, learn how to build and run the machines. The market is based on the Law of Nature. Natural Law we will never change. Most politicians think they can defy Natural Law. It is the deceit and vanity of people who seek power. If politicians could, they would outlaw gravity if their constituents complained enough about not being able to fly on their own.

A democracy is a collective "me-first" society. Alexis de Tocqueville warned that "the American Republic will endure until the day Congress discovers that it can bribe the public with the public's money," and the country would be in peril as Americans discover if they have control of the largess, they will vote themselves into prosperity.[204] It is our demands as a perceived majority that fuels the expansion of government. Politicians are always obliged to spend more of someone else's money on the shopping spree for their constituents. Fortunately, for the politicians, there is no accountability. No liability. Their argument is always they were just doing what their constituents wanted.

The American people wanted a balanced budget, so Bill Clinton gave them one. The fact that he borrowed the money from Social Security taxes to get the job done seems to be unbeknownst to the corporate media.[205] As Special Effects artist and netizen news site owner, Michael Rivero, wrote on his blog:[206]

> *Here is the problem. Starting back in the 1980s, our Social Security*
> *Taxes were raised to build up a lump of cash to cover the expected*
> *increase in costs as the Baby Boomers retired, and we all went along*
> *with that tax increase because many of us ARE Baby Boomers. But the*
> *problem is that Presidents, especially Clinton, looted the Social Security*
> *trust fund to balance the Federal Government's books. In Clinton's case,*
> *it was the Social Security money that allowed him to declare that his*
> *budget had a surplus. The problem is that now the Baby Boomers are*

---

[204]   Tocqueville, Alexis. *Democracy in America, Vols. I and II* (Charlottesville, Va. University of Virginia Library, 2000)

[205]   US braces for baby boom retirement wave

[206]   www.whatreallyhappened.com/archives/cat_economy.html, (12-26-07)

> *starting to retire, and the Social Security Trust Fund (along with the Native American trust fund, the Federal Employees Retirement trust fund) are empty, filled with government IOUs. We The People are already taxed more than we can pay, as is evidenced by the flood of TV commercials for "Tax Resolution" services. Clinton "borrowed" his cash from the Social Security fund at a time when it was claimed the economy was booming. Obviously, if one has to borrow when the economy is good, there will never be a time when repayment is possible, and with the economy tanking now, certainly the government has to choose between denying the benefits we already paid for, or trying to tax us all a second time for those benefits.*
>
> *Guess which they will choose.*

We haven't yet seen the impending catastrophe waiting for us when the government is going to need 50 trillion dollars to pay off the boomers who will be flooding the role of government *consumers*, strapping the next two generations, or more, with the bill. As Ron Paul's campaign showed, a number of young people are beginning to get it

The crisis of the day for the corporate media to exploit is the mortgage crisis and impending economic meltdown. No one in the media considers the bailouts inflationary, the ultimate destroyer of the economy. Printing money out of thin air seems to be a logical mechanism to prosperity for the political class We all know how silly and unrealistic the idea of *money growing on trees* is.

> *5* Then the devil took Him up into the holy city, set Him on the pinnacle of the temple, *6* and said to Him, "If You are the Son of God, throw Yourself down. For it is written: 'He shall give His angels charge over you,' and, 'In their hands they shall bear you up, Lest you dash your foot against a stone.' " [E13] *7* Jesus said to him, "It is written again, 'You shall not tempt the Lord your God.' " [E14] *8 Again, the devil took Him up on an exceedingly high mountain, and showed Him all the kingdoms of the world and their glory. 9* And he said to Him, "All these things I will give You if You will fall down and worship me." *10* Then Jesus said to him, "Away with you, [E15] Satan! For it is written, 'You shall worship the Lord your God, and Him only you shall serve.' " [E16]
> (Matthew 4:5-11)

Has there ever been a time in Western history when social order was controlled by a religious entity interested in promoting the principles of liberty and justice? Has there ever been a government, secular or sectarian for that matter, that understood its limitations of power and governed accordingly? Why is it that sectarian authority?

In the sixteenth century, Aztec Emperor Moctezuma II mistook the arrival of Hernán Cortés de Monroy y Pizarro Altamirano for the second coming of their deity,

Quetzalcoatl. Cortés used the emperor's misapprehension to advance his plans for conquest in the New World. Sometimes people get things wrong, collectively, many times with devastating results.[207]

In the 1840s, Protestants began using local and state governments to wrestle control of education from private, mostly Catholic institutions to a public setting controlled by the state (see the next chapter). Ironically, it is now the Protestants of the so-called Religious Right who are clammering about state-controlled education and running politicians who will abolish the federal Department of Education and establish school vouchers to send more kids to private schools.

Again, it can't be said enough: the only feasible role for government in a *free* society can only be to protect the rights and liberties of its citizenry, whosoever chose to abide be the strictures within the boundaries of that government's jurisdiction. The rights mentioned above would be the fundamental rights to life, liberty and the pursuit of happiness. The political class has nearly destroyed those fundamentals and at an alarming rate will have transformed a relatively free republic into an imperial police state. This didn't happen by accident.

The theory expounded by such groups as the John Birch Society and the 911 truth movement that warn of an impending one world government conspired by international bankers and industrialists is in its final steps can no longer be ridiculed as a "conspiracy theory." Thirty years ago the Geo HW Bush, the first Bush president, admitted, almost glorifyingly, that with the victory in the first Gulf War, and the collapse of the Soviet Union, success had brought the US into a "New World Order" with America the sole superpower. But in 1992, America rejected Bush's ideals and voted for a Blue Dog Democrat from Arkansas, Bill Clinton to utilize the so-called peace dividend the country could save not having to defend itself from the Soviet empire.

During the 1990s, America witnessed tremendous prosperity by virtue of the dotcom revolution. Clinton's success rode on the wave of this economic, technological phenomenon, and his Classical Liberal hands-off approach to letting this fledgling industry grow reaped tremendous success in the polls in 1996, against two Texans with two entirely opposite world views.

Democracy is just an easy way for people to make change in the world and not get their fingernails dirty. In just one day casting a vote, people think can fight

---

[207] Mayan Gods and Godesses http://www.crystalinks.com/mayangods.html

poverty, get an education, beat up nations that don't play along, or get along, protect the global climate, and provide for a one-size-fits-all "social security" to meet the needs of all who play by the rules. Indeed, we live in an incredible time! We now have all the information available to us to understand that all the "benefits" of government activity I described above can be easily refuted with the facts

No one mixes religion with the state more than the Jews and Muslims. In 1948, after six million Jews were exterminated by the German state, coincidently like the prophetic six million killed and burned found in the Torah. Israel today is a theological police state, where whole cultures and creeds of people have color-coded license plates and have little to say about the heavy-handed treatment of Palestinians by the IDF, Israel's military police. A name given to the indigenous tribes of the fertile crescent by the Romans, the Palestinians in the twentieth Century were systematically ghettoized by the Israelis. Christians in the West who followed the End Times prophesy ignored the fundamentally cruel treatment as acceptable.

Before 1948, Jews, Muslims and Christians lived in relative peace throughout the Middle East. After 1948, the Jewish state, made up primarily of immigrants, began purging the Muslims and Christians from the land given to them and sanctioned by the UN. Many of the Muslim states forced the Jews out and took their properties. The wars began after 1948. Colonial wars. Israelis began terrorizing the British and Palestinians

The Hypocrisy of "Campaign Reform"

> *"Every election is a sort of advance auction sale of stolen goods."* -- H.L. Mencken

Everyone who understands the inner workings of politics knows the sole purpose of campaign reform was to give the illusion that politics are driven by Big Money and reform was needed to curtail lobbyist manipulation of politicians through uncompetitive huge campaign contributions. But it never reformed anything. In fact, the wealthy benefited the most, allowing them to out-compete lower incomes for power using <u>less</u> of their lobbying resources (eliminating soft money) and forcing their competitors to shell out the same limits, as well. The rich and powerful will still hedge his bets by contributing to both candidates. If major campaigns were truly reformed why are campaigns now hauling in even more money than they did in

2002, when the _Bipartisan Campaign Reform Act of 2002_ was passed in Congress and signed by "small government conservative" George W. Bush?

Never mind the fact that BCRT was blatantly unconstitutional in two or three different ways, it soothed the cynical sentiment of the governed towards their masters in Washington. What was important was the perception, that _boobus Americanus,_ as H. L. Menken called them, would have a better feeling about the illusion that their "representatives" were working for them and not the rich and powerful.

Piracy

Piracy. This is an interesting term. The word conjures up the thought of lawless people brutally attacking and pilfering innocent dwellers of their peace and prosperity. The news lately has been covering pirating off the coast of Somalia, Africa. Pirates   have been attacked commercial ships passing by and confiscating manifests on board.

Is it even moral to ask a thieving government, one that exists only because it forces people to pay for it, to enforce the intellectual property laws? Two wrongs hardly make a right. Asking a criminal government, one that exists by theft and brutality, to punish someone who stole the property of ideas and creativity from someone else is the height of hypocrisy.

Yet, when governments stick guns in the faces of workers, businesses and homeowners, and take billions of dollars in property and income taxes from them, defenders of the state call it "duty" and "sharing responsibility."   So, I am supposed to share responsibility with someone ten miles away who I don't even know. I don't think so! Who is being robbed here and who is really the pirate?

One has to wonder what the world is thinking when they learn the United States has condoned torture and murder, even before the 9-11 attacks gave the military and political tyrants what turned out to be a convenient cover for all kinds of malicious deeds in the name of US citizens everywhere.

> _The torturers from the start had said that the United States supported them and that was what counted." -- Amnesty International report on Greece in the 1960s under US--supported dictator George Papadoupolus_

What Happens when the People have Enough

What happened when ordinary people are driven to the brink by a heartless, soulless elite class that openly exploits the workers by over-taxing and other freedom-robbing misdeeds? One only has to look at what happened in England towards the end of the 14[208] Century. When the poor classes of countryside merged with the rebellious peasants in the towns and villages, they took to the street indefensible by sheer numbers. Mayors, Dukes, rich merchants, hundreds up and down the ladder were summarily executed by guillotine or murdered by angry mobs across England.

American colonists in the late 18th Century, finally fed up with the King's exorbitant taxes, more the 10-fold less than Americans are taxed today, totally (~47% average), went to war with the British to secede from tyranny.

The social disconnect of our federal legislators with their constituents is appalling. Legislators rarely read, or have sufficient time to read, the bills they vote. The fact that they have no idea what these laws could do to our economy and liberties borders the line of treason. The House of Representatives passed the Waxman-Markey carbon-cap bill without the bill even been prepared yet. According to a Hill reporter, David Freddoso, "The House started debating the bill before even one copy of it was available, and while clerks were inserting another 300-page, last-minute amendment."[209]

The political class of politicians, banksters, and lobbyists have is easy. They live in gated communities with private protection far from the masses they are screwing over. A little more than two hundred years ago, especially after the con-job bank bailouts they pulled off in 2008 and 2009, they would have been rounded up and hanged or guillotined. Now, as a result of decades of public complacency and apathy, politicians get re-elected and banksters get promoted or, worse, made Commerce or Treasury Secretary.

Face the fact: There is no such thing as collective rights or liberties, not that your various governments try to make it that way. These values do not come from governments. You are born with them and they are taken away by the state. Even in

---

[208]   Jones, Dan, "Revolution in the air," British Broadcasting Company, May 2009. http://news.bbc.co.uk/today/hi/today/newsid_8061000/8061725.stm

[209]   Freddoso, David, On the House Floor, The Washington Examiner, June 26, 2009.http://www.washingtonexaminer.com/opinion/blogs/beltway-confidential/wheres-the-bill-49208987.html

a democracy, there can be no collective right or liberty that isn't watered down by the perceptions and manipulations of millions of other people acting on millions of others in the system. The only way you can have complete rights and liberties is in a free society, free from governmental coercion and oppression. Henry David Thoreau understood this: "The law will never make men free; it is men who have got to make the law free."

One of the true ironies the past decade is how a Marxist such as the President Barak Obama could surround himself with so many "czars," nearly thirty,[210] in such a short time. Regulatory Czar, Banking and Finance Czar, to name a few have been appointed shortly after Obama's inauguration.

The recent, highly political annual propaganda stunt, the Nobel prize awards, took hypocrisy and absurdity to a new level when the Nobel committee awarded President Barak Obama the Nobel Peace Prize. Obama was in office days, for fresh off the campaign trail of promises, when on February 1st, 2009, he was nominated for the prize. On October 9th, after eight months of bombing Pakistan, escalating the presence of American troops in Afghanistan and rattling his sabre at Iran, the Nobel committee announced our peace-loving president took the trophy. And war is peace.

This wasn't a surprise to anyone who follows the total hypocrisy of social engineers and bizarre institutional façades. A good number of warmongering presidents won the esteemed award years ago. Woodrow Wilson, the candidate who promised to keep the US out of the European Theater and soon after elected, sent thousands of troops to England and France, won the award in 1919, after establishing the ineffective and now-defunct League of Nations. It was the League of Nations and its various treaties that isolated Germany, destroying its currency that led to the rise of Adolf Hitler.

The political class, with the help of a sycophantic media, has always had the means to manipulate historical events.

Interestingly, a recent Rasmussen poll revealed that "nearly half of American adults see the government today as a threat to individual rights rather than a protector of those rights."[211] Surprisingly, 74% of the Republicans believe

---

[210] Vlahos, Kelley Beaucar, Obama *Regulatory Czar's Confirmation Held Up by Hunting Rights Proponent*http://www.foxnews.com/politics/2009/07/15/obamas-czars-draw-criticism-sides-political-aisle/, July 22, 2009.

[211] Rasmussen Reports. "48% See Government Today As A Threat to Individual Rights." June24,2010http://www.rasmussenreports.com/public_content/politics/general_politics/june_2010/48_see

government is a threat to individual rights. Not surprisingly, 64% of the Democrats see the government protector of rights. The general rule is that Democrats want to regulate business (economic oppression), and Republicans have shown they have no problem regulating the individual (e.g., they support outlawing abortion and some drugs). Neither most Republicans nor Democrats realize how loathsome they have become in the eyes of true freedom-loving individuals.

The American public has fallen into the trap of the left-right paradigm in political discourse. The elite political class has created this paradigm to keep people believing if their side wins, they will be in control of America's destiny. The elite political class supports both sides with campaign money and an army of lobbyist . Politicians are just puppets, sideshow tools in a giant sleight of hand. FDR said that History never happens by accident. Two hundred years ago most bankers, financiers and politicians would have been strung up or guillotined had they pulled off the unconstitutional and criminal shenanigans they foisted on taxpayers and future taxpayers today

The United States is at a fork in history, as it was at the turn of the last century. The US then took the wrong turn, supporting a national tax and establishing the Federal Reserve, two elements of tyranny that has wreaked untold mischief around the world. They have been a curse on generations to come that would have to fight world wars they financed with a national treasure and printing press, propping up dictators like Josef Stalin and Adolf Hitler[212] and creating catastrophic economic bubbles around the planet.

A freedom movement has snowballed, large in part beginning with the presidential candidacy of Rep. Ron Paul (R-TX), a response to the inane corruption of lobbyists and central planners in Washington, D.C. From Paul's candidacy sprang a national "Tea Party" movement of senior citizens, young people, working class families, independents, libertarians, constitutionalist, all brought together by one simple thread, Freedom, against a Ruling Class spinning out of control from its own contemptible inertia.

Until people give up their obsessive dependence on the mythical social mores that only governments can solve huge problems, usually problems created by government policies, can we as humankind move forward to freedom, peace and

---

_government_today_as_a_threat_to_individual_rights

[212] "The Bankers behind Hitler, Stalin and Israel." Vols. 1-6, September 12, 2011. https://www.youtube.com/watch?v=1cL6jtR5c0g

prosperity. Franklin Roosevelt said that history doesn't happen by accident. There is geological history, natural occurrences beyond our control, and then history created by human interactions.

The Bretton Woods Meltdown

Seventy years this week in July, during the heat of the 1944 European and Pacific campaigns of World War II, delegates from the U.S. and over 40 allied nations converged on Bretton Woods, New Hampshire to put together a new economic system to be rolled out after the war. The system would create, for much of the world, a universal currency using the U.S. dollar as the primary means of exchange. Other nations would purchase the U.S. dollar with gold ($35/oz) which would be held in American banks. The dollar would be used by all for trade. The deal would ensure that all oil, for instance, would be purchased with what would become known as the "petrodollar". After the war, America initiated a treaty with Middle East oil-producing nations stipulating that if these countries would sell their oil for petrodollars, the United States would in turn provide them protection from the Soviet Union and Communist China.

Fast forward to today: "After years of railing against the Western-dominated global financial order, a powerful bloc of the world's emerging economies has finally done something about it."[213] I suppose all the saber rattling between East and West lately has nothing to do with these developments. And now back to the airliner shot down over Ukraine. Spam meet fan.

After the war, America was the only superpower in the world with an intact industrial infrastructure. Factories, along with whole communities, were destroyed in bombing raids over Europe and Asia. The American economy exploded in production and growth as America's industrial might led the charge to put the world back together. Two generations later

Your Vote Doesn't Count

A false dichotomy has been going for a long time to make us think we have a choice. Over time both parties have slowly eroded our rights and liberties, in turn destroying our ability to escape the plantation. They know that if they keep us

---

[213] Pizzi, Michael, "BRICS announce $200B challenge to world financial order." Aljazeera America, July 15, 2014. http://america.aljazeera.com/articles/2014/7/15/brics-bank-announced.html

fighting each other, we won't be fighting them. People like Libertarian presidential candidate Gary Johnson and former house representative Ron Paul (R-TX) throw a monkey wrench into their plans. So the media, for one, try to ignore them, calling them "fringe." Funny how ideals like liberty and individualism, a free market economy, and peace have become fringe elements out of step with mainstream society. The tumultuous election for US president in 2016 did nothing but (hopefully) expose the creepy underbelly of national politics. From my viewpoint I don't believe Hillary Clinton had proven herself to be anything but untrustworthy and diabolical.

Trump is a throw of the dice, politically. Johnson was a pretty good governor and leans libertarian. I don't like his VP pick at all. Statistically, with national and state populations as they are, your vote doesn't count anyway. So vote early, vote often.

EDUCATION INDUSTRIAL COMPLEX

Democracy 101: PEOPLE can't be trusted to govern themselves, so they elect PEOPLE to govern for them. Make sense now?

The BLS also estimates that <u>*approximately   136,000*</u> <u>*professors are employed in the*</u> <u>*social sciences as a whole.*</u> *At 17.5% held constant, there are about   23,800   self-described Marxist social science professors in the United States.*[214]

History of public education

Istorically, for the most part Catholic schools educated kids in the United States of America up until the 1840's, when Unitarians figured out a way to take control of education from the Catholics and Calvinists, first at Harvard University then on to the states.[215] Twenty years earlier, in Boston, Massachusetts, the first government-owned, and -operated, public high school began a new approach to education that eventually was federalized in modern times with subsidies to states, and an education department that contributed six percent funding to local schools but demanded 100 percent adherence to federal policies established over many decades. Into the 1850s states were already juggling with secular-sectarian control for the pedagogy of a community parents' children. By 1926, the State of Massachusetts legislated a mandate for all towns within the state

---

[214] Magnus, Phil. *The Marxist Devil and Free Speech on Campus* . Areo Magazine (online) May 9, 2017.

[215] Blumenfeld, Samual L. *Is Public Education Necessary?* (American Vision, 1981)

to establish a committee to oversee a new centralized public education system. Other states in the Northeast followed suit with modified programs such as "tuitioning students" (i.e., allowing districts that decided not to own/operate public schools to use public funds to pay costs of a district students' schooling at a private, parochial, or religious school of parents' choice).

Prussian military-style

By the mid-nineteenth century the American elite ruling class became more and more interested in the Prussian military-style pedagogy that emphasized obedience and rote instruction over the development of critical thinking and problem-solving strategies. By the early part of the Twentieth Century the Prussian style of pedagogy manifested whole generations of a citizenry that didn't question the nefarious agendas of tyrants who managed to ram through legislation that established such monstrosities as a central bank (the Federal Reserve), imposition of a federal income tax, while taking over huge swaths of land around the country, especially the western states. The public lacked the critical thinking even to resist a constitutional amendment to outlaw alcoholic beverages nationwide, which lasted for nearly 14 chaotic years before being repealed by another amendment. The Prussian military-style of teaching worked nearly perfectly well for the U.S. ruling class.

Do kids really learn anything?

"A previous evaluation of student drug testing programs conducted by the Robert Wood Johnson Foundation concluded, "Drug testing, as practiced in recent years in American secondary schools, does not prevent or inhibit student drug use." Investigators collected data from 894 schools and 94,000 students and found that at every grade level studied -- 8, 10, and 12 -- students reported using illicit drugs at virtually identical rates in schools that drug tested versus those that did not." [216]

Remediation programs have become an academic requirement for incoming freshmen at most community colleges. Allie Bidwell, staff writer for USA News wrote[217]t hat more than "half of community college freshmen are told they aren't ready for college-level work." A uniform mode of teaching leads to a uniform result of failure. A system of teaching as it is taught in the United States cannot possibly benefit the

---

[216]   http://www.rwjf.org/research/researchdetail.jsp?id=1234&ia=131

[217]   Bidwell, Allie, How to Fix Americas's College Remediation Issue." US. News and World Report. July 3, 2014. http://www.usnews.com/news/articles/2014/07/03/schools-and-colleges-still-struggle-to-reduce-the-need-for-remedial-education

students (and parents) when more emphasis towards discipline and obedience is practiced instead of critical and creative thinking, as well as an appreciation for the fundamental values of reading, writing and arithmetic. These values have been precipitously eroded by Hollywood and the entertainment industry that reinforce the idea that an education is somehow an impediment to happiness and a libertine lifestyle. Smart students are derided as geeky, squares and boring.

"... (A) music teacher for many years in Madison, WI, reports being at the end of her rope. What has been, and should be, a joyful experience has been made increasingly tedious by regulation, standardization, assessment rubrics and other nonsense that adds nothing."[218] Even the paragons of progressivism understand that the centralized U.S. education system is perilously in decline. This promotion of a centralized education system has not resulted in any significant improvement in low test scores for over a century.

No Child Left Behind

Possibly there is no better example of the way "compromise" between political and institutional adversaries can negatively affect the intellectual and creative fundamentals of a society than the "bi-partisan" No Child Left Behind Act written by Democrat senator Ted Kennedy and signed into law by Republican president George W. Bush.   In 2001, Federal intrusion into the states' authority to regulate public education had never been more evident than since the institution of a Federal Department of Education initiated during the Carter administration.   During the trepidation of a fledgling Bush presidency that lost the popular vote months earlier in a bizarre electoral contest and vote recount, four senior senators and representatives began work on what would turn out to be one of the worst pieces of legislation in recent history. Senators Ted Kennedy and Judd Gregg and Representatives George Miller and John Boehner, at the behest of Bush Administration's domestic advisers' Margaret Spelling and Sandy Kress, began to federally reform[219] and nationalize the American education system with a program coined "No Child Left Behind." The purpose of this 2001 congressional bipartisan act was "(a)n act to close the achievement gap with accountability, flexibility, and choice, so that no child is left behind."

---

[218]   Nelson, Steve. Education Reform Is Making All Public Schools Worse." Huffington Post January 13, 2015 http://www.huffingtonpost.com/steve-nelson/education-reform-public-schools_b_6457414.html

[219]   McKenzie, William, "Ted Kennedy and No Child Left Behind," The Dallas Morning News, August 27, 2009. http://educationfrontblog.dallasnews.com/2009/08/ted-kennedy-and-no-child-left.html/

Of course, as with most legislation, the law of unintended consequences kicked in and by 2015, NCLB Act was replaced with a more state-friendly "Every Student Succeeds Act" that stripped away much of the national features of No Child Left Behind.

Never understanding the logic of such statements as "there would be utter chaos, anarchy, if government education was turned over to the private sector." Or "what would happen to our work force if parents were in charge of their kids' education." Yet, parents decide what food their children eat and chose which grocery store to buy that food.   Utter Chaos, Anarchy?   Nearly every neighborhood has a food mart nearby.   Food is inexpensive, readily available and best of all, privately distributed. Yet, people aren't in the streets rioting.   Where are the burning tires and broken shop windows?

If we had a system of food distribution similar to government programs such as education or the war on drugs, our children, along with us, or at least a good share of us, would practically starve to death.   Pick any socialized food distribution state around the world and you will see either severe shortages or worse, mass starvation. In fact, the worst form of totalitarianism is the one where the state controls food supplies. The Soviet Union's bread lines and China's Cultural Revolution, where millions of Chinese were intentionally starved to death, are two of many examples. So, why is it that parents can trust private food supplies for their children's nutrition and health, but they can't spend the money they spend on property taxes to <u>choose</u> the best education for them?   Unfortunately, as long as the various governments continue to educate our children, then I guess we'll never know.   Or, so the autocrats hope.

Some kids, most more than ever, are absolutely not ready for the world when they graduate from high school. Education is about self-reliance and taking the initiative to understand the world. A student will never succeed in learning if he does not, or cannot, read. Students who do not read, who have no inclination or no desire to open a book, should not be in school. The viable solution for them is an alternative to academic reading, math and writing: vocational school where they are exposed to hands-on instruction by rote demonstration. Americans waste billions of dollars a year trying to "educate" individuals who really have no desire to investigate how the universe works, and rules such as Natural Law or the Laws of Thermodynamics that impact our very existence.   Instead, children are taught obedience, to obey authority and accept it without question. Or, again, so the autocrats hope.

Veteran teachers have reported that in their careers they have witnessed a tragic decline in student cognitive skills.[220]   Television and video games have wiped out whole generations of kids whose neurological anomalies are brought on by a half-decade of pre-school- blunted neuroplasticity and learning before they even enter school at age five.   In school, they are fidgety and inattentive. This is a tragedy. Schools, in turn, deal with it by drugging these students with stimulants, such as Ritalin, that seem to paradoxically induce a mild stupor, or "mellowness," rendering the student more relaxed and focused. Of course, long-term use of these stimulants manifests severe and long-lasting neurological and psychological problems.

Kids in the U.S. today are coddled. They are no longer taught the classics, have no understanding of history, and are generally incapable of understanding even the fundamental principles of market economics.   Instead, students are given a perpetual drone of sensitivity classes involving cultural, race, LGBT and religious (other than Christian) indoctrination. They are taught that without the state, they would no longer be safe nor free. They learn that that by voting, the state will continue to care for them, so they can enjoy an abundant food supply and sleep safely at night knowing the sun will rise on their ambitions and dreams. The state can do no harm, of course unless 67890-
-*/it is necessary inflict it, for which they have the authority that the citizenry is denied and jailed.

For thousands of years girls were married off shortly after puberty and had children before they were fifteen. Women were considered Old Maids if into their twenties they hadn't experienced childbirth. In most places around the world this is still the case. In the U.S., with the help of birth control, women usually wait until later in life to have children and it is unacceptable, usually illegal in most states, for people to have sex before 18 years of age. In some countries of European Union, child pornography standards are years lower than American standards. Ironically, American standards are not the norm, globally speaking.

Most kids today are expected to stay in school and stay at home until they are nearly twenty. The reason for that is usually economic, as their education leads them into dependency on government programs, requiring a post-secondary education, a prerequisite to becoming financially independent and stable, eventually.   After all, the government and corporations run the economy, so why concern themselves with making a living the old-fashioned way?

---

[220]   Morford, Mark. First published October 24, 2007. SF (San Francisco) Gate http://www.serendipity.li/more/american_kids.htm

Special Education

Special Education is an integrated array of educational programs targeting kids with physical and mental impairments. These would include functionally nonambulatory, as well as cognitive and emotional impairments. Although an inordinate amount of money is spent educating these kids, little progress is made.[221] As Karen Klein writes:

> As a result, year after year, Eve has gone on to the next grade without actually having learned much of anything. She is atrociously behind in basic skills — computations and reading fluency trip her up — but she is able to quickly grasp complex concepts when she puts her mind to it. This is, unfortunately, the case for a large number of my special education students. It is more common for them to be identified as "emotionally disturbed" than "learning disabled."
>
> Yet while that emotional state tends to affect work ethic more than cognitive potential, students with this classification are given an adjusted promotional criteria just as those students who are learning disabled are.
>
> And so frequently I look at the I.E.P. of a student who has proven himself to be gifted in one way or another, and be startled to find that he is only expected to be able to master 30 percent of the standards. And so they do. Set your standards low, and people won't fail to meet them. But why don't we demand more?
>
> It's no wonder that students graduate from high school without learning to read; we enable them to underperform. Indeed, simply by being classified as emotionally disturbed, they can fail all of their classes starting in kindergarten, and still be promoted each year.

As is usually the case, education bureaucrats believe that throwing more money at a social or educational problem will fix it. But for much of the time these problems can be solved by addressing the fundamental, underlying problem with the resources they already have instead of blaming the problem on underfunding.

State Lotteries Sold as a Way to Fund Education

In 2002, two state lotteries nearly back-to-back, 11 winners shared $192 million in winnings. On September 7, seven FLORIDA LOTTO™ players share the third highest jackpot, of $87.81 million, created from a record of 10 rollovers. Each player used personal numbers to select the winning numbers. Then on December 14, the second highest FLORIDA LOTTO™ jackpot estimated at $104.85 million is shared between

---

[221]   Klein, Karen, "The Special Education Problems We Aren't Solving." New York Public Radio. July 23, 2012.   http://www.wnyc.org/story/301679-the-special-education-problems-we-arent-solving/

four winning tickets.

The chances of seven people choosing the correct numbers is 1/(17,000,000) to the seventh power. That's 1 to 17 million times 1 to 17 million out seven times! The chances of seven people hitting the same correct numbers out of 53 is one to an astronomical number. May as well say "infinity," as we know it. I doubt if there is even a word for a number that has that many zeros after it. In other words, the chance of seven people having the same six correct numbers out of 53 is nil.

Another clue to how corrupt the state lotteries are (or maybe just Florida's) is when one of the six balls that get coughed up by the "random ball–number generator" gets stuck in the machine and is called out anyway![222]

Does funding from state lotteries really go to schools? Well, yes and no. Most of the public believe state lotteries help fund education, especially K through 12, but the public has been sold a bait–and–switch scheme by the politicians. Although funds from state lotteries do fund education, money that is earmarked for education usually goes to fund other things.[223]

The Indoctrination of Race Sensitivity

The "ugly collectivism," as Rep. Dr. Ron Paul wrote, of racism is nowhere more prevalent in the American landscape, other than in government edicts and regulation, as is the prevalence of anti–"racism" indoctrination in the public school system and universities. For the past 25 years, especially, schools have bombarded students with straw dog correlations of economic failures or success to genetic predisposition. Teachers are quick to blame white success and minority failures to group misfortune

Racism doesn't adhere to Rand's thinking, because racism is not compatible with her philosophical proclivity for individualism. She wrote,

> *Racism is the lowest, most crudely primitive form of collectivism. It is the notion of ascribing moral, social or political significance to a man's genetic lineage—the notion that a man's intellectual and characterological traits are produced and transmitted by his internal body chemistry. Which means, in practice, that a man is to be judged,*

---

[222]   http://www.orlandosentinel.com/news/local/orl-florida-lotto-malfunction-082409,0,1152298.story

[223]   Strauss, Valerie. Mega Millions: Do lotteries really benefit public school? The Washington Post, March 30, 2012. https://www.washingtonpost.com/blogs/answer-sheet/post/mega-millions-do-lotteries-really-benefit-public-schools/2012/03/30/gIQAbTUNlS_blog.html?utm_term=.b153fe25b6f2

not by his own character and actions, but by the characters and actions of a collective of ancestors.

Racism claims that the content of a man's mind (not his cognitive apparatus, but its content) is inherited; that a man's convictions, values and character are determined before he is born, by physical factors beyond his control. This is the caveman's version of the doctrine of innate ideas—or of inherited knowledge—which has been thoroughly refuted by philosophy and science. Racism is a doctrine of, by and for brutes. It is a barnyard or stock-farm version of collectivism, appropriate to a mentality that differentiates between various breeds of animals, but not between animals and men.

Like every form of determinism, racism invalidates the specific attribute which distinguishes man from all other living species: his rational faculty. Racism negates two aspects of man's life: reason and choice, or mind and morality, replacing them with chemical predestination.

MAKE-WORK-INDUSTRIAL COMPLEX (REGULATIONS; E.G., CITY CODE INSPECTORS)

Would You Pay $100,000 a Foot for A Wheelchair Ramp?

I probably would not. But the generous taxpayers in San Francisco would*:*
Thanks to a maze of bureaucratic indecision and historic restrictions, taxpayers may shell out $100,000 per foot to make the Board of Supervisors president's perch in the historic chambers accessible to the disabled.

What's more, the little remodel job that planners first thought would take three months has stretched into more than four years - and will probably mean the supervisors will have to move out of their hallowed hall for five months while the work is done.
Says the director of the Office of Disability: "It's crazy. But this is just the price of doing business in a historic building."

Enough said. ~ Posted by Manuel Lora at February 27, 2008 05:13 PM
LewRockwell.com

City Code Inspectors

T hen there is the story of the Assemblywoman from Westchester County, New York, who plans to introduce legislation to regulate volume levels at movie theaters after a visit to a local theater to watch a movie during the holiday season. Of course, enforcement of this regulation would require a legion of inspectors to keep an eye - or should I say *ear?* - on every theater throughout the state of New York.[224] There is a quicker way to regulate the volume in a movie theater: Talk to the manager.

Anyone who has grown up in the mid-to-late Twentieth Century remembers raising money in the summer by selling lemonade on the curb in front of their parents' house, or the house of a friend. A high-traffic area could bring in enough money to save for the fair or a trip to the beach or movies. But those were the good old days. The 21st century has seen a seismic shift in regulation in a number of cities around the country that heavily regulate lemonade stands, sometimes out of existence. The police have shut down lemonade stands, of course, for public safety reasons. Probably someone, somewhere in the universe developed an acute stomach ache from drinking lemonade from a neighborhood stand. That is all it takes for some bureaucrat to find a reason for shutting stands down. I don't recall anyone getting sick from neighborhood stands but you can be sure far more people got sick from all the fluoride and other toxins they put in the public water system. And rest assured the collectivists at City Hall were not happy about being denied their "fair share" in sales tax!

Just recently in Toronto, Canada, a retired mechanic took upon himself the job to build a stairway on a slope in a community park that had become a fall hazard for some people walking the pathway. One person actually broke a wrist falling on the slope. Adi Asti, with the funds raised by neighbors, bought the materials and built the stairs for about $550. The City of Toronto made arrangements to install a stairway for a whopping cost of $65,000 to $150,000 to city taxpayers. Asti thought that the city was going to install an escalator for that price! Not to be outpriced, and

---

[224]   Lower Hundson Online, The Journal News (Gannett Co. Inc.), December 29, 2007. http://lohud.com/apps/pbcs.dll/article?AID=/20071229/NEWS01/712290347

defying all logic, the city has taped off the stairway while city officials decide what to do about it.

Public parks and other public facilities are a no-man's land. Everybody owns them and nobody owns them. The Left loves to go on about how public property belongs to everyone and how it fosters social togetherness for the community. Of course, public property belongs to everyone until everyone wants to stay after curfew, barbeque in the park, make a campfire, play amplified music, pick wild flowers, park the car in the wrong place, run your dog without a leash, smoke a cigarette, or drink an alcohol beverage. Sidewalks belong to the public, unless of course someone is hurt on the sidewalk in front of your house, or the sidewalk needs costly repair. Then it belongs to you.

Immigration Laws

Since 2000, immigration in the U.S. has exploded with the assistance of the U.S. government primarily for the corporations that are looking for cheaper labor. Since the 2007-2008 economic crash, legal and illegal immigrants both have enjoyed complete participation, regarding new job growth, as job growth for native-born Americans declined proportionately.[225] The number of H-1B visas for foreign technical workers exploded in recent years from 117,828 for FY2010 to 135,991 for FY2012, a 15.4% increase in two years for technical visas alone.[226] Economist Milton Friedman equated the H-1B visa program as a subsidy for corporations. High-tech companies have lobbied Congress for an increase in H-1B visas, despite evidence to the contrary that there is no shortage of qualified American workers. Wage depression is the major complaint by critics of the H-1B program. Workers immigrating to the U.S. are paid significantly less than U.S. workers. In an article from Center for Immigration Studies, John Miano found in 2007 that despite technology sector employer claims of highly skilled workers shortages in the United States, "employers classify most of their H-1B workers as being relatively low-skilled for the jobs they are filling."[227] The end result is that companies get low-skilled workers for lower wages at the expense of skilled American workers, who before getting laid off or retired out sometimes have to train the lower skilled workers. Milton Friedman was right: a subsidy for corporations.

---

[225] Camarote, S.A. and Zeigler, "Despite recent job growth native employment still below 2007: BLS data show all net employment growth has gone to immigrants.." Center for Immigration Studies, December 2014, pp. 1-10.

[226] http://en.wikipedia.org/wiki/H-1B_visa

[227] Miano, John. "Low salaries for low Skills: Wages and skill levels for H-1B computers workers, 2005." Center for Immigration Studies, April 2007, pp. 1-12.

Outlawing the outrageous act of backing into "your" driveway

To tackle the city blight problem in Jacksonville, Fla, and not being able to identify abandoned vehicles parked indefinitely in the driveways of run-down properties, the Jacksonville city council, in all its wisdom, decided to take up the suggestion to force the people of Jacksonville to park their vehicles' backside towards the street so that the city inspectors could read the license plates without having to come onto the property. That would take an extra effort as well as possibly a warrant. Note: Florida requires a license on the back of the vehicle only, not both ends.

The Underground Economy

Measuring the size of a nation's underground economy is obviously a specious undertaking. One could analogize this to trying to prove a negative. Needless to say, man was not going to be denied walking on the moon, some economist took the challenge to research and estimate the fraction of the U.S. economy involved in these so-called underground economic activities. Friedrich Schneider, a professor of economics in Germany, reported that not including criminal activities, the U.S. economy not reported to the various agencies that follow economic activities to be about 7.2% in 2007.[228] As illegal immigration employment continues to grow in the U.S., one could assume this fraction of underground activity has increased the past decade. But this paltry 7.2% underground economy is nothing compared to the top-ten national economies with markets in the shadows.[229]

Country	Average(%)
Bolivia 66.1	
Georgia 65.8	
Panama 63.5	
Zimbabwe	61.8
Azerbaijan	58.0
Peru	58.0
Haiti	56.4
Tanzania	56.4

[228] Schneider, Friedrich. "The Shadow Economy and Work in the Shadow: What Do We (Not) Know?" IZA Discussion Papers No. 6423. March 2012.

[229] Ibid., pp. 61-64.

| Nigeria 56.2 | |
| Thailand | 50.6 |

Table 3

Interestingly, of the ten nations with highest underground economies in Table 3, most are unitary presidential-constitutional republics (6), one is a federal presidential-republic; one is a dominant party-presidential-republic; one is a unitary dominant party-republic and one is a unitary parliamentary-constitutional monarchy. By contrast the United States remains a federal presidential-constitutional republic. The isolationistic Democratic People's Republic of Korea (North Korea) has a unitary socialist one-party state (totalitarian dictatorship). As a result of its closed-state system no data were available.

Federal Employees are obligated to not work

Prior to a *Salmonella* outbreak, USDA was told about unsanitary conditions by Iowa egg plant employees. The federal inspectors in charge of "grading" egg size claim it wasn't in their job description.

> *FRIDAY, Sept. 3 (HealthDay News) -- Two former workers at one of the two Iowa egg farms implicated in the massive recall of salmonella-contaminated eggs said federal inspectors who worked at the two farms ignored complaints about conditions at one of the sites, the Associated Press reported Friday.*
>
> *The two workers, employed at Wright County Egg facilities, said they reported problems such as leaking manure and dead chickens to U.S. Department of Agriculture employees, but nothing was done, the news service reported.*
>
> *A spokesman for the Agriculture Department, Caleb Weaver, said the federal employees' main duties were "grading" the eggs and they weren't primarily responsible for looking for health problems.*[230]

[230] Amanda Gardner, "Former Egg Farm Employees Say Their Complaints Were Ignored: Report" BusinessWeek.com, September 3, 2010. http://www.businessweek.com/lifestyle/content/healthday/642815.html

[231] PatriotRising.com, "20,642 New Regulations Added in the Obama Presicency." May, 23, 2016 http://patriotrising.com/2016/05/23/20642-new-regulations-added-obama-presidency/

Explosion of Federal regulations under just two presidencies

In eight years of the Obama administration 20,642 new regulations were added to the books at a cost of over $100 billion a year.[231] In 2015 alone, more than $22 billion a year in new regulations were dumped on American consumers and taxpayers. Most of these regulations will do nothing to solve the problems they address, but conveniently add thousands more federal bureaucrats and functionaries to oversee the meddling and destruction these regulations create. As PatriotRising.com stated, "The (EPA's 'Clean Power Plan') represents the first direct regulation of so-called greenhouse gas emissions from power plants, at a cost of $7.2 billion a year (and far more according to critics). Despite the huge costs, the plan will do nothing to mitigate global warming."

To be fair to Democrats, Obama's predecessor George W. Bush contributed to the regulation pool with a combined cost of $176 billion for already overburdened Americans who saw an increase of more than 2,000 new regulations in 2016, as well. The insurmountable damage to the fragile American economy will not be realized for years as these new regulations slowly rot the remaining foundation of a fragile to failing economy.

What licenses and permits really are

In 2014, 210 million Americans held a license to drive on American public roads. Licenses and permits are a way the various governments take your rights away and then sell them back to you. Freedom and "rights" are not the privilege or responsibility of governments to allocate to the people. Before a person became a citizen he was already free and already had natural rights. Limitations to one's freedom occur immediately after birth. People in the U.S. are assigned a social security number at birth, and will require that assigned number to eventually enter school or the workplace. People cannot work without a certain occupational license, or licenses. In this way, the government has the authority to decide who work and who do not. Building permits, repair and installation permits, and gun ownership are all ways to control the citizenry and harass political outsiders and opponents.

In the state of Florida there are nearly 30 divisions within the Florida Department of Business and Professional Regulation that issue licenses in just about every sector of employment in the state. The argument for their existence, of course, is that without licensed workers and professionals, the public would be at risk. These licenses do little to protect the public, but instead create monopolies for established companies and trade unions by limiting the number of permits or licenses. Nowhere is this more true than in New York City, where a permit to run a cab service in that city used to cost $150,000. This ensures a near-competition-free market for established taxi companies at the expense of both riders' costs and the nascent drivers of companies who are trying to enter the market in New York City. It nowhere protects the consumer, who is eventually gouged by the monopoly of cab drivers who can keep the price of cab service artificially, and ridiculously, high without the downward pressure of competition. The list of below shows the number of divisions that protect the established businesses that lobby for stifling competition and provide jobs for inspectors and paper-shuffling bureaucrats.

Alcoholic Beverages and Tobacco

Architects

Asbestos Contractors and Consultants

Athlete Agents

Auctioneers

Barbers

Boxing, Kickboxing and Mixed Martial Arts

Building Code Administrators and Inspectors

Certified Public Accounting

Community Association Managers

Construction Industry

Cosmetology

Drugs, Devices and Cosmetics Program

Electrical and Alarm Contractors

Elevators and Other Conveyances, Technicians, Inspectors and Companies

Employee Leasing Companies

Geologists

Harbor Pilots

Home Inspectors

Hotels, Motels, Apartments and other lodging

Interior Design

Landscape Architecture

Mold-Related Services

Pari-Mutuel Wagering Facilities

Real Estate

Restaurants, Take-outs, Delivery, Caterers and Mobile Food Vendors

Talent Agencies

Veterinary Medicine

ENVIRONMENT-INDUSTRIAL COMPLEX

Common Misconception

O n December 12, 1970, Republican President Richard Nixon introduced to Congress a proposal to establish the Environmental Protection Agency (EPA) to oversee regulation of national pollution and other environmental standards, such as energy efficiencies and endangered species protection. The EPA now employs over 15,000 full-time federal employees with an annual (2016) budget of over eight billion dollars.[232] The EPA headquarters remains in Washington, D.C., with 27 laboratories in ten regional offices.   Half of the EPA consists of engineers, scientists and environmental protection specialist. The remaining bureaucratic departments execute legal, financial and IT responsibilities, and public affairs.

Environmental regulations stifle productivity and job growth all the while guaranteeing a failure in holding industry here in the United States. The EPA was created to secure great swaths of land in Western US to be placed under federal jurisdiction, and subsequently "protected" for collateral to secure loans (debt) from foreign banks.[233,234] These loans served the purpose of paying for a plethora of new government programs and for the mounting debt from the Vietnam War. The empire needed money for policing a diminished hold on strategic geopolitical realms, such as the Middle East and Africa.

---

[232] EPA's Budget and Spending. https://www.epa.gov/planandbudget/budget

[233] Brownfield, Derry. Our Land: Collateral for the National Debt. News with Views Aug. 17, 2007 https://www.newswithviews.com/brownfield/brownfield59.htm

[234] https://www.peakprosperity.com/forum/our-land-collateral-national-debt/38295

Environmental regulations do not necessarily protect people and the environment from hazardous and unhealthy byproducts of human productivity, but instead allow what the EPA considers to be "acceptable" standards of pollution within the various aspects of human productivity. These standards are usually set by industry insiders brought in by the various bureaucracies of government. These bureaucracies are usually duplicitous at the state and federal level to appease the environmental activists and the politicians elected to represent them. The politician's job is to find money for these bureaucracies.

In 2015, the EPA caused a spillage of hundreds of times over the EPA's own established limits of six toxic heavy metals from a botched Gold King Mine cleanup in Colorado.[235,236] Not one EPA official was held accountable, even as the agency helped convict 185 other Americans of environmental "crimes" that very same year. The convictions resulted in "levying more than $88 million in fines, $112 million in restitution and $4 billion in court-ordered environmental projects."

People in academic and governmental positions who become vocally contentious about the central dogma of environmentalism are ridiculed and sometimes find themselves unemployed. When the University of Ottawa caught wind of Professor Denis Rancourt's academic views of environmentalism, especially the anthropocentric, pedagogic, but scientifically flawed canon of man-made climate change, the university began a campaign to smear him. Charging him with "academic squatting," when he changed a course to study "not just how science impacts everyday life, but how it relates to greater power structures."[237,238,239] Eventually, Rancourt drew global attention about the scientific scam of climate change, charging United Nation's Intergovernmental Panel on Climate Change scientists as "named by governments, they are scientists who accept to serve a

[235]   2015   Gold   King   Mine   waste   water   spill. https://en.wikipedia.org/wiki/2015_Gold_King_Mine_waste_water_spill

[236] Barker, Daniel, "After releasiong toxic pollution into rivers with zero accountability, the EPA convicts 185 other Americans for 'environmental crimes.'" Investment Watch, January 11, 2016. http://investmentwatchblog.com/after-releasing-toxic-pollution-into-rivers-with-zero-accountability-the-epa-convicts-185-other-americans-for-environmental-crimes/

237 Trew, Stuart, Understanding power, *Ottawa Xpress*, January 5, 2006.

[238] Tam, Pauline, Students rally around controversial professor, *The Ottawa Citizen*, February 15, 2006

[239] Teaching Science Through Social Activism is Protected by Academic Freedom, Arbitrator Rules. *College and University Employment Law E-Bulletin*, Issue No.23. February 17, 2009.

political role. Their mission is to write a report [that] is meant to be used by government. Their goal is [to] find a conclusion…it is a political process."

The environment isn't necessarily good for us. The environment in most cases will kill us. And we can only defend ourselves to what we can think. Mowing the lawn, kicking up dust, and pathogenic organisms are all related. Nature is sometimes deadly. Much of mammalian survival depends on the individual idiosyncrasies of the immune system and other biological functions. But fortunately for humans we have an incredible ability to adapt and survive.

An environmentalist is someone who blames global cooling on global warming. There's no arguing with these people. They hit so many branches on the way down the ignorant tree that they've knocked themselves intellectually unconscious. While former Vice President Al Gore, high priest of the environmental movement, preaches to us about rising oceans as the polar ice caps melt from global warming, he buys an expensive oceanside mansion in Montecito, California, formerly owned by singer Tom Jones and entertainer Dean Martin.[240,241] Actress and singer Barbara Streisand, a proponent of radical environmental legislation, "spends $22,000 a year watering her lawn and gardens, requests 120 bath-size towels upon arrival at production offices, jets around the world in a private jet, and uses thirteen, 53-foot semi-trailers at her concerts," according to Human Events.[242] Evidently, these troublemakers haven't got the memo that the planet has been cooling since about 1998.

---

[240]   Ocean's   rising,   why   is   Al   Gore   in   Montecito?   August   22,   2013. http://www.sgvtribune.com/opinion/20130822/if-oceans-rising-why-is-al-gore-in-montecito

[241] Beale, Lauran. Al Gore buys $8.9 million ocean-view villa. World Property Journal, May 13, 2010.

[242]   Human   Events.   "The   top   10   Hollywood   hypocrits."   March   631,   2012. http://humanevents.com/2012/03/31/the-top-10-hollywood-hypocrites/

Just recently, a global warming study in Canada was cancelled because the ice breaker ship carrying 40 scientists on a study team couldn't continue because the ship was needed elsewhere in the southern waters around eastern Canada! As the title of the Winnipeg Free Press comically pointed out, and I noted above, "U. of M. climate change study postponed due to climate change."[243] Because the climate has been cooling for nearly two decades, climatologists have had to change the nomenclature of their global-warming ruse to keep people believing that human existence is the primary cause of any and all weather anomalies on the planet.

The Flint, Michigan Water Crisis

In 2014, the city of Flint, Michigan began using the Flint River as a water source to cut costs. It previously relied on Detroit's proximity to Lake Huron. As it turns out, the city of Flint is now in a crisis, where the corrosive river water has destroyed the water lines and made the city's water contaminated with toxic heavy metals and other crud sequestered from the pipes. Naturally, the so-called liberal media directed attacks against the Republican governor and other Republicans, whereas the EPA knew about the problem and never warned the city or state about high levels of metals and other toxins.

Fluoridation and Public Water Systems

> Now declassified files of the Manhattan Project and the Atomic Energy Commission show that the toxicology department at the University of Rochester – which was under the direction of Harold Hodge – was asked to produce medical information about fluoride that could help defend the government against lawsuits where they were charged with fluoride pollution.
>
> It is now clear that if water fluoridation were declared harmful to human health, the U.S. nuclear bomb program, as well as many other fluoride-polluting industries such as aluminum plants and fertilizer manufacturers, would have been left open to massive litigation.[244]

So how do certain industries remove toxic fluoridation by-products from their waste streams? It's simple: have government officials declare fluoride beneficial and put it in public water systems! Declassified files of the Manhattan Project and the

[243] Rollason, Kevin, U of M climate change study postponed due to climate change." Winnipeg Free Press, June 12, 2017. http://www.winnipegfreepress.com/local/u-of-m-climate-change-study-postponed-due-to-climate-change-428030543.html

[244] Mercola, Joseph. "Lead Poisoning Alert: This Widely Used Drink Is Dangerous." http://lewrockwell.com/mercola/mercola156.html

Atomic Energy Commission revealed that the reason behind promoting fluoride and water fluoridation in the U.S. was to protect the bomb and aluminum industries from liability.

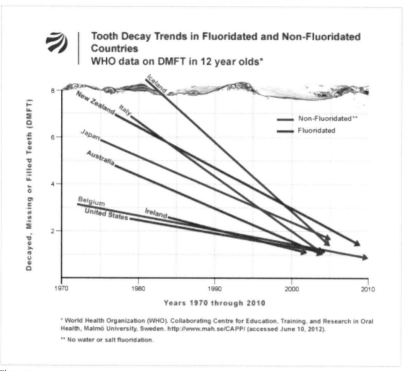

Figure 13

The graph above, published from data collected by the World Health Organization and Sweden's Malmö University, shows no difference in reduction of decayed, missing or filled teeth of twelve-year-old patients in eight countries that had fluoridated or non–fluoridated public water and salt.[245] In fact, tooth decay declined faster in two non–fluoridated countries, Iceland and Italy.

A movement has sprung up around the world in recent years to ban water fluoridation.   Countries that banned, or never had, fluoridation of their water systems include Israel, Germany, Denmark, Sweden, Norway, and Hungary. On January 18, 2011, New York City councilor Peter Vallone, Jr. introduced legislation

---

[245] Flouride Action Network, August 7, 2012. http://fluoridealert.org/articles/50-reasons/who_data01/

"prohibiting the addition of fluoride to the water supply." As of 2014, 76.0% of New Yorkers still receive fluoridated water from the city.

Evidence that fluoridation of water does not contribute to the prevention of dental caries was established recently in a review by Cochrane Oral Health Group.[246] The study revealed that despite evidence showing a reduction of caries levels in both deciduous and permanent dentition in children, study designs, high risk of bias, and the applicability of evidence to current lifestyles highly confounded the conclusions presented forty years ago. But "a significant association between dental fluorosis and fluoride level" in the drinking water corroborated recent evidence that over-exposure of fluoride can cause substantial deterioration in tooth enamel.

> "Frankly, this is pretty shocking," says Thomas Zoeller, a scientist at UMass-Amherst uninvolved in the work. "This study does not support the use of fluoride in drinking water." Trevor Sheldon concurred. Sheldon is the dean of the Hull York Medical School in the United Kingdom who led the advisory board that conducted a systematic review of water fluoridation in 2000, that came to similar conclusions as the Cochrane review. The lack of good evidence of effectiveness has shocked him. "I had assumed because of everything I'd heard that water fluoridation reduces cavities but I was completely amazed by the lack of evidence," he says. "My prior view was completely reversed."[247]

Science reaching back to the 1920s has shown fluoride is an endocrine disruptor and a recent study out of England has shown that fluoride can induce hypothyroidism in communities with drinking water fluoride levels greater than 0.7 parts per million. Water fluoridation is now being linked to a higher prevalence of attention deficit hyperactivity disorder (ADHD) amongst children and adolescents in the United States.

Keeping an Open Mind in a Closed Environment

---

[246] Iheozor-Ejiofor, Zipporah, et al. "Water fluoridation for the prevention of dental carries." The Cochrane Collaboration, June 18, 2015. http://onlinelibrary.wiley.com/doi/10.1002/14651858.CD010856.pub2/abstract

[247] "Fluoridation May Not Prevent Cavities, Scientific Review Shows." Washington Blog, June 29, 2015 http://www.washingtonsblog.com/2015/06/fluoridation-may-not-prevent-cavities-scientific-review-shows.html

Figure 14

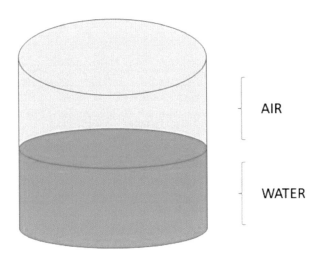

The image above symbolizes the title of this book. The container is neither half-full nor half-empty. Keeping an open mind will help you realize that the container is 100% full. Perspective is important when understanding the world around you. If you close your mind to new ideas, substantiated facts, and the opinions of others, you will perpetuate the static, stubborn and regressive environment of a failed society.

Tyranny is everywhere now, not only in the U.S. but around the planet. It silently creeps into every aspect of our so-called civilization, primarily through the advancement of modern technology. Tyranny is the dark matter to the light matter of liberty in our social universe. Freedom can still exist wherever people hold it tight in their hearts and minds. Instead of succumbing to the dark forces, people must keep their minds open to their own potential and to the potential of those who share the same values.

Possibly one of the easiest ways to change the incestuous and closed environment of corporate-government destruction of our planet is to refuse to participate. Riding a bike, using solar, buying things second-hand or made locally, collecting your own water, growing your own food are all ways to vote with your feet and get off the grid. In some states, in turn, getting off the grid has become not only an act of defiance but incredibly a criminal act. Cities in states as politically diverse as Florida, Alabama and California have gone after people for just trying to get off the grid.[248] Laws are in place around the U.S. that force residents to hook up to city water and electric grids, or face fines, even jail time. Reasons to force people onto the grid plantations can be as insidious as keeping them on the tax and fee rolls to as scientifically debatable as protecting the environment. Recently in Florida, a lobbyist for Florida Power and Light was caught writing anti-solar legislation for a Fort Myers state representative, who took $15,000 campaign contributions from FPL that year.[249] The law requires that people must shut off their solar power to their house after losing power to their homes after a storm. This, of course, is to protect FPL linemen while they work on restoring power, even if the homeowner has a switch to block power from leaving the house (back feed). Protecting linemen is a reasonable concern, but denying people the right to provide themselves power to their house is totally unacceptable. People off the grid are of course more difficult to control. And anyone who can live their lives independent of the corporate-state is a huge threat to the existence of it. This government power, whether local, state or federal, is antithetical to the very core of what America is supposed to represent.

Protecting the environment comes down to an individual effort. We have seen for years how environmentalism has become Big Business, making people with spurious causes and agendas incredibly wealthy at the expense of those who suffer unnecessary inconveniences, unemployment, and the higher costs of an overregulated economy. Leading up to the Paris Climate Change Conference and culminating in the so-called Paris Climate Agreement, which Barak Obama signed on, Christiana Figueres, executive secretary of U.N.'s Framework Convention on Climate Change, admitted that the reason for a global imposition on fossil fuel emission in the industrial world of the West (China and India were exempt) was not so much to control the climate, a nearly impossible undertaking, but to destroy capitalism[250] and to redistribute wealth into a globalist slush fund similar to the IMF.

---

[248] "Is it illegal to live off the grid?" The Alternative Daily, May 2016. http://www.thealternativedaily.com/illegal-to-live-off-grid/

[249] Doctorow, Corey. "Florida Power and Light lobbyist made it illegal to use solar duting outages." Boing Boing   September 18, 2017. https://boingboing.net/2017/09/18/rep-ray-rodrigues.html

[250] "U.N. official reveals real reason behind warming scare." Investor's Business Daily, February 10, 2015. http://www.investors.com/politics/editorials/climate-change-scare-tool-to-destroy-capitalism/

INFORMATION-MEDIA-INDUSTRIAL COMPLEX

"The Central Intelligence Agency owns everyone of any significance in the major media." ~William Colby, Former Director, CIA

"Our job is to give people not what they want, but what we decide they ought to have." ~Richard M. Cohen, former Senior Producer of CBS political news

"... he's (Donald Trump's) trying to undermine the media ... he can actually control what people think. And that is our job ...." ~Mika Brzezinski, co-host of MSNBC's Morning Joe, explaining her role with the Fourth Estate.

"Truth is treason in the empire of lies." ~former U.S. Rep. Dr. Ron Paul

Corporate Media

Decades ago, before Al Gore created the Internet[251] (his words, not mine), I used to believe I was well-informed about history, politics and the current events. I read newspapers and watched the morning and evening news daily. Most of the book reading I did during this time, when I was in college especially, was text books and other books related to my studies, which were primarily related to math and science. At that time, like most Americans, I believed that journalists were reporting to us an objective overview of what was happening in the world. On cable TV shows we were given a historical perspective that the wars that our American

---

[251]   "During my service in the United States Congress, I took the initiative in creating the Internet." Senator Al Gore, Jr., a Wolf Blitzer interview on CNN's *Late Edition*, Cnn.com, March 9, 1999. http://www.cnn.com/ALLPOLITICS/stories/1999/03/09/president.2000/transcript.gore/

ancestors fought were righteous and honorable. Although I believed that most politicians and other government higher ups were greedy, self-absorbed megalomaniacs, I thought many, many years ago that most TV reporters and journalists to be watchdogs protecting our interests as a free society.

In 2002, a book called *Into the Buzzsaw: Leading Journalists Expose the Myth of a Free Press*[252] was published that changed my world-view of mainstream media forever. Decades before that, as I became more and more a libertarian skeptic of our society, I began suspecting an incestuous relationship behind the corporate state and corporate media, both scheming to rob us of our treasures and liberties. *Buzzsaw* solidified that perception. It cleared the air about literally decades of rumor and charges of "conspiracy theories" about corporate-government malfeasance. The various media outlets (i.e., which are corporations) are literally poisoning us, lying to us and robbing us in so many ways that it's difficult to keep track.

Corporate media operatives, from the local newspaper to the national news networks, have always been cheerleaders for the state. The idea that the journalist was a "watchdog" of government was a fantasy of the Left.[253] The media's pundits and professional "experts" are now nearly always former government bureaucrats, politicians, military leaders, or members of ominous elitist organizations of the political class such as the Council on Foreign Relations. As former CIA director William Colby admitted, many in the media were (are) from the CIA. In other words, these are individuals with a vested interest in all-things government. Radaronline.com reported[254] that CNN anchor Anderson Cooper spent summer internships with the CIA following his sophomore and junior year at Yale, a well-known recruiting ground for the CIA. And then there is the 1975 congressional hearing revealing that the CIA in fact paid out a billion dollars to broadcasters, editors and the like in mass media of TV magazines and newspapers

And then there is the "incestuous" relationship, as the Breitbart author John Nolte calls in a Washington Post article,[255] between media and certain government

---

[252]   Borjesson, Kristina, ed., <u>Into the Buzzsaw: Leading Journalists Expose the Myth of a Free Press</u> (New York: Prometheus Books, 2002)

[253]   Brasch, Walterm *Toothless: The watchdog press that became the government's lapdog.* The Online Journal http://onlinejournal.com/artman/publish/article_4389.shtml Februrary 20, 2009

[254]   Bercovici, Jeff, "Anderson Cooper's CIA Secret." The Constantine Institute for Advanced Media Studies May 16, 2008. http://constantineinstitute.blogspot.com/2008/05/anderson-coopers-cia-secret.html from http://www.radaronline.com/exclusives/2006/09/anderson-coopers-cia-secret.php

[255] Nolte, John, "Wahington Post: Family Relations between Media, Obama Officials does not affect coverage." Brietbart, June 13, 2013. http://www.breitbart.com/big-journalism/2013/06/13/washington-

officials. The table below, taken from the Nolte article, shows the close connection media and government officials have, and the degree of collusion and conflicts of interest of those we are told to trust and depend upon for keeping us informed.

- ABC News President Ben Sherwood, who is the brother of Elizabeth Sherwood-Randall, a top national-security adviser to President Obama.

- His counterpart at CBS, news division president David Rhodes, is the brother of Benjamin Rhodes, a key foreign-policy specialist.

- CNN's deputy Washington bureau chief, Virginia Moseley, is married to Tom Nides, who until earlier this year was deputy secretary of state under Hillary Rodham Clinton.

- White House press secretary Jay Carney's wife is Claire Shipman, a veteran reporter for ABC.

- NPR's White House correspondent, Ari Shapiro, is married to a lawyer, Michael Gottlieb, who joined the White House counsel's office in April.

- The *Post*'s Justice Department reporter, Sari Horwitz, is married to William B. Schultz, the general counsel of the Department of Human Services.

- [VP] Biden's current communications director, Shailagh Murray (a former *Post* congressional reporter), is married to Neil King, one of the *Wall Street Journal*'s top political reporters.

Rarely will viewers and readers see someone with a point of view that is countermand to issues involving government solutions. Rarely will you see someone with a libertarian outlook on life asked his or her opinion. When a libertarian is dragged out for an interview, or whenever a libertarian point-of-view is scrutinized, it will nearly always be someone with a unique, fundamentally libertine lifestyle, such as Howard Stern, or some other controversial individual who philosophically resides far outside the social norms of the viewing/reading public. This tactic is intended to reinforce in the viewer's mind the idea that the words *libertarian* and *libertine* are synonymous. You will rarely see someone like a Llewellyn Rockwell or a Tom Woods, Jr., or a Ron Paul, someone who is intellectually grounded in social and economic issues of the day, be asked to participate in a roundtable discussion on Fox's *The Five* or CNN's *Crossfire*. It will not happen. Any "libertarians" these shows highlight are usually what has been called "liberventionists," (thank you, Joseph Stromberg[256]) someone who thinks marijuana should be legalized (and taxed, of course) but also wants to see more military interventionism overseas and funding for strategic allies such as Israel and Saudi Arabia.

---

post-family-relations-between-media-obama-officials-does-not-affect-coverage/

[256] Stromberg, Joseph R. "Liberventionim Rides Again: the Twisted Tree of Liberty – Indeed." April 13, 2002. http://www.antiwar.com/stromberg/s041302.html

Despite American voters that consistently identify themselves to be more libertarian-leaning than either conservative or liberal,[257] voters continue to place crooks and authoritarians into political office from local to federal. Studies have shown over many decades that the U.S. Congress has consistently polled shamefully low in the minds of most Americans, around 10% favorability, yet its members consistently get re-elected at a rate of 90 percent! Mainstream media have much to do with this by reporting one-sided stories favoring the incumbent, while scrutinizing the opponent. Political ads are expensive providing the well-funded incumbent a clear pecuniary advantage over the opponent(s). Slanted reporting in turn provides the journalist or news outlet easy access to the office of the incumbent.

Of course, because the rooster crows before sunrise, the rooster crow must cause the sun to rise in the morning. So it is with media: even as drug war violence has become an unintended consequence of bad government policy, the media blame guns and drugs. Never mind the fact that you never see beer distributors shooting each other in the streets, because they can sell their product safely, cheaply and legally to consenting adults. Despite the fact that alcohol is far more addictive and destructive than marijuana, alcohol is still revered to be America's drug of choice. And despite American tax-funded programs like education and military adventurism receiving enormous funding, the folly they create is blamed on illiteracy and foreign aggression and resistance. And, of course, a perception of liberty by someone who is free to shop at the mall or go to church on Sunday may be quite different than an atheistic IT guy who shops tax-free online and spends his Sunday programming and compiling data.

Despite the normal, nearly 100% libertarian decisions and actions of an American civilian public every day, the media continue to perpetuate a perception that the public needs an omnipotent State to protect them from every social and natural aberration under the sun. In the case of the drug war, or the FDA, or the USDA, or the economy, for that matter, we are told that even though together we make trillions of moral, anarchistic decisions every day, the world would start spinning out of control if not for government intervention. Those who fail to make moral, anarchistic decisions we see in the news, where life-molding perceptions are made.

This all came to a head in 2008 when The Center for Media Democracy and Free Press exposed an epidemic of fake news infiltrating local television broadcasts across the country. At a press conference in Washington with FCC Commissioner Jonathan

---

[257] Goodman, John C., Libertarians Outnumber both Liberals and Conservatives." Townhall, April 18, 2015 http://townhall.com/columnists/johncgoodman/2015/04/18/libertarians-outnumber-both-liberals-and-conservatives-n1986898

S. Adelstein, the group called for a crackdown on stations that present corporate-sponsored videos as genuine news to an unsuspecting audience.[258] It is no wonder more Americans are abandoning newspapers and network news, especially, for the internet.[259]

Writes Bill Anderson, PhD:

> ... my first "real" job after I was graduated from college 33 years ago was working for a daily newspaper. It was a typical statist publication, and most of the "beats" were covering different government agencies. Of course, that meant that the reporters were chummy with officials, both elected and "appointed."
>
> The police beat reporter, for example, always took the police line as being the unvarnished truth, and he was backed up by his bosses. He later took a job as the publicity officer for the local sheriff. (I almost was fired for making the "shocking" statement to someone that police officers often lie in court proceedings and elsewhere.)
>
> I wrote my doctoral dissertation on newspapers, and have published some academic papers as well as other articles on the relationship between journalists and government. While journalists are fond of saying that they are the "watchdogs" of government, that is a bald-faced lie.
>
> When the New York Slimes performs its "watchdog" tricks on government, it usually is to castigate the government for not using more force, either in regulating private economic affairs or coercing people to do what the lefties at the Slimes are demanding. For example, we have heard a series of whines from the editors at the Times that the Bush administration did not "do enough" on the "global warming" front, and that government needs to impose taxes and other rules on the rest of us to keep us from driving automobiles as much as we would like.
>
> I would challenge any reader to show me one time -- one time -- when the editorial page of a newspaper has *not* advocated increases in state power, either on the right (invade or bomb another country or ratchet up the drug war) and on the left (stop global warming, or we need more government regulations of business). There is no greater advocate of the totalitarian state than the typical journalist, so we should not be surprised when journalists begin to demand that the government bail them out, too.
>
> Jim Bennett of George Mason University once told me that "technology undermines government," and it seems that technology also undermines

---

[258] Diane Farsetta,   John Stauber and Craig Aaron   "Fake TV News: News Release"   Center for Democracy and Free Press, November 14, 2008. http://www.prwatch.org/fakenews/release

[259]   Americans abandon newspapers for the internet. Telegraph, December 26, 2008.
http://www.telegraph.co.uk/news/worldnews/northamerica/usa/3966307/Americans-abandon-newspapers-for-the-internet.html

> newspapers. Since newspapers and government pretty much are joined at the hip, we should not be surprised to see that these "freedom-loving" journalists are going to demand censorship against competitors.
>
> Don't forget that the NY Slimes and Washington Post were at the forefront of demanding passage of the execrable McCain-Feingold Act which criminalizes political speech from entities *other than newspapers*. That is right; journalists already are on the record demanding arrest and imprisonment of their competitors. Why should we not be surprised?

Some things you will never read in the print media or hear on the radio or TV news channels: Apparently, in Michigan, more voters approved legalization of medical marijuana use with 63 percent, outnumbering voters for President-elect Barak Obama. More evidence comes at the time in mid-summer, 2009, when Barak Obama was struggling with moving his agenda of healthcare reform, when he made an off-color statement about the way policemen handled the arrest of a Harvard professor for trying to "break into" his own house during the night. This story caught fire in the media as another of many examples of police discrimination and treatment toward blacks. Of course, the "conservative" blowhards on Fox News and Clear Channel talk shows exploited this controversy to keep the media's attention on the story and not what Obama had to propagandize about his healthcare plan, which surely did bankrupt the taxpayers and consumers with billions of added tax liabilities, premiums, and deductibles on healthcare.

United, the Elite Divide

For decades the ruling class, with the help of moles within the corporate media, has manipulated the mindset of the masses with division, to the elitists' benefit. The long-time Republican-Democrat paradigm has provided the entertainment of bread and circuses to distract people long enough to rob them silly. Now, people are beginning to understand that representation for the voters is rarely met with the appropriate actions of the politicians of Washington. So, recently the division has been diverted to the groupthink of generational differences. The American society is headed for a major conflict where waves of baby boomer retirees are met with a younger generation of workers who increasingly believes it owes no one social security other than its future self. Retirees have found that the government has spent their social security long ago on debt, wars and inflation, and that there is no social security "lock box."

The elites have realized a long time ago that as long as they keep the masses fighting amongst themselves, they won't have to fight the masses. The only time the two major parties get together is when they are robbing the rest of us of our liberties and treasure.

The Reagan Lie

The media has always made President Ronald Reagan's presidency a symbolic victory over communism, especially the collapse of the Soviet Union.   If anything, though, Reagan's policies toward the Soviets prolonged their eventual demise by giving the Soviets reasonable nationalistic propaganda and keeping the Union states together to protect themselves from Reagan's well-known military escalation.   Of course, any country whose leader openly antagonizes and demonizes a failed socioeconomic system, such as the Soviets had, that was so poor[260] it couldn't even afford to put a whole naval fleet out on the ocean, already won the Cold War. Most of the Soviet protection was in its submarine fleet which dwarfed in comparison with America's towering naval and air might.

Brezhnev admitted as much in the early 1970s,[261,262,263] long before Reagan was president. The media's role in perpetuating the Soviet threat myth was blatantly obvious. It wasn't difficult for the Republicans, especially, to turn the media's feeding frenzy with Reagan's popularity (he was a likable guy who happened to be a Republican) into some kind of uber-national super hero who defeated the Soviets single-handedly. It was well-known to anyone who saw through the baloney of partisan politics that the Soviet Empire was near collapse. So, as mentioned earlier, while Reagan propagandized the Soviet military "threat," the Soviet government was so broke it could barely put a full fleet of war ships on the high seas.

How the Media Lie about War

In 2008, the Pentagon suspended briefings to a platoon of military analysts whose job it was on the various television news networks to promote the wars in the Middle East. As David Barstow from the New York Times put it:[264]

> A spokesman for the Pentagon said the briefings and all other

---

[260]   *The Soviet Union Disintegrates* http://www.fsmitha.com/h2/ch33.htm

[261]   Kotkin,   S.   *Armageddon   Averted: The   Soviet   Collapse,   1970–2000* (2001).http://books.google.com/books?id=ONxZ3eSVMJsC&dq=kotkin+s+armageddon+averted+the+soviet+collapse+1970+2000+2001&pg=PP1&ots=DprRFZCnlo&sig=pMzTpLsILGd7fgAtI2z4MqZ-9WA&hl=en&prev=http://www.google.com/search%3Fhl%3Den%26q%3DKotkin,%2BS.%2B%2BArmageddon%2BAverted:%2BThe%2BSoviet%2BCollapse,%2B1970%25E2%2580%25932000%2B(2001%26btnG%3DSearch&sa=X&oi=print&ct=title&cad=one-book-with-thumbnail

[262]   http://www.answers.com/topic/union-of-soviet-socialist-republics

[263]   http://en.wikibooks.org/wiki/European_History/Europe:_1945_to_Present

[264]   Barstow, D. Pentagon Suspends Briefings for Analysts. The New York Times. April 26, 2008.

> interactions with the military analysts had been suspended
> indefinitely pending an internal review.
> On Sunday, The New York Times reported that since 2002 the
> Pentagon has cultivated several dozen military analysts in a
> campaign to generate favorable coverage of the administration's
> wartime performance. The retired officers have made tens of
> thousands of appearances for television and radio networks,
> holding forth on Iraq, Afghanistan, detainee issues and terrorism
> in general.
> Records and interviews show that the Bush administration
> worked to transform the analysts into an instrument intended to
> shape coverage from inside the major networks.

Possibly, the most ardent cheerleader for Bush's war in Iraq, other than Fox News, of course, was the late Tim Russert of *Meet the Press*. Here was a guy who, probably more than any other manipulator in mass media, used his show to perpetuate the many myths coming from the non-stop propaganda organ for the administration, specifically Vice President Dick Cheney. Justin Raimondo, an authentic journalist, frankly put it,

> Oh yes, Russert did his research, all right, but he only utilized it to the
> War Party's advantage. He sucked up to power and was little more than a
> stenographer for high government officials whose confidence he coveted. He
> was, in short, a great journalist, at least by today's standards, and that's why
> the media blowhards are turning his death into a celebration of... themselves.
> Because they're virtually all the same – shameless, sycophantic suck-ups
> who will do anything to advance their careers and could care less about
> where it takes the country.[265]

Had it not dawned on anyone in the media on the blatant complicity they all had in selling the Big Lie about Iraq? Shouldn't someone in the media had argued that if Mr. Smith comes over to your house and punches you in the face, you don't go over to Mr. Jones' house and kill his family, just because he goes to the same church as Mr. Smith? Leading up to the Iraq war, where was the media, someone, anyone arguing that the aftermath would be as tragic as, well, it turned out years later, a hellhole and quagmire of unimaginable proportions? No one in either print or television media argued that position. Liberation? No one believes that anymore, other than hundreds of thousands of Iraqis who were liberated from their bodies, permanently.

For centuries, religious authority and monarchies controlled the flow of information to control the mindset of their subjects, the masses. For a long time, for

---

[265] Raimondo, J. Enough Already! The eulogies for Tim Russert ignore his role as the War Party's sounding board. June 8, 2008. http://antiwar.com/justin/?articleid=13006

example, common people in the Christian cultures were denied the chance to read the Bible by virtue of the lack of Bibles available. Prior to Johann Gutenberg's printing press in the early-mid fifteenth century, only clergy and royalty could afford to own the scarce scrolls and parchments with hand-written Bible text. By 1500, printing presses spread throughout Western Europe printing more than 20 million volumes.[266] In time liberalism and enlightenment changed how the flow of societal information was controlled and directed. These ideals of liberty put the individual in the driver's seat. The religious authority and kings became an obstacle to the pursuit of knowledge and self-governance. Eventually kings, especially, became irrelevant and were overthrown, such as in 18th Century France and the American colonies.

The Computer Age has brought the world to the point that even government and corporate media have become irrelevant. People no longer rely on expensive daily newspapers and the corporate-state propaganda from commercial-laden television news networks. Even the universities are feeling threatened, as individuals can, with persistent effort, become an authority on any subject. Self-educated becomes self-governance and personal responsibility.

Calculations are difficult to ascertain in politics. Poll numbers become a gauge for social engineers to keep the governmental fires and steam working for their benefit and the benefit of their allies. Most calculations are based on assumptions (e.g., "say half of ...") that may not be historically correct. In real science calculations are still based on assumptions. And even if assumptions are historically correct, they may not really reflect actual voter intent because, as we all know too painfully, the elections are corrupted. One could easily have said, "Say the polls were rigged ... ."

You see, the way the elections work is this: The media polls are distributed before an election as a kind of self-fulfilled prophecy to legitimize the results. The media do the polls, or purchase polls from firms like Zogby. Then with enough conditioning by the media over months of propaganda, a private media conglomerate, Voter News Services,[267] tabulates the results on election night. Nice and neat.

---

[266] Febvre, Lucien; Martin, Henri-Jean. <u>The Coming of the Book: The Impact of Printing 1450-1800</u> (London, New Left Books, 1976)

[267] Collier, V. Your stolen vote—the missing piece of the puzzle, The Online Journal, May 2000 http://www.onlinejournal.com/evoting/020801Collier/020801collier.html

In the past, I hoped a Ron Paul win would disprove my arguments, but I think people are being naïve if they think that those in power are just going to roll over and let Ron Paul take away their multitrillion-dollar slush fund. Regardless of a win, Ron Paul has done a great service to the world in spreading his (our) message of Liberty! Doctor Paul's message resonated long after the elections of 2008 and 2012, especially with young people, bringing optimism to millions of people such as myself who have spent much energy trying to spread the message of liberty for not only Americans, but people around the planet.

Elections are so corrupted by the media and the political class. After the 2008 New Hampshire primary, allegations of fraud were becoming increasingly apparent to people in watch groups that follow this kind of thing.[268],[269] The media reported projected winners in New Hampshire 17 minutes after the polls closed at 7 PM EST. Many of the precincts with Diebold optical scanning machines, of which the majority votes were cast (75%), never reported their results until nearly midnight. For the Obama-Clinton race there was a gigantic discrepancy between hand-counted votes versus those cast on electronic machines relative to the exit poll results. Hand-counted numbers were closer to the exit polls, where Obama won by five percentage points over Clinton.

The Internet and Net Neutrality

The consensus in the photosphere of the Internet is that the Internet will be consumed by the same fascistic elements in the corporate political circles that ruined the quality of information disseminating from both television and the press. What makes the Internet different and less controllable than the old media is the fact that viewers now have a comparable control of media dissemination, as well as control of the broad spectrum of *genre* they chose to watch and read. The powers-that-be in media, which are nothing more than an organ of the political class, no longer control content and it is driving them crazy.

Polls and hard market realities have shown that the dead wood press and magazine media of the 20th Century have consistently lost circulation numbers for years recently.[270] And they are not getting them back. It won't be long when cable

---

[268]   Moriarty, Judith   Who Counts Your Vote? Only The Shadow Knows, January 13, 2008 http://www.rense.com/general80/mdro.htm

[269]   Hart, Len . Princeton University Reveals How the GOP Steals Election,   January 12, 2008 http://www.opednews.com/articles/opedne_len_hart_080112_princeton_university.htm

[270]   Snyder, Michael, *Is the Mainstream Media Dying?* Infowars.com, May 20, 2014 http://www.infowars.com/is-the-mainstream-media-dying/   and   Watson,   Paul   Joseph

and network news shows, as well as political talk shows, will have gone the road of newspapers as serious, non-bias ways of informing the public.   The trends are already happening.   The Internet rules, and already the powers-to-be are conniving ways to take the cyber world away from us. People are waking up to the fact that "(a)bout 90 percent of the 'information' that is endlessly pumped into our heads through our televisions is controlled by just six gigantic media corporations," as Michael Snyder wrote in his article *Is the Mainstream Media Dying?*

The latest scheme to get control of information back in the hands of the political class is so-called "Net Neutrality."[271] As with most government schemes, Net Neutrality will be anything but neutral and will burden ISPs and other Internet users with higher fees and more regulations (less freedom).

Recently the media networks and websites have integrated popular websites such as YouTube and Facebook to connect with the millions who are shedding off the corporate propagandists and following alternative news sites. People don't take corporate news seriously anymore,[272] especially after cheer leading the propaganda blitz perpetuated by a lying Bush administration leading up to the invasion of Iraq in 2003.   Now, during this most-recent recession, we know how Americans were bilked into believing the FDR administration was "doing everything it could" to get the economy going again, because we're seeing it played out again live on TV and the Internet. We know now that it was the mischievous meddling of the federal government and its Fourth Branch, the Federal Reserve, that created the bubble during the Clinton and both Bush administrations that enriched the bankers and other politically connected at the expense of other taxpayers. It is, for all practical circumstances, a rectification of the kinds of devastating governmental policies of the 1930s that will drag the US through a possible decade of stagnation and high unemployment worse than we experienced through the 1970s.

History Revisionism

> Isn't "revisionism" just a synonym for learning? When we
> discover something we didn't previously know, hasn't our prior

---

http://www.globalresearch.ca/mainstream-media-decline-are-fox-news-cnn-and-msnbc-losing-the-information-war/5375493

[271]   Babcock, Grant, *Net Neutrality – and Obama's Scheme for the Internet – Are Lousy Ideas.* Reason.com November 12, 2014. http://reason.com/archives/2014/11/12/net-neutrality-is-a-lousy-idea?utm_campaign=naytev&utm_content=54edcf13e4b03233ace34c9e&fb_ref=Default

[272]   Shafer, Jack, *Democracy's Cheat Sheet? It's time to kill the idea that newspapers are essential   for democracy.* Slate. March 27, 2009 http://www.slate.com/id/2214724/pagenum/all/

learning been "revised"? The war against revisionism, in other
words, is nothing more than a war against a freely-inquiring
mind. ~ Butler Shafer, law professor and author

History revisionism is a big topic amongst discussion circles on the Internet and recently on radio and TV talk shows. In fact, on the latter, history revision is treated with as much vile as denial of the holocaust Jews and other minorities experienced in Nazi Germany. Revisionism of topics sacred to the monopolistic and secretive information of the state that supports the state's ability to control perception of reality is treated like treason. United States Representative Ron Paul wrote, "Truth is treason in the empire of lies."

Court historians through the 20th Century distorted information disseminating from textbooks and taught in government schools. War crimes, for instance, committed by US officials were always whitewashed with rationale based on faulty or contrived reasoning and facts.[273]

Mesmorization

Ever notice how, in the media, whatever bleeds leads?

In the Orwellian world of corporate media, bad is good; a sad story is better than a happy ending and every crime is motivated by a simpleton's explanation that the criminal was on drugs or had a tabooed tattoo or was in a gang. Here in the city I live, a shoplifter from the mall was chased down through the streets by two cops (there's a public police station inside the mall, of course, where the majority of mall customers are minorities). Gunfire erupted. A cop was seriously injured and the shoplifter was killed.   Later, an autopsy revealed the shoplifter had marijuana (gasp!) in his system.   Of course, the analysis by the media was: shoplifter bad. And pot made him do it. Never mind the probable fact is that the vast majority of pot smokers do not shoplift, lead normal lives and certainly do not shoot at cops.

Never in the media will you hear a statement like no drugs were found on the criminal.   Or that the criminal had cigar smoke and booze on his breath. To perpetuate the lunacies of the drug war, the media always reinforces the notion that drugs cause crime by including any irrelevant information connected to drugs and

---

[273] Suskind, Ron.   http://www.ronsuskind.com/thewayoftheworld/transcripts/

weapons. Again, never will you hear or read that drugs and weapons were NOT involved. And rarely, if at all, will you find out that guns were used to protect the victim from a crime, only that guns were used during a criminal offense, or that guns were found on the criminal. No one knows all the stories of guns protecting lives unless extensive research is done.

The length to which news media distorts and manipulates the elections is astounding. During the primary season of 2008, as well as the Republican primary and the general election of 2016, media polls in some races were way off, by nearly ten percentage point. And the lack of reporting allegations, and sometime downright proof of election fraud, has been shameful to say the least. In some New Hampshire precincts where paper ballots were still counted by hand (80 percent of votes are cast on voting machines in the U.S. now), bulk bags carrying the paper ballots were torn into, while the certified seal that keeps the bag shut was still locked up.

People in New York were told by precinct workers that Ron Paul had dropped out of the race and they shouldn't waste their vote on him. In other precincts, Ron Paul's name was crossed off the ballot! Ron Paul was legally registered as a candidate in the state of New York. He was legally registered in all 50 states. When I voted in the Florida primary, the precinct worker behind the table who checked me in forgot to remind me to sign my name before getting my ballot. The vote wouldn't have counted. Well, actually, mathematically it really doesn't count anyway. But we are encouraged to believe the illusion, according to the media pundits and cheerleaders, to feel good about our "freedom". A better system would be those who don't vote get to keep all their tax money, since they share no representation. Voting only encourages the state to proceed with its agenda no matter which side wins. Voting legitimizes the state.

The so-called surprise presidential election of Donald Trump in 2016 exposed the media for what it really is: A cheerleader and propaganda arm of the state. During the Republican primary elections, and then after the summer conventions, the mainstream media pounded on Trump by reporting anything that would instill a negative impression of him in the voter's mind. Every negative ad run by his opponent(s) was reinforced by news broadcasting and punditry that would reiterate and regurgitate the talking points of the negative ads. It became crystal clear in the minds of many voters who the favored candidate of the media and establishment types in national political circles. Voters were reminded that Ronald Reagan trailed Jimmy Carter by nearly 10 percentage points with two weeks left (mid-October) in the 1980 presidential election.[274] Reagan won with 90.9 percent of the electoral votes.

Lies about gun laws

> Myth No. 3: Guns are of little help in defending against criminals. In fact, guns are a big help. Each year, potential victims kill from 2,000 to 3,000 criminals and wound an additional 9,000 to 17,000. And mishaps are rare. Private citizens mistakenly kill innocent people only 30 times a year, compared with about 330 mistaken killings by police. Criminals succeed in taking a gun away from an armed victim less than 1 [sic] percent of the time.[275]

> And while *guns* are *used to prevent* some *crimes* they are *used* far more often to commit *crimes.*[276]

To be fair, one has to admit that the number of gun victims far outnumber the number of times a victim protects oneself from a crime. But that is only reasonable, considering that the gun rights of potential victims are so restrictive as to put the gun-toting criminal at a huge advantage over the law-abiding, defenseless victim.

> "There was another student rampage at the Appalachian School of Law, just a few miles from the Virginia Tech campus. But this shooting did not make the news because the Appalachian School of Law, unlike Virginia Tech, unlike the Northern Illinois University, is NOT a gun free zone, and a student, armed with a legally owned firearm and trained to use it, stopped the killing.

> "Get this into your heads, people. The police do not PREVENT crime. They do not STOP crimes in progress. The police, when they are not busy harassing political protesters, show up AFTER the crime is all over, the body already dead, the woman already raped, the valuables already taken, and act all official, promising revenge somewhere down the road, a revenge which according to statistics, as about a 1 in 40 chance of ever actually happening." M. Rivero WRH.com

[274] May, Donald R. "gallop Poll: Jimmy Carter 47—Ronald Reagun 39," Lubbock Avalanche-Journal, September 19, 20012. http://lubbockonline.com/interact/blog-post/may/2012-09-20/gallop-poll-jimmy-carter-47-ronald-reagan-39#.WEBk_-S7pes

[275] Reynolds, M.O. and Caruth, W.W. III. *Myths About Gun Control* National Center for Policy Amalysis Policy Report No. 176, ISBN 0-943802-99-7. December, 1992.

[276] http://www.opposingviews.com/counters/gary-kleck-numbers-often-disputed

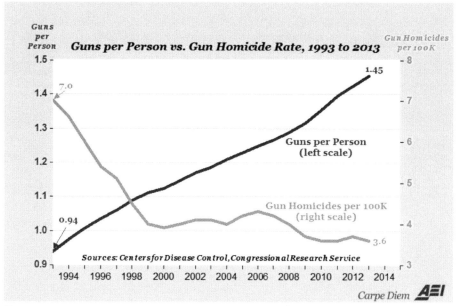

Figure 15

The graph above from the American Enterprise Institute compares the number of gun homicides in the United States to the number of gun sales in the same span of time. The data are normalized to *per capita* population (100,000 people). Clearly, even as gun sales increased steadily, fifty percent in 20 years, gun homicides dropped precipitously, tapering off to one-half the number of homicides as in 1994.

In California for over a decade, violent crime dropped dramatically as handgun ownership increased (graph below). In other places that have instead banned guns, homicide rates have increased. The Welch and English saw a marked increase in homicides after their 1997 handgun ban.[277] Other island nations such as Jamaica and Ireland suffered the same fate as well. In the case of gun bans in Chicago and Washington, D.C., homicide numbers where declining up until the gun ban and then began to rise as people were giving up their guns!

---

[277] "Murder and homicide rates before and after gun bans." Crime Prevention Research Center, December 1, 2013. https://crimeresearch.org/2013/12/murder-and-homicide-rates-before-and-after-gun-bans/

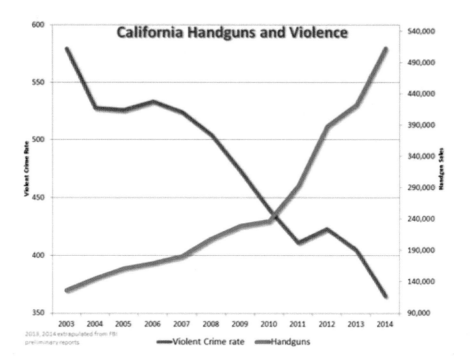

Figure 16

Figure 17

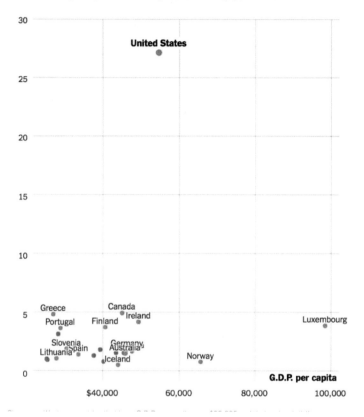

No Other Rich Western Country Comes Close
Gun homicides per day if each country had the same population as the U.S.

Shown are Western countries that have G.D.P. per capita over $25,000 and that make statistics on gun homicides available.

Sources: Small Arms Survey (2007–12 average); World Bank

Figure 18

The graph above deceptively labels the data as gun homicides without identifying whether the guns were legal or illegal. Assuming the majority of gun victims were killed by illegal guns, the data is tarnished by the fact that gun laws on the bocks did not deter homicides. More gun laws, or confiscating guns from law-abiding citizens, will not significantly keep people safer, nor would they in turn diminish gun deaths in the United States

Guns = Violence and Forks = Obesity

Of course, obesity kills far more people in the U.S. than gun violence, but no one would recommend restricting the rights to own eating utensils. One in five people die from being overweight according to *American Journal of Public Health* (2013), more than three times earlier data suggested. In 2011 assault rifles held by humans killed 323 humans in the United States, fewer than hammers (496), knives (650), drunk drivers (~12,000) or medical malpractice (~195,000).

Besides the 9/11 terrorist attack on the U.S., possibly the worst job media reporters have done regarding investigation into mass killings was the Sandy Hook Elementary incident that allegedly left 17 students and adults dead and an all-out frontal attack on guns and high-capacity ammunition clips. All the evidence of newsreel clips and still shots suggest the whole incident was a staged drill with actors posing as parents, students and concerned bystanders. Of course, all this evidence was ignored by the media that has consistently pushed the left-wing gun control agenda for many decades.

The media has shaped public opinion in so many ways it would be nearly impossible to cover all of it in one book. For decades, the media has scorned us and lectured us about a plethora of politically incorrect stereotypes that permeate our society still today from centuries ago. We are constantly bombarded with group-think and mesmerized with various classifications, about what is cool and what isn't, what is deviant and what isn't, without even a superficial examination of certain people who gravitate towards these anomalies. For example, nearly all the school shootings that have occurred the past decade were carried out by young people medicated for ADHD, depression and social anxiety.[278]

As we have all seen or heard, fans of Star Trek, or people proficient on computers, are nearly always referred as "geeks," but someone who spends his Sunday morning dressing up in a Halloween costume for the afternoon NFL game is respected as a loyal fan and participating in community or team spirit.   I could never figure that one out, other than the media has successfully indoctrinated people

---

[278] Corsi, Jerome R. 'Psych Meds linked to 90% of School Shootings." World Net Daily, December 18, 2012   http://www.wnd.com/2012/12/psych-meds-linked-to-90-of-school-shootings/

into thinking frivolous activities are better than disciplined study habits and hard work.

Media Complicity in Gun-Grabbing

> Willie
> It must be nice to go through life convinced that you have all the answers, even when you don't. I used to live in Los Angeles. I, lived through the Rodney King riots. **I watched the cops run like hell** (my emphasis). I watched law-abiding citizens go to gun stores to buy protection and were blocked by California's waiting period. I watched as criminals who did not already have guns simply smashed the windows of gun stores and abandoned police cars and steal the guns they wanted. And I watched a store keeper standing on the roof of his store, with his AK-47, keeping the looters at bay when the police were nowhere to be found. So, you tell us all why it would have been preferable for this law abiding [sic] store owner, whose entire life was invested in his business, to not have that AK-47 to protect his business when the cops ran like hell. You just try to explain that one.
> ~ Michael Rivero (Hollywood special effects and graphics artist)

The majority in media have been solidly behind gun control in the United States for decades. How long have we heard the tired, old stories about the original intent of the Second Amendment of the Bill of Rights? After the plethora of school shootings in America, the media, for the most part, refuses to discuss more attenable solutions other than gun confiscation to reduce the recent plague of mass killings in various public places

The Media and Political Campaigns

Government apologies for inhumane policies represent:

Acknowledgment of wrongdoings	26%	27142
Political posturing	47%	48701
Dredging up irrelevant history	27%	28474
Total Votes:		104317

CNN.com July 29, 2008

There is something fundamentally wrong, and telling, with the results of the poll above. The operative word in the question was, of course, the word *inhumane.* The idea that nearly half of the respondents consider *inhumane* policies to be merely political posturing boggles the imagination! Do we live in a society where two thirds of the population believe politicians and their governments are above accountability and humility? So according to our new-found tyrannous majority, the inhumane policies from the likes of a Stalin or a Hitler, two sides of a socialist coin, are merely *political posturing!* In other words, torture and willy-nilly hubris are merely political posturing. Yes, of course, our leaders torture and ignore the Constitution they swore to defend to win votes.   It is all very clear: People in Middle America love torture and a runaway government. This is why it is called *The Heartland*! Maybe, there are just degrees of inhumanity that could be acceptable to those in The Heartland who are fond of torture and tyranny. And someday it will be perfectly acceptable for football to be so violent that one or two deaths during a game would be a minimum of acceptability. It will be like Rome was thousands of years ago. Bread and Circuses. Nothing changes.

The incredible theater we see at major political conventions has unfortunately become more reminiscent of the Nuremburg rallies in Nazi Germany than what they should be: A good old American celebration of our rights and liberties and an expectation to improve on them in the future.   Instead, we are inundated with nationalist fervor and a determination to exact their perception of "justice" and "prosperity," at any cost, of course. As the torches burn throughout the mob, politicians stand on uber-podiums of network television, on giant screens reminiscent of an Orwell novel, promising the moon and stars to a crowd of what seems like giggling, gullible teenage girls at a Justin Bieber concert. And, like clockwork, it is the same moon and stars they promised last election.

Corporate media, apparently allergic to the truth, loves this theater and augments the already distorted worldview that feeds the nationalistic fervor of these pathetic dreamers of power lust. During the 2008 presidential primaries a study was done to track candidate popularity versus media coverage.[279] What they found was astounding! While media lap dogs were gushing about media darling John McCain's 19,000-plus videos, Hillary Clinton had over 72,000 and Barak Obama had more with almost 85,000. Ron Paul, whose candidacy was all but completely suppressed by the mainstream news, had a whopping 117,000 in the third week of April 2008 all the while Google media trackers were showing a disparity of three-to-one coverage of Barak Obama over Ron Paul. Meanwhile, Fox News, not to be outdone and falsifying information about candidates, showed around-the-clock a video of Obama's pastor,

---

[279]   Media   Caught   Lying,   Version   2,   posted   by   "minivanjack",   April   19,   2009 http://www.youtube.com/watch?v=7iW5kOB1pmg

Reverend Wright, denigrating the United States and white people. The truth was, of course, Wright was quoting a white man, Ambassador Edward Peck:[280]

> Fox news doctored and falsified the video of Obama's pastor Wright. Wright did not preach those words himself. He was quoting a White Man.; Ambassador Edward Peck. And he is a retired, white, career U.S. diplomat who served 32-years in the U.S. Foreign Service and was chief of the U.S mission to Iraq under Jimmy Carter. The complete video below will show that Pastor Wright is telling his audience that "I will tell you what a white man named Ambassador Peck said". And then he will quote Mr. Peck. And he ends by reminding his congregation "A white man said this, I didn't say it". Fox didn't show that because they wanted people to think it came from Pastor Wright.   M. Rivero WRH

Media Self-Glorification

Nothing personifies the ugly, self-interested pandering and self-importance of the media than what it displayed with the passing of NBC *Meet the Press* host Tim Russert. His tough journalist persona he foisted on the public weekly oozed pus like a festered boil the week he interviewed Republican presidential candidate Congressman Ron Paul after Paul's phenomenal six million-dollar "money bomb" raised in one day. Russert was known amongst the other statists and apologists in media as a hardballer, although that title was officially taken by another left-wing establishmentarian, Chris Mathews.

---

[280] FOX Lies!! Irresponsible Media! Barack Obama Pastor Wright

FOX Lies!! Irresponsible Media! Barack Obama Pastor Wright...Posted whatreallyhappened.com **Apr 23, 2008.**

The media has enjoyed near-total control of information. As discussed in the *Political-Industrial Complex* chapter, the left-right paradigm of politics, established and exploited by the corporate media, ensured fidelity towards news-making policies established in Washington by equally faithful elected officials and their army of bureaucrats and functionaries. The left-right paradigm ensures power. And because the ruling Republicans and Democratic elite want power, the growing welfare-warfare state continues to consume more and more wealth and freedom from the private sector.   All of destruction is channeled through the corporate media daily in newspapers and the network news shows and portrayed as a problem originating within the private sector. Of course, it is the politicians and government bureaucracies that gallantly save the day for the damsel citizenry in distress.

Libertarian trajectory follows above the left-right, liberal-conservative two-dimensional plane, forming a triangle, still two-dimensional, but adding another trajectory in thinking. What became the Nolan quiz, named after political scientist David Nolan in the 1970s, is a diamond formed when adding an angle representing an authoritarian paradigm below the right-left plane. With the Nolan quiz designed to question fundamental sociopolitical philosophies, people could plot their political leanings in a way that would refine their general perceptions of politics. Surprising to many, people would consistently plot above the left-right plane, towards the Libertarian midpoint.   Millions of these Nolan quizzes have been distributed by groups such as the Libertarian Party and Advocates for Self-Government, Inc., that were projecting a grass roots end-around the interests of the Establishment and its media enablers.

With the onset of the Internet and a more decentralized form of information dissemination, the corporate media have become irrelevant to many people, not only in the US but around the planet.[281]

Amateur Media and the Internet

> Alexander Wolfe of *Information Week* notes that the largest and most timely source of information coming out of Mumbai was from amateurs using social media like Twitter:
>
> I'd add that Mumbai is likely to be viewed in hindsight as the first instance of the paradigmatic shift in crisis coverage: namely, journalists will henceforth no longer be the first to bring

---

[281]   Wolfe, A. "Twitter In Controversial Spotlight Amid Mumbai Attacks." InformationWeek, Business Technology   Network.   November   29,   2008 http://www.informationweek.com/blog/main/archives/2008/11/twitter_in_cont.html

us information. Rather, they will be a conduit for the stream of images and video shot by a mix of amateurs and professionals on scene.

> 36 hours ago, a look at Twitter postings about Mumbai revealed some of the best on-the-ground information about what was going on. The news channels offered nothing but the usual endless chit-chat about President Bush and other irrelevant topics.
> The Wired blog also has an interesting entry on the role of social media in the crises.[282]

In a ground-breaking research article about an undercurrent of internet discussions of alternative theories surrounding the tragic events of 9/11, psychologists Michael Wood and Karen Douglas[283] revealed interesting data about the psychology of conspiracy beliefs as they relate to public dialog and debate about the putative "official" conspiracy, as well as the subsequent investigations, that 19 Arab zealots with limited pilot experience flew jet airliners into the Twin Towers, the Pentagon, and a field in Pennsylvania.

Psychology has been criticized in the past for being a tool for states to incarcerate political malcontents. In the former Soviet Union, for example, its political machine used psychology to suppress political dissent.[284] The charge was called "psychopathological mechanisms" of dissent, a psychiatric disorder. How many times in social media discussions have we seen someone state "liberalism is a mental disease" or those "crazy right-wing nut jobs" or "Tea Party wingnuts"? Of course, this is the ultimate distillation of statists with no principled political acumen, nor qualification as a psychologist.

Media Complicity in Propagandizing the 911 Terror Myth

Of course, rowing with everyone else is always easier than rowing against everyone else. This is a reason why those who row against are thrown overboard, or in the real world are castigated, fired from their jobs, even executed for contrived treasons of ideology, depending on the degree of state control. Politicians know

---

[282] McMaken, Ryan W. "Twitter and Flickr replace 'official' news outlets in Mumbai." www.lewrockwell.com   November 30, 2008.

[283] Wood, M.J. and Douglas, K.M. (2013) "'What about building 7?' A social psychological study of online discussion of 9/11 conspiracy theories." Frontiers in Psychology, 4:1-9.

[284] KONDRATEV, FEDOR [ФЁДОР КОНДРАТЬЕВ]. *Судьбы больных шизофренией: клинико-социальный и судебно-психиатрический аспекты [The fates of the ill with schizophrenia: clinico-social and forensico-psychiatric aspects]*. Moscow: ЗАО Юстицинформ [Closed joint-stock company Justitsinform]; 2010. Russian.

this. Hence, they do not lead but go along. They are called leaders and even followed as leaders, but they are merely going along with the rowing regime, even if the boat is headed for a steep waterfall. An anarchist in this environment, in order to survive, must find a way off the boat and get on dry land.

Violence and terrorism give the government more power. Possibly the biggest, and most successful, propaganda blitz ever perpetrated on the American people was the official government conspiracy theory surrounding the attacks on September 11, 2001. According to this theory, 19 or 20 Middle Eastern nationals, armed with razor box cutters, hijacked four transcontinental airlines and successfully crashed three of the four into buildings in New York and Washington, District of Columbia. Within hours, these perpetrators were identified and the ringleader, Saudi Arabian Osama bin Laden, was publicly indicted in the media. Despite government officials, such as the president of the United States, claiming they had no idea someone would hijack airliners and fly them into buildings, the media had this information available to them within minutes to a few hours after the attack!

In psychology, first impressions are usually the solidifying memory event in future perspectives and belief systems people develop in the months after such a traumatic event. Soon after the attack, the media began focusing in on the hijackers and the ringleader, Saudi Arabian Osama bin Laden, solidifying in people's minds that they were the enemy and that we can confidently support a war against them. All this despite solid evidence that the attack scenario even happened the way the media described it.

Despite the two months after 911 the FBI never listed the attack on its official www.fbi.gov website listing OBL as the leader of al Qaeda and the mastermind of 911. Even upper echelon FBI bureaucrats would admit they had no definitive evidence OBL was behind the attacks. Yet the media obsessed on bin Laden night and day in its 24/7 reports on al Qaeda and bin Laden. A simple check on the official FBI website would demonstrate that what the corporate news outlets were reporting was blatantly false.

To survive the info wars, you must turn off the network news station, cable news shows, first and foremost forget the newspapers. A key to survival is to disassociate yourself from systems that are working against your very survival. Newscasters are misinformed and scripted, just as politicians are. The media can no better control the chaotic masses in society any more than the government can. As law professor Butler Shaffer wrote;

> Former White House Press Secretary Dana Perino's
> admission that she was not familiar with the Cuban missile crisis
> is but one more example of how chaos theory negates the state's
> claims to be able to create programs and policies to effectively
> deal with complex problems. The capacity to predict the
> outcomes of complex systems is impossible, due to the inability
> to be aware of all the variables at work upon events. The rationale
> for the exercise of state power (i.e., the ability to amass
> information not available to the rest of us) depends upon this
> "sensitivity to initial conditions," which the "butterfly effect"
> completely disrupts. Government officials who have never heard
> of the Cuban missile crisis, or are unfamiliar with the dynamics
> of the business cycle, or, worse yet, are formulating policies on
> the basis of lies and other deceptions, are bound to create more
> dysfunctional consequences. Should Boobus ever grasp this
> fundamental fact (i.e., that the state is the creator of the very
> problems it then insists upon correcting, with an escalation of
> further problems) he/she may begin walking away from this
> most insidious and vicious racket

The corporate media has melded with government like no time in U.S. history, other than when major wars broke out. The nationalist fervor in the US since 9-11 is frightening. When the media are perpetrating lies, in line with the lies of the politicians, instead of fact checking-based investigations, then we have nothing more than a propaganda machine in Washington that has no more credibility than the former Soviet Union's Pravda had. Ordinary people in the USSR used to ridicule the lies coming from Pravda propaganda.

BANKSTER-INDUSTRIAL COMPLEX

The best way to rob a bank is to own one. ~ William Black

Good for Ron (Paul) for stirring these two establishment mullahs to oppose him. But forget their official arguments, which are always a smokescreen in the state-bankster world. Remember that Greenspan was a J.P. Morgan (i.e., Rockefeller) economist before he ascended to the Fed. Now he works for hedge funds and big banks in NYC. Volcker was vice chairman of Rockefeller's Chase Manhattan Bank before his apotheosis. Now he runs the J. Rothschild investment bank on Wall Street. Power-elite analysis is what we need. As Murray Rothbard always said, look to where high state officials come from, and where they go after their terms in office. This is criticized as conspiracy-theorizing, since men like Greenspan and Volcker are guided only by their view of the common good. Hah! Who lines their pockets, and what are their goals? That is what we always want to know for actual political science, let alone Fed analysis. ~ Llewellyn Rockwell, Jr.

Why does it take 30 years or more for most people in this country to pay off their home, a house? Two simple answers: inflation and the Federal Reserve[285] (but I repeat myself). The system has been gamed to the benefit of the banks since early in the 20th Century, when the federal government took control of our incomes and currency system through a federal income tax (the 16th Amendment), regulations and public financing. The federal government extracts 15% or more of our incomes and the incomes of our employers, through income and excise taxes. These do not include taxes for retirement "insurance" and medical care paid to the Social Security Administration.   Those who liberated us from British

---

[285] Griffin, G. Edward, <u>The Creature from Jekyll Island: A Second Look at the Federal Reserve</u> (Boca Raton, Fla.: American Media, 2002).

bankster Rothchild's Imperial Army, over two centuries ago, went to war over tariffs amounting to far less than the taxes we pay today. These tariffs were imposed by the British crown to make imports (e.g., sugar, tea) from countries in the West Indies or the Far East more expensive than those in Great Britain and the American colonies. Modern-day federal taxes go to the Federal Reserve for debt incurred by a bloated federal government through years of spending binges for government programs, foreign military adventures and diplomatic interventions, and things we aren't even told the government is doing.

Number one, start with taxes. American workers and business people pay on average nearly 50 per cent of their incomes in various taxes (local, state and federal). Add to that the cost of regulation and inflation, more than 50 percent of our income (property) is taken by government collectors. Higher income earners pay considerably more. The very poor still must pay sales taxes, property taxes (or through rent), et cetera. So, right off the bat, you can see that home mortgages that take 30 years to pay off could be paid off in less than half the time, if not for the ridiculously high cost of government meddling.

Government sympathizers will argue that people want police, firefighters, teachers, and, of course, the military, as well as a myriad of government programs their political representatives create that provide incomes for both recipients and bureaucrats and other beneficiaries. Government is a huge make-work program for millions of people who would otherwise be employed in the private sector. Note, too, that in downturns of our economy, only private sector jobs suffer, and are usually the first to go. Government jobs are rarely cut. In fact, many times, government jobs are increased to take care of the influx of people in need when they become unemployed! The money in turn at the federal level is simply printed and borrowed from the Federal Reserve. This creates inflation that further damages one's ability to save or to pay off debts. Statists prefer instability in society as well as a preference in central planning because the federal government can simply print money and put the cost of debt and inflation on future taxpayers. States and cities cannot print money out of thin air. That is why big-government advocates want a strong central government that has the authority to print money that the unconstitutionally subjugated states and cities do not have.

A lack of savings is another reason why most people have difficulty paying off a mortgage. Because the central banksters have artificially set interest rates so low, people, especially the younger generations, who have never been exposed to the virtues of thrift and savings, flat out refuse to account for down payments. Interest rates are so low, people along with investors are borrowing money to leverage investments, creating bubbles in the markets and wrecking retirement pensions and IRAs.

Thirdly, wages have never kept up with inflation, compounding the difficulty people have with paying off debt. Every time the central banksters print more money, they devaluate the currency, wrecking both savings and income improvements (bonuses, raises, etc.).

All of these insults to personal prosperity are brought about by a manipulating banking system, the Federal Reserve and its collection agency, the Internal Revenue Service. Bubbles are created by people investing and purchasing artificially contrived economic targets keeping people in debt and behind the curve their whole lives. I first wanted to include the banksters in the Political-Industrial Complex chapter because banksters are intimately connected to the power structures of Washington, D.C., whether Democrat or Republican. The U.S. Treasury, for example, is literally a revolving door between the financiers on Wall Street and the United States government.

The reason illegal aliens are illegal is not because they are here illegally (they can walk through the gate at the border like everyone else), but because they *work* here illegally. Once here they are afforded all the accommodations the U.S. citizenry has. The banks like this system of taxpayer-funded subsidies for cheap, foreign labor because the federal government must borrow the money to subsidize it. The politicians get accolades for having the compassion to help poor immigrants, while providing the corporations with cheap labor. Everybody in the Ruling Class is happy, while the standards of living for the Middle Class and poor deteriorate.

Banksters, like government bureaucrats, want drug regulations because the banks make billions laundering drug money for the cartels and clandestine government agencies, e.g., the CIA, the two major suppliers of illicit drugs that come into the United States. The CIA in turn agitates civil wars and border disputes in third and second world countries so that these countries need to borrow money from the banks for arms and more security (mercenaries) to put down unrest and to fight their wars.

But back to illicit drugs: those on the Left want to legalize drugs, so the government can tax users. The Left likes it because - it believes – drug legalization promotes "freedom" while feeding power to their beloved Leviathan. Of course, this would be promoting "freedom" for all the wrong reasons, although this system would be better than how it is now. Like alcohol regulation, the drugs would be available, but users would be penalized with a user fee. Those on the right who are sympathetic to the Nanny State in these matters want drug regulation because it punishes people who maintain different lifestyles than them. They believe illicit drugs threaten the health and well-being of their youth. Like alcohol prohibition, children have no problem obtaining illicit drugs if they want them. In American schools today, drug and alcohol abuse is widespread. By grade 12, one of three students have tried marijuana.   Their so-called morality laws to protect people from themselves eventually create an immoral environment of corruption and unintended consequences akin to Prohibition in the 1920s.

Again, if you are to survive being victims of the criminal bankster-industrial class, robbing you every day by inflation, debt and taxation, you must divest yourself of their influences and manipulations. Pay off your credit cards, cut them off and throw them into the garbage where they belong. Companies make shredders, like the one I have, that will shred cards along with paper! At the very least, if you must own a credit card - and there are logical reasons, such as for vacations, business trips where hotels and the like will not reserve rooms, rental cars, etc., without a credit card number and down payment - use the credit card wisely and pay off the balance as soon as possible. In fact, to be financially sound, never make a credit card purchase without having at least double the amount in savings to cover the purchase.

A good way to avoid inflation is to purchase items you need from dollar stores and resale places such as flea markets and garage sales. Television shows are now trumpeting the virtues of resale places that sometimes hold valuable and vintage vestiges of profitable property.

World Peace

History has shown that the concept of *World Peace* will never be realized, because bad people always gravitate to positions of power, a kind of Peter principle where excrement rises to the top. As for the monotheistic religions of the West, until good Christians/Jews/Muslims can somehow rid the world of bad Christians/Jews/Muslims, there will be no world peace, certainly in the Middle East. Neither in the secular world will people realize *World Peace* as long as they continue to put their *faith* in unprincipled government entities that rob, murder, trespass, and kidnap their citizenry and others around the world.

America is becoming a closed system in many ways hence the title *Keeping an Open Mind in a Closed System* was chosen for this book. Unlike China[286] which has gone from a closed system with open minds to an open system with closed minds, America has slowly degenerated into a China-like closed system with closed minds unwilling to think outside the box with regards to terrorism, trade freedom and individualism.

> The libertarian tears off the mask of the state, revealing it as the wealth-destroying, poverty-enhancing instrument of terror and expropriation it is. The advances that constitute civilization, libertarians argue, have resulted not from the orders of hangmen and other executioners, or the social planning of bureaucrats and academics, but from human beings cooperating voluntarily in ways that will amaze and astonish anyone who opens his eyes to see them.
>
> And that makes libertarianism the most liberating political philosophy of all.[287]

Libertarians and anarchist aspire to live in an open system with an open mind. Humans, as most higher animal species, function better with a certain amount of order and uniformity in their lives. Even governments, militaries and businesses rely on normalcy to function efficiently. When these random acts of violence, and the continued systematic attacks on our liberties, shatter our balance, it's nearly impossible to make any sense of it. Governments create calculated, or controlled, chaos for a reason.[288] In order for people to keep in line with the agenda of government, full-spectrum control of information and the actions of those controlled by the information perpetuate the destructive cycle of oppression. This cost is realized by those in power to take considerable time and resources to maintain order and remain in their control. The best way to achieve that is to have the masses pay for it. This power is best achieved by convincing the very people it controls by obedience to accept it as normal and the "cost of freedom."

---

[286] McGregor, James. "China went from being a closed system with open minds to an open system with closed minds." Quartz, December 3, 2012. http://qz.com/33449/china-went-from-being-a-closed-system-with-open-minds-to-an-open-system-with-closed-minds/

[287] Rockwell, Lewellyn H. "Who are the Champions of the Common Man?" September 19, 2013 https://www.lewrockwell.com/2013/09/lew-rockwell/who-are-the-champions-of-the-common-man

[288] Shaffer, Butler. *Calculated Chaos: Institutional Threats to Peace and Human Survival (Plantation, FL, LJumina Press, 2004)*

Made in the USA
Middletown, DE
29 November 2021

53713554R00113